THE BREAD BUILDERS

THE BREAD BUILDERS

HEARTH LOAVES *and* MASONRY OVENS

DANIEL WING *and* ALAN SCOTT

CHELSEA GREEN PUBLISHING COMPANY

White River Junction, Vermont

Cover photo: The Bay Village Bakery, Point Reyes Station, California (see chapter 11). Chad Robertson's naturally leavened loaves really pop. They have great oven spring and a well developed and fully baked crust that shows the full range of colors from tan to nearly black.

Frontispiece: Bread oven in Point Reyes Station, California. Oven dome by Alan Scott; oven stonework by George Gonzalez; flanking wall by others.

Designed by Ann Aspell.

Printed in the United States.

10 9 8 7   05 06 07 08

First printing, April 1999

Library of Congress Cataloging-in-Publication Data
Scott, Alan, 1936–
    The bread builders : hearth loaves and masonry ovens / Alan Scott
and Daniel Wing.
      p. cm.
    Includes bibliographical references and index.
    ISBN 1-890132-05-5 (alk. paper)
    1. Bread 2. Stoves. I. Wing, Daniel, 1948– . II. Title.
TX769.S397 1999
    641.8'15—dc21   98-46016

Chelsea Green Publishing Company
Post Office Box 428
White River Junction, VT 05001
(800) 639-4099
www.chelseagreen.com

for Dina DuBois—who is always ready to visit another bakery,

and Gladys Littlefield, lifelong baker

≈

ACKNOWLEDGMENTS

With thanks to David Auerbach, Albie Barden, Laurence Baudelet, Graham Beck, Greg Borchelt, Anne Bourget, Sue Conley, Pierre Delacretaz, Theresa and Richard D-Litzenberger, Michael Gänzle, Al and Keith Giusto, Maggie Glezer, George Gonzales, Gerard Grabowski, Dale Hisler, R. Carl Hoseney, John House, Nancy Iott, Philip Johnson, Chris Kump and Margaret Fox, Rachael Kuo, Heather Leavitt, Lothar Lilge, David Lyle, John McChesney-Young, Pat Manley, Gina Piccolino, Laurent Pouget, Christian Pozzar, Helen and Jules Rabin, Chad Robertson and Elizabeth Prueitt, Laurel Robertson, Frank and Brinna Sands, Rani and Keith, Jim Sargent and Amy Bernhardt, Alan Ricker, George Schenk, Steve Schwab, Joe and Nan Schwartzman, Andrea Smith, Norbert Senf, Susan Sibbet, Tom Stroud, Tina Subasic, Steve Sutcher, Michel Suas, Pam Taylor, Doug Volkmer, Kathleen and Ed Weber, and Doug Wood

CONTENTS

PREFACE

I first met Dan Wing when he showed up on my doorstep and generously offered to help me with whatever would further the cause of "Ovencrafters." Dan had come to California to be with his wife, who relocated for a while to Berkeley to be nearer her grandchild. Temporarily un-harnessed from his profession as a doctor, and far from their Vermont home and his beloved workshop, Dan was hot to find a worthwhile local project to which he could apply his talents, and which would tap his abundant energy and enthusiasm. My often started but never completed book about masonry ovens and the Flemish "Desem" bread was one project that immediately appealed.

Dan quickly found his feet on familiar ground; as a bread baker, an oven builder, and an already published author, he was qualified for the task ahead. It was not long before every book, file, and photo in my office was unearthed, scrutinized, and absorbed by this dynamic new "super appren-tice" from the East. For some considerable time after that the place retained the distinct feeling of the starting line of the Indianapolis 500 after the racers had sped off. More visits followed in succession, as Dan lapped the course, flying by in hot pursuit of his quest. Ovencrafters would never again be that quiet, rural, home-based, one-man, not-for-profit (by default, that is) business it once was. Never.

My path to California was different. After growing up in Australia and living for a time in Denmark, I came here from two very different "democracies," both small, both very socialized if a little restrictive personally. California is anything but restrictive for the individual, since private venture is king. And yet outside of one's home environment, and apart from the region's natural splendor, farms and park lands, California tends to be a rather stark wasteland dominated by the automobile. Small-town America had already been brushed aside in the rush to profitable

Alan Scott baking and teaching at Rani and Keith's. Notice how convenient it is to have a roof overhead and a counter that comes out from the side of the oven, in front. Alan is squeezing water from the hearth mop (or scuffle) before cleaning the last ashes off the floor of the oven.

"development"—or had it? Fortunately I discovered the small, rural townships of western Marin County, and moved into a comfortable renovated barn on half an acre at the edge of one of them. My determination to live and work in a small community, to be always on hand for family and friends, meant honing up on appropriate survival skills: renovations in exchange for rent, a grain mill, an outdoor oven, two milk goats, a large vegetable garden, a corn patch, and a few fruit trees. For cash and community service, I had a welding and fix-it shop at the front gate. Life was grand.

All too soon, however, I was ejected from the garden into the real world of single parenting, of "soccer mums," of house hunting, of first and last month's rent, shared child care, and job searching. But better than a job I eventually salvaged the bread baking part of my former life and took this to the next level. Necessity again

proven to be the mother of invention, so was born a successful baking business based on one bread alone. I built a commercial oven and bakery at home for less than a month's pay, gathered firewood free from the neighboring farms, and baked and delivered warm bread to friends and neighbors on two days each week. One pound of organic wheat at seventeen cents, with almost zero overhead, became a loaf of bread worth three dollars. As little as 250 loaves a week paid the basic bills.

However it was not just any bread. What I learnt from Laurel Robertson, a neighbor, was two lessons: how to make the venerable Flemish "Desem" bread, and what an astounding difference it makes to bake the loaves in a brick oven.

The Desem bread is also a story of rebirth. Desem is a bread researched and developed in Belgium after World War Two to meet the demand for a healthier diet, a "brown" bread, the European equivalent of the fashionable but imported "brown" rice. Besides utilizing the whole grain or "brown" flour, this bread was made out of a thoroughly fermented dough using the ambient microorganisms of the flour itself as the leavening agents. The starter dough was called "Desem." The return to the age-old practice of natural fermentation put this bread on the map. At last, here was the real thing, truly a staff of life dating back millennia. I knew that this "new age" bread was popular both in Europe and now on the east coast of the U.S., so it promised to be an easy sell here too, but not unless it was baked in the right oven.

"Health" breads tend to get overly ponderous, if not downright stodgy, but the

Desem bread even with health credentials enough to sink a ship became dark, delectable, and simply irresistible when baked in a brick oven.

Natural fermentation has been key to the paradigm shift that has sparked the new bread revolution in North America today, no matter what flours are used. I do enjoy a lighter loaf of "artisan" bread occasionally, but it has to be a mature loaf thoroughly fermented by a natural starter, and of course baked in the inimitable heat of a brick oven. This book contains heaps of my enthusiasm for the success stories of those true baker-artisans who have gotten their many ducks in a row, and who are now successful family and community nurturers. Without nurture I do not think that there can be nutrition, since nutrients, numbers, and other heady stuff can lack heart whereas nurture, being from the heart, is the more powerful mover and shaker. And yet, although it was the freshly ground wheat-flour Flemish Desem bread that energized me in the early 1980s to create the appropriate ovens to bake in, and that became a cornerstone of my vegetarian diet, the Desem remains a bread with relatively narrow appeal. Now, nearly twenty years later, it has become obvious that the nurturing qualities of the artisan process, even when directed toward production of perhaps less nutritional breads, are what is energizing this new generation of successful bakers.

A warning, though: Any obvious success in the marketplace using commercial flours will not go unchallenged, for even as I write this, the so-called "artisan" breads that are energetically being produced by big industry could soon swamp the market in a flood of look-a-likes at throwaway prices. These breads will be skillfully compromised to fit the established supermarket system of food distribution—precisely that which promotes the civic poverty I bemoan.

There is such a growing need to encourage the family and community baker/ nurturer, that rather than delay the process any further with lectures on whole grain to unwilling ears (good advice thrust down unwilling throats), I have endorsed the course that this book has taken, including some concessions toward commercial flours. I feel certain that whole grain breads have a secure place in the scheme of things now, and will have a more important role in the future than their industrialized cousins, but the train has already left the station. How could anyone not make better choices given a good command of the facts?

Thanks to the meticulous research by my dauntless partner in this book, I for one have seen some of my wildest intuitions about my cherished Desem bread substantiated by solid science, much to everyone's relief. Armed with these facts, I feel much more secure now about the how and why of the bread I bake, and even about the who I bake it for. I hope that the information in this book will seem as digestible and attractive as the breads now appearing on our tables. I hope too that this valuable knowledge and the skills to implement it will add substantially to our capacity to serve our families, friends, and communities.

—Alan Scott

LOOKING *for* REAL BREAD, FINDING MASONRY OVENS

I have baked bread for thirty years. Not professionally, but regularly: I made a lot of bread in all those years. Most of the bread I baked was not as good as the best bread I have ever eaten, though. It was better than any bread I could buy, but only because few bakeries in this country were making bread that was better, none of them were nearby, and bread is perishable.

Don't get me wrong: I had fun baking, and everyone liked my bread. But when my bread was only okay I could still see and taste in my mind the bread I wanted to bake—a hearth loaf with an open crumb and a resilient crust, full of flavor. Bread that would stay fresh for days without added sugar, milk, or fat. For years I just couldn't seem to make bread like that. Now I do, almost every time I bake. My success surprises me a little, even though I know it is my own bread coming out of my own oven, and of course I know exactly what I did to make it. Each time I open the oven door and I see

and smell the loaves, my heart jumps and swells a little.

Learning to bake that way didn't come without a lot of flailing around, because I was walking in the dark at first. The steps I eventually took to learn to make the kind of bread I like are ones that you can take more easily with the help of this book. Although a first-time baker will get plenty from this book, he or she may not realize the value of the information I have collected. People who have baked before—but never *really* understood what they were doing—are going to get the most out of it. That is especially true for people who want to make wonderful rustic loaves, and haven't been able to.

To do that, you must first learn to ferment your dough naturally (using what most Americans call a sourdough starter) and you have to understand fermentation well enough so you control it, not the other way around. That is how you make a full-flavored loaf that honors the remarkable grain it's made from, that delights the eye, and holds whatever degree of sourness you seek—a little or a lot. In this book you will learn how and why rye flour, or whole wheat flour, or machine kneading, or a hot day, or many other factors will change the dough you make and the bread you bake. Controlling natural fermentation is the first big step on the path to creating great bread.

The second big step is to bake your bread in hot masonry. The reasons for this will become clear as you read the book, but take it as a given for now. "Hot masonry" means you can bake many loaves at a time in a masonry oven or you can bake one loaf at a time in a ceramic cloche in a conventional oven. (Bread from a cloche is not actually the same as bread from a masonry oven, but is so close that you almost need the two loaves in front of you to tell the difference.) Only by baking in masonry can the home or small commercial baker get a loaf that looks, chews, and tastes right. That is true even if the dough is perfectly made before it is baked.

If the secrets of good bread baking are so simple (fermentation, hearth baking), why do so many people have trouble making good bread? There are four reasons for our failures: The first is that most of us have tried to learn the process from books, and there haven't been books in English that adequately explained fermentation or discussed masonry ovens. The second reason is simple confusion—the best described sourdough baking technique in this country (using a sour starter to react with baking soda to raise flapjacks and quick breads) is not similar to the process for making good "European" naturally leavened bread. Americans tend to maintain sourdough starters in a way that does not

produce consistent results when baking bread, but would be fine for pancakes. The third reason is that for more than seventy-five years bakers have been taught to equate successful baking with fast baking—witness the profusion of instant yeast brands—while the opposite is true. The impetus for speeding up the process of making bread was first reflected in advertising that yeast companies directed to commercial bakeries (the familiar "time equals money" equation). Faster baking was then presented as a lifestyle improvement to home bakers who did not realize what speeding up baking would do to their bread. Although the amount of time spent mixing, kneading, slashing, and baking is only marginally longer for good bread than poor bread, the number of hours over which the steps occur is much longer for good bread, regardless of whether the dough is raised with small doses of commercial yeast or from a natural leaven. The fourth reason? The ovens—most people are trying to bake hearth breads in kitchen ovens.

You can gauge the extent of the confusion about natural fermentation by reading the questions posted to Internet Usenet newsgroups such as rec.food.sourdough and rec.food.baking. Many of the people who post questions to these groups are experienced (often professional) bakers who encounter difficulty changing from speed-baking with store-bought yeast to baking with a natural leaven. These otherwise able people don't understand the principles of natural fermentation because those principles have not been laid out—the lessons of research in cereal chemistry, dough microbiology, and so forth have not been explored to any extent

My trailer-borne oven is a strange hybrid: a thin dome makes it light enough to be mounted on wheels. There is no chimney, again to keep the structure lightweight (photo: Dina DuBois).

in popular books on baking, while specialized seminars and videos about sourdough are expensive, costing hundreds of dollars. Baking books give elaborate and intimidating descriptions of how to start and maintain a leaven when it would be more enlightening to describe in detail what is happening in the sourdough process and to consider the properties of sourdough ingredients—water, flour, salt, wild yeast, and bacteria. Methods and rules are not as useful as *understanding*. A baker who understands the process is liberated—free to create new recipes and to manipulate the determinants of bread quality in pursuit of his or her perfect loaf. This book is short on recipes (on purpose, as there are many excellent sources of recipes) but long

on the background information you need to make the kind of bread you want, either by adapting an existing recipe you like, or making up a new one.

"Fermentation." "Cereal chemistry." "Nutrition." All of this sounds intimidating to the non-scientist. To be truthful, it is even intimidating to a scientist—but you don't need to be a scientist to understand it. You just have to want to learn. Since I knew little of the "science" of fermentation or cereal grains when I set out, the information I found was new to me, and I hope that it seems fresh as I relay it to you. Although most of it has been published somewhere, no source I could find includes it all, or digests it for consumption by the committed layperson. I hope that the "bread" half of this book will teach you the characteristics of sourdough hearth bread and the factors (that you can control) that determine those characteristics.

The other half of this book is about building and using masonry ovens. Simple retained-heat ovens (in which a fire is built in the same chamber where the bread will be baked after the fire is removed) are what I actually started out to write about. Masonry ovens have great historical appeal because they are the way bread was baked for millennia, but they are being built now out of more than a purely historical interest. They are built for the unique way they bake: masonry ovens "shock" dough with a massive transfer of heat when the bread is first put in, and they preserve the dough's moisture when the crust is first forming and the loaf is expanding.

I had never seen a masonry oven until 1992 or 1993, but that first experience (an oven inauguration at the house of Heather and Randy Leavitt in East Barnard, Vermont) produced such wonderful bread from the same natural leavened dough I had been making for years that my course was set. I visited Alan Scott—America's preeminent masonry oven builder, renowned sourdough baker, and my partner in this book—for advice and went home to build my oven. Over the next year Alan and I decided that since he cannot spend half a day with every baker in the country (and I have blocks of time in which I am not practicing medicine), I should help Alan produce a book devoted to the history and principles of masonry ovens, and to oven planning, oven building, and oven management. Because there is little

useful literature on most of these topics, the "oven" sections in this book are based on basic principles and direct experience—Alan's, mine, and that of many bakers I visited while writing this book.

I want to state again that much of what I learned and discuss here about ovens I learned from Alan or from sources (manuscripts, publications, articles, and introductions) that he provided. The plans in this book are Alan's plans, the photographs are of Alan's ovens or of ovens built to his plans (except where noted), and the research on managing a wood-burning oven was done with equipment that he provided. In addition to his technical and organizational involvement in this book, he has been its major spiritual influence. Although I am not totally without spirit, mine is the kind that gets one

RIGHT: Sue Conley's oven, built by Alan Scott, is in an outdoor kitchen overlooking Tomales Bay, California.

kept after school. Alan, on the other hand, is a deep thinker, and he thinks about things from first principles. Alan follows a spiritual teacher, he practices meditation every day, and he has made a life that is congruent with his spiritual knowledge.

That spiritual life is part of what he contributes to this book, and is one thing that makes it more than a "how-to" manual. Alan became on oven builder in the early 1980s when he did the forge work for the iron fittings for the first oven built for Laurel Robertson and her community. As a participant in their pursuit of good bread (which resulted in the *Laurel's Kitchen Bread Book*) he went on to become an oven builder, a baker, and a teacher in his own right—a man people travel hundreds of miles to meet and bake with, as I did. Alan and I both believe that baking in a masonry oven makes the best possible bread, though, as you can see from the Preface, we came to this book by different paths and the bread we make is different.

I began this book to help Alan get the word out about masonry ovens, and neither of us thought we would be doing original research on the thermal characteristics of ovens, or that the book would have more than a little in it about bread and baking—there are already so many books on the shelves about bread and baking. But the more I read, the more I learned, the deeper I dug into scientific journals and correspondence with other bakers, the more I realized that much of what one reads in popular baking books is misleading, especially about natural fermentation. As I added more and more to the "baking" side, the book became balanced, almost unintentionally: it now contains a lot about baking *and* a lot about ovens. It is vastly more researched and detailed than we anticipated, and will answer questions that occur to even very experienced bakers.

To introduce you to these subjects I will first describe the differences between good bread and insipid bread and delineate the factors responsible for those differences. As I make this exploration I will define terms and topics. Then I will tell you exactly what I do when I make dough and then bake it, and what Alan Scott does and talks about when he makes dough and bakes it. After that I will present chapters that progress through the book from grain to finished bread, using a fairly linear approach. Each chapter is followed by one or more "visits" that profile people and companies dedicated to hearth baking: restaurants, consultants, suppliers, bakers. I hope that the good versus insipid bread review and the breadmaking section will give you enough perspective to carry you through any potentially dry spots, and that the visits will give you some perspective about how natural fermentation of dough and brick oven baking work in the world of the professional artisan baker.

—*Daniel Wing*

CHAPTER ONE

NATURALLY FERMENTED

HEARTH BREAD

Why would anyone build a wood-fired brick oven and bake in it, in this day and age? And why bother to bake with a natural leaven (sourdough culture) that hangs around in the refrigerator and has to be resuscitated before it is used? I want to persuade you to do the extra work that it takes to bake with natural leavens and to build and bake with a masonry oven. First, though, I need to convince you that there is enough difference between what I might call good bread and insipid bread to justify your exertions.

Pretend you have two slices of bread, one in each hand. Take a bite from one slice, chew, swallow, have a sip of water. Take a bite from the other one, chew, and swallow. One bite is from a slice of factory-made "sandwich" bread, "French" bread, or "Italian" bread, a loaf you brought home from the supermarket in a plastic bag. The other one is from a naturally fermented, hearth-baked loaf. How can two pieces of bread *be* so different? Be-cause almost every step in their formation was different—they were baked, proofed (raised by the action of yeast), formed (made into loaves), fermented, kneaded, and mixed differently, from ingredients that were similar in some respects, and completely unlike in others. What are these differences you can see, smell, feel, and taste? Are they going to change the way your body digests the bread?

Supermarket Bread

Let's start with what you can *see:* the crust of the supermarket loaf is a uniform brownish tan, because there was enough sugar in it when it was baked to make it brown easily at a relatively low temperature. The crust never ripped open anywhere because the dough was very soft and full of water, and because just enough steam was injected into the oven to keep the crust pliable as it baked. Look at how thin the crust is on this bread. The dough was relatively low in starch—which forms the structure of the crust—and relatively high in fat, protein, and air.

Now look at the inside of the loaf. This is the **crumb**, but in this bread it is not in the least crumbly. (See the glossary for definitions of words set in bold type.) Because the water content is high, the crumb is gummy and spongy. The water content is high because the bread was made with very "springy" high-protein flour, and the dough was fortified with sweeteners, **amylase** (an enzyme that converts starch to sugar, and produces as a byproduct **dextrins**, short chains of sugar that hold on to water in the dough), and other conditioners that make a crumb that is soft and stays that way for a long time. All the little cells of the bread are the same size—you can hardly see them. The walls of these cells are thin, the cells nearly closed and perfectly round. Hold the slice to a bright light and there is a translucent glow, but no bright sparks of light shine through. The crumb itself is starkly white because the flour used to make it was bleached with oxidizing compounds and then overmixed (mixed beyond ideal conditioning of the gluten in the dough) to incorporate excess oxygen that further bleached the dough. This is not done just to make it white, but to make the flour proteins more manageable, allowing an increase in the speed of mixing and the omission of fermentation. Traditionally, bread is fermented twice, before and after the loaves are formed. The first cycle of fermentation is called "primary fermentation" (or "first rising") while the second is called "proof" ("second rising"). But the first fermentation stage is omitted when factory bread is "whipped" as it is mixed. This process increases factory efficiency, but unfortunately vitamins, fats, and other constituents of the dough get oxidized and degraded along the way.

Let's try the *smell*: this is a moist, sweet, flat, vaguely chemical smell, pungent and cloying—with the sweetness coming from added sugar and some of the chemical overtones coming from the large percentage of commercial yeast added to the dough. Commercial yeast fermentation products are high in alcohol and strong-smelling isobutyric acid, but low in acetic and lactic acids, which give traditional breads their flavor and bite. Some of the pungency of supermarket bread is from the fermentation products produced by the yeast, but the rest is from fatty acids that became oxidized and malodorous due to excessive aeration of the dough. There is no "bottom" to this supermarket bread's aroma, no binder to hold it together, no bouquet.

Try the *feel* of the supermarket bread: the crust is a little rubbery because the bread has been in a plastic bag and couldn't breathe. The crust (dry at the end of baking) took on water from the crumb until the stiff starch gels in the crust became pliable again. The crust is smooth because the dough was relatively rich (containing fat and sugar) and because the dough proteins were so conditioned by mechanical mixing that no ripping or shredding occurred, even as the bread was springing up in the oven. (A few percent of added fat increases the volume of bread loaves by about 10 percent. It makes them larger and lighter, but spongier.) The dough was nearly neutral in pH (a measure of acidity), so there was little clumping of gluten strands in the dough, as there would be in an acidic dough. The crumb is soft because the walls of the gas cells are thin and flexible—squeeze it a little too much between your fingers and it collapses, never to spring back. Put it in a bowl of hot soup and it instantly dissolves. Bite it and you can see a little rim of collapse in the crumb where your teeth have caught and crushed it. Chew it and it is gone—a moist plug of paste that slides down the throat on its own moisture, having failed to stimulate a flow of saliva in its short stay in your mouth.

And *taste*? This supermarket bread taste is vapid, neutral. There is not really a taste of wheat, and only a little of caramel (unless caramel was added to the dough, as in commercial "wheat" bread). No taste of acid—mostly the taste is of sugar, and of yeast: it would be nearly the same if a paste of flour and water had just been boiled.

Even without considering digestion and nutrition, supermarket loaves (whether "white" or "wheat") are like insipid students passed from grade to grade and then out into the world—unable to read or figure, ignorant and showing no signs of how they spent the last twelve years. The bread doesn't really taste of wheat, of fermentation, or of baking. Unfortunately, attempts to create a partial solution to the supermarket bread problem (by adding a little whole grain flour to yeasted bread baked in the oven of a household range, or adding molasses, or forming the loaves into "French" bread) don't work well. You are sending dull students to vocational school where they will fail to learn welding as they have previously failed to learn the history of colonial America.

Nutritionally, there is little fiber or ash (minerals) left in the factory bread, and even if some whole wheat flour and caramel color were added, the short fermentation the factory bread received was not enough to unlock the nutrients in the bran. It contains carbohydrate of course, protein, fat, and the vitamins that were added by federal law. But nutritionally, there is not much else in the supermarket loaf but water.

Naturally Fermented Hearth Bread

What about the slice of naturally fermented bread, from a masonry oven—how is it different?

Well, starting with *looks*, the crust of the hearth loaf has three different colors. First, there is a rich brown over most of it, formed by heat-driven chemical reactions. To get this brown color the crust had to get hotter than the factory bread crust did. It tolerated

A well-baked loaf of sesame hearth bread resting at the side of Chad Robertson's oven. The color of the crust goes from tan to brown to nearly black.

a hotter oven in part because the naturally fermented dough did not have extra sugar in it and was therefore more resistant to burning. Because the oven was hotter, the crust dried out more as it baked, and strongly flavored chemicals began to form, chemicals that leave a little "bite" of flavor and a deep brown color. The acid that fermentation brought to the dough catalyzed the development of this color and flavor. The second color on a hearth loaf is a light tan, found in the rough, shredded area of the slash, where the protein net of the loaf stretched and pulled apart as the loaf sprang up in the oven. This part of the crust wasn't exposed to the oven's heat for as long, so its color is less intense. The last color in this crust is a dark, dark brown, almost black, where the lifted lip of the slash has gotten hotter than the rest of the loaf, and almost started to burn. Brown, tan, and dark brown—these three colors are the external signs of what makes a hearth loaf look "rustic" and irregular.

The open crumb of naturally fermented hearth bread. Note how the gas cells stream away from the heat of the masonry. The walls of the cells are glossy and ranslucent.

Just under the crust is a tan layer about one-eighth-inch thick that represents a transition from the crust to the crumb. This layer was missing altogether in the supermarket bread: the crust there was as thin as a layer of paint. The inner crust is starch that was first heavily gelatinized, as heated starch soaked water greedily from its surrounding milieu, then dried out as it cooked to a temperature above the boiling point of water. This inner crust formed as a result of several conditions. First, there was just enough water present in the dough and the oven air to keep the crust moist when it was starting to bake. Second, the fully fermented dough contained enough acid and other fermentation products to help "set" the starch and help it darken. Third, the webs of the cellular structure of the loaf were thick. Finally, oven heat and oven moisture fell off some at the end of baking, which thoroughly dried out the crust.

The crumb of the hearth loaf is irregular, with cells of all sizes. Many of them are elongated, and they seem to stream away from the bottom of the loaf, as if gas bubbles were trying to get away from the intense heat of the hearth when the bread was first loaded into the oven. The largest cells are about three-eighths of an inch across and have a glossy inner surface where starch and starch byproducts made by the fermentation culture have been baked into place. Some of these holes link up, one with another. The structure of the crumb is maintained by columns of cooked dough, not only by trapped gas. These columns formed (in part) because the naturally fermented dough was acid in pH, and some of the gluten strands clumped together. When compressed, this crumb will spring back part way; if you hold the slice to the light, bright spots will shine through places in the crumb where the gas cells line up.

Naturally fermented bread is going to *smell* of wheat (more or less, depending whether it is made of whole wheat flour, white flour, or a mixture of flours) because prolonged natural fermentation released aromatic compounds from the grain. And it is going to smell fermented—a little acid, alcoholic, and aromatic—from the compounds produced by the yeast and bacteria in the natural leaven. It will not have the pungent smell of excessive yeast common in factory bread.

The crust is going to *feel* dry, firm, and springy, and both the crust and the crumb are going to be chewy without being gummy. You can slice this bread with a knife when it has cooled after baking and it will not crush, because it gets much of its structure from the strength of its starch gels, not only from trapped gas. It will *not* dissolve in hot soup, and it won't dissolve in your mouth, either, until you have chewed it for a while and are ready to swallow it.

The *taste* of this bread is not neutral. It will be a little acid, and the crust just a little bitter. The crumb will taste sweet and smooth, though I did not add any sugar or oil. An aromatic bouquet of fermentation products that are neither "chemical" or cloying will make it taste clean and honest. This bread can be eaten without accompaniment, but will also stand up to and enhance the tastes of soup, butter, cheese, or jam.

Nutritionally, this bread will exercise your digestive system from your teeth and tongue to your colon. The yeast and bacteria from the sour leaven will provide B vi-

This slice of cracked-wheat hearth bread is full of irregular, oval-shaped gas cells.

tamins and biotin (important if you follow a vegan diet containing no animal products). If the bread contains whole grain flour, the soluble and insoluble fiber in the bran will help control the absorption of fats and cholesterol, and will reduce the rate at which sugars are absorbed after a meal. Bran will retain water in the gut and stimulate the bowel, increasing transit speed and reducing the gut wall's exposure to toxins, some of which will be detoxified by antioxidants from the bran and germ. Natural fermentation pre-digests bran so that its minerals and vitamins are more available for absorption, despite the increased bowel transit rate.

Breadmaking: How I Make Bread

I take a jar of **leaven** out of the refrigerator. It has been there a week, so it is "old" and acid. I take out **300** grams of the leaven (which I call the "storage leaven"), and expand it by putting it in a bowl with twice as much water by weight (600 grams) and twice as much flour by weight (600 grams) as the amount of leaven I started with. Weight is more convenient and accurate than volume for measuring ingredients and is universally used in bakeries. Electronic scales can be set back to zero after each ingredient is added, which is a huge convenience when the next item is to be weighed into the same bowl. The metric system is convenient because it is decimal and easy to manipulate using the "baker's percentage" system.

I have now made 1,500 grams of leaven sponge, but it isn't ripe yet, and it isn't very active. I am calling it a leaven sponge because there is no acknowledged word for this expanded intermediate leaven in English. It could be called the first leaven sponge, to parallel the term in French. It could be called an intermediate leaven sponge, to imply that it is a stage between the storage sponge and the dough.

I let the leaven sponge sit out on the counter for eight to twelve hours, fermenting. It will then be quite ripe. It is not active enough yet for baking, though, because the organisms in the culture are still slightly inhibited by their long storage in the refrigerator. There also remains some excess acidity in this first intermediate sponge, carried over from the storage leaven. When the intermediate sponge is ripe, though, it is a tenacious, airy, slightly sour sponge containing billions of yeast and beneficial bacterial cells.

I triple it by mixing it with its weight of water and its weight of flour, to make 4,500 grams of unripe leaven. (I triple it because that is how much leaven sponge I want to have, but I could have increased it by more, by a factor of five as I did with the first leaven, or even by a factor of eight, if I needed that much. The microorganisms are so prolific that they reproduce faster when they face no competition, a process that is complete in about eight hours for tripled leaven, or twelve hours for higher multiples. Cell counts

NAMES *for* LEAVENS

French	German	English
chef	*Anstellgut*	storage leaven
levain premiere	*Anstellsauer*	first leaven sponge
levain seconde	*Grundsauer*	second leaven sponge
levain à tout point	*Vollsauer*	ripe leaven sponge

Not all European bakers use stiff storage leavens and a sequence of expanded leavens, though that is the traditional method. Many have begun to use a semi-liquid leaven that is propagated in vats that are heated, cooled, and stirred automatically to develop and then store a leaven until it is used to make a dough.

in a leaven sponge are more closely related to the time it was inoculated and to the temperature at which it is kept than to the size of the inoculation.) Let's call this the second leaven sponge. As soon as I mix it, I take out 300 grams. I let this ferment one to four hours in my storage leaven jar before I put it in the refrigerator. It will continue to ferment slowly there until I need it next week. Putting it away before it ferments fully will help it stay as sweet (low acid) and active as possible in storage.

Note that I had only left my storage leaven in the refrigerator for a week before I made my expanded first intermediate leaven. Leavens can handle a week of storage well if they are not ripe when put in storage. But if I had left it there several weeks, I would have to treat it a little differently when I expanded it. I would have started with a smaller volume (say 50 grams) and would have expanded it several extra times, first to 150 grams, then to 300 grams. That would have given it more chance to become fully active and completely balanced in terms of yeast and bacterial cell counts as well as acid content. If I had known when I put it away that I would be leaving it for a long time (a couple of months, maybe) I would have stored it in a drier form (see chapter 3 for information on storing and reviving starters).

The other 4,200 grams (4,500−300) will be ripe and active in seven or eight hours. Now *this* is an active leaven. It is more airy, more fragrant, and less sour than the last one was when it got ripe. I know that under typical conditions of kitchen temperature a dough should be made of 20 to 40 percent leaven by weight, with the remaining 60 to 80 percent consisting of the flour, water, and salt that is added when the dough is mixed. (This leaven percentage in dough can vary from 20 to 40 percent depending on the temperature at which the fermentation of the dough will take place. More leaven is used in colder weather.) The 4,200 grams of leaven I have made will be enough for 10.5 kg of dough made with 40 percent leaven in cooler weather. That will make fourteen typical small loaves (750 gm each), but it would be only ten medium or seven large ones. I get a better loaf with a better crust when my oven is at least half full, and this batch will be just large enough. Usually if I am making all large loaves I will make 20 kg of dough, the most I can bake in my oven in one load. I start with the same amount of storage leaven but I either expand it one more time (I make a third leaven sponge) or expand it twice as much at one step, then let it ferment a few extra hours.

THE BAKER'S PERCENTAGE

Now I am going to explore a concept that is hard to understand. You may experience mild confusion, but it will soon clear. I am going to explore the concept of the "baker's percentage," which is used to calculate the ingredients in a dough formula, and I think the sensible way to do it is to explain what I see as the reason behind it, then give you an example.

You realize that bakeries deal in large quantities. For instance, commercial mixers are often referred to as one-sack, two-sack, or five-sack mixers. They consume flour in large amounts, like 100 or 500 pounds a mix. The baker may not even weigh the flour, since it is weighed at the mill. What he or she wants to know, then, is how much of the other ingredients are going to go in, such as water, yeast, and salt. The baker's percentage system measures all ingredients **relative to the weight of the flour in the recipe.** You might want to read that last sentence again: "The baker's percentage system measures all ingredients relative to the weight of the flour in the recipe." A common formula starts with 100 pounds of flour and has 65 pounds of water, so it is called a 65 percent dough; the dough is said to have 65 percent hydration. Of course, in conventional terms the percentage of water is 65 parts to 165 parts, or 39 percent. Similarly, the percentage of flour is 100 to 165, or 61 percent, but those figures are not as convenient for deciding how much water or salt to add.

Typically the percentage of water is 60 to 75 percent of the weight of the flour in a bread recipe. A lower percentage of water is used with low-protein flour (60 percent of the flour weight) and a higher figure (75 percent) with higher-gluten wheat flour. In this case I am going to mix two flours together, an unbleached white all-purpose wheat flour that will form a moderate level of gluten, and a fresh rye flour that will not form gluten but that will absorb extra water because of its high pentosan content.* I will use one-tenth rye, two-tenths cracked soft wheat berries, and seven-tenths good-quality all-purpose unbleached white flour. I know from experience that this combination will tolerate more than 64 percent hydration. Starting with a 64 percent dough will allow me to add more water near the end

*Pentosans are a type of gum-forming polymer found in both wheat and rye but present at over twice the proportion in rye, compared to wheat. They are very hygroscopic, that is, they soak up a lot of water. Doughs containing rye may require extra water, though they can be too sticky to handle if too wet.

The bakers's percentage system measures all ingredients relative to the weight of the flour in the recipe.

of kneading, to adjust the consistency of the dough perfectly.

Now, I know that the quantity of flour is always 100 percent in the baker's percentage, and that the water is going to be 64 percent of the flour weight. (I ignore the salt altogether and I ignore the fact that there is a lot of water and a lot of flour in the leaven sponge that I will add—I will account for these later, as I am looking at totals only, now.) The total flour and the total water add up to 164 percent, so I divide the 10.5 kg (10,500 grams) of dough I want by 164, multiply by 100, and find that I need 6,402 grams of rye flour, wheat flour, and cracked wheat. That equals 640 grams of rye flour, 1,280 grams of cracked wheat, and 4,480 grams of unbleached white flour. The same division product (64.02) multiplied by 64 is 4,097 grams of water. Let's check: 6,402 + 4,097 = 10,499. This is close enough, since I rounded up and down, since my scale is only accurate to 5 grams anyway, and since the humidity level in the air (and moisture in the flour) will lead to greater variability than my measurements permit, no matter how precise they are.

What is especially nice about weighing ingredients by baker's percentage is that I don't have to measure out volume quantities, cup by cup. If I find my dough is too stiff, it is easy to add a little water. I can then plan to make a 66 percent hydration dough next time. If I want to make 18 kg of dough, or 3 kg of dough, I can do it easily, without having to divide quantities into half-cups,

THE 100 PERCENT LEAVEN

Some bakers use thicker leavens (the consistency of dough) and others use thinner leavens. I have just said that my leaven is half water and half flour or, as the baker's percentage, a 100 percent hydration leaven. I use that percentage for several reasons:

- It makes it easy to measure water and flour into it when I increase it: always the same weight of each.
- It is thin enough that it can be stirred with a spoon, so I don't have to knead it and then wash up when I increase it.
- It is thin enough to ferment to ripeness in about eight hours at kitchen temperatures, while thick leavens may take longer.
- It is thick enough that it does not sour too quickly in the refrigerator, as long as it is placed there before it is ripe.

tablespoons, or whatever. I just refigure the percentages with my calculator.

Just knowing that the finished dough will have 6,402 grams of "flour" and 4,097 grams of water in it is not quite enough to begin mixing. Remember that there is one set of calculations still to do: the starter already contains both water and flour, and the amounts it contributes count toward the total for my recipe. I am going to have to subtract those amounts from the amount I calculated for my dough.

In the case at hand, I have 4,200 grams of leaven sponge, which consists of 2,100 grams of water and 2,100 grams of flour. I subtract 2,100 from 6,402 and I find I must add 4,302 grams of "flour" (approximately) when I make my dough. This will reduce the amount of white flour I add to 2,380 grams. Similarly, 4,097 minus 2,100 means that I add about 1,997 grams of water. I will still add 128 grams of salt (2 percent times 64). I

put a bowl on the scale, add my leaven, zero the scale, add my water, zero the scale, add my salt and mix it in a little, zero the scale, and add my "flour," one type at a time. I now have almost the exact proportions that I know will make great bread, though I can add more water or flour as I work the dough, if I want.

KNEADING, ROUNDING, AND PROOFING

I am going to mix and knead this mass for ten to fifteen minutes, if I work by hand; a little less time if my mix has more rye, which doesn't tolerate excessive kneading, a little more time if I use high-protein wheat flour, which requires more kneading. My preference is to err on the side of a slightly stiff dough initially, then to add a little water toward the end of kneading, a process known in French as *bassinage*. Making your initial mix a little stiff, then adjusting the consistency of

*I have a cheap electronic timer from Radio Shack that will time two different events for up to 100 hours each, simultaneously, and also tell me the time. It will act as a stopwatch (from 0 to 100 hours by seconds) without an alarm or it will beep to alert me. I have found a timer like this to be essential to my baking.

the dough by adding water—instead of routinely making a dough that is too soft and adding flour—has several advantages:

- because the water is the matrix of the dough, added water redistributes more readily throughout the dough than does added flour. All you need to do is flatten the dough into a disc, poke wells into it with your fingers, pour a small quantity of water over it, and work it in a little before rolling it up and kneading it again until it has a uniform consistency, which takes less than a minute.

- although it is physically easier to knead a dough that is too soft, the action of that kneading is less effective. Flour particles are not broken down as quickly and gluten is not conditioned as quickly. Of course, this is true only within limits—it does not make sense to mix a stiff dough on purpose.

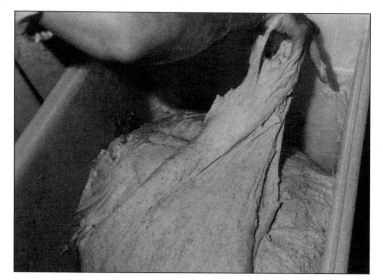

Kneading well-hydrated doughs is often easier in wooden or plastic troughs. See how stretchy this "wet" whole wheat dough is?

I know that my dough is finished when it is smooth, resilient, consistent, only a little tacky (not sticky), able to stretch without tearing, soft enough to flow beneath my hands, and stiff enough to hold its shape when made up into loaves and set to rise.

Once I am finished kneading and the dough is fermenting in a large covered vessel, I should start my timer.* I know I will start to bake in about seven hours if I don't "retard" the dough in a refrigerator at any point. Since my oven likes to be heated for at least three and one-half hours and to equilibrate for about one hour before I bake, I will need to light my fire about two and one-half hours after I finish kneading. (I have a fairly low-mass oven, light enough to be built on a trailer. Many ovens need to be fired longer than this, so they must be lit sooner.) At kitchen temperatures my dough will rise quite a bit in three hours of fermentation, which is also about the time it takes for the bacteria in the dough to multiply to a steady population. I want these bacteria to thrive, because they contribute greatly to the flavor of the bread. The yeast take almost twice that long, but still will be fully propagated by the time the bread is ready to bake.

I usually start to mix and knead my dough about 6 A.M. on Saturday morning. Between measuring ingredients, kneading, and washing up, I am usually done at about 7 A.M. That's a good time to have breakfast and get to the trash transfer station (still called the dump in these parts, though it is just an idling garbage truck parked next to the recycling bins) and back before 9 A.M., which is about when I should light the oven. In Vermont, "Car Talk" is on our public radio station at 10 A.M. on Saturday and that is a good time to be in the kitchen dividing the dough and making loaves.

My oven is mounted on wheels, and I usually park it on a little rise just in back of the house so the hearth is at a convenient height. Next to it I maintain a pile of softwood sawmill slabs that I cut to four-foot lengths. Because I have a friend with a portable mill who does custom sawing, I always know where I can get the small quantities of slabs I need, and the softwood lights easily, burns rapidly and vigorously, makes a bright flame, and doesn't make an excessive amount of persistent coals. Even though I bake in the same chamber where the fire has burned, the type of fuel used does not affect the flavor of bread baked in my oven, since all of the coals are removed before the bread is baked. If I only had access to thin hardwood logs or bundles of hardwood twigs (the traditional European fuel) I could use those just as well, especially for pizza.

I start the fire by crumpling about four double sheets of newspaper loosely and placing them about 18 inches back from the doorway of the oven. I cover these with six to ten sticks of softwood kindling, and light the paper. Within a couple of minutes the kindling is burning briskly and I can start to pile on the slabs, leaving enough airspace between them to encourage combustion. I nearly fill the oven with loosely packed slabs, even though the fire is only at the front. I know that as the wood in the front is consumed, the fire will sweep slowly to the rear of the oven, burning all the wood in its path. That takes two and a half to three hours if the oven was quite full of wood.

Back to the dough!

Remember that I left the dough to ferment some time ago? After three hours, at about 10 A.M., it is time to divide the dough and round the loaves. Let me expand on this terminology a little: **dividing** means cutting my big fermented doughball into loaf-sized lumps, using a metal-bladed scraper (also called a baker's knife). **Rounding** means forming that lump into a loaf-sized ball, putting slight tension on the gluten structure of the loaf. **Resting** means waiting after rounding until some of that tension is relaxed. **Shaping** means building quite a bit of gluten tension when I form the loaf to its final shape.

To start dividing, I deflate my big doughball somewhat by pressing it in the center and freeing its perimeter from contact with the bowl. Then I turn it out on the table and cut off hunks, either weighing them or dividing the entire mass by eye. I usually weigh the hunks, and of course I would have to if I planned to sell the finished loaves.

To round a loaf, I flatten the doughball a little, roll it up part way, then pull it toward me, dragging the lower surface against the table a little as I form it into a ball by tucking in its behind. The friction of the table helps tighten it up, stretching the structure of the dough without ripping it. When the ball is formed I turn it a little sideways so its tail is under my right hand, then I use that hand to roll and wipe the tail toward me until the outside of the doughball is tense but not ripping, and the tail of the ball is all sealed up. This set of actions is hard to describe and some people have a lot of trouble learning it. But you have to learn it, or some similar action, if you want to make a good hearth loaf. (*The Laurel's Kitchen Bread Book* has illustrations that detail one way of doing this.) After

*There is not as much benefit to separate rounding and shaping steps for loaves containing more than about 20 percent rye flour. The high pentosans and low gluten content of such doughs makes them more plastic than elastic, and they will not benefit as much from stretching the dough structure in shaping.

I round the loaves I let them rest on a dusting of flour on the table for fifteen to twenty minutes. They have to be relaxed to take the stress I will put into them when they are shaped.* Shaping is a repeat of rounding, only gentler. I barely flatten out the doughball, and then repeat the rolling, dragging, tucking, and tail sealing to make a nice round ball.

The final rise of a loaf of bread is called the **proof**. It essentially proves that what you have been doing works! At kitchen temperatures proofing takes about three hours and a half with my particular starter, medium-gluten dough, and with the degree of hydration I favor. I like to proof my round hearth loaves in plastic colanders lined with linen cloth. Linen proof cloths are less linty than cotton and will not stick to the proofed loaves when you turn the colanders (or baskets) upside down to flip the loaf onto a **peel** (a long-handled board used to move bread in and out of the oven).

Round loaves do not need to be proofed in baskets. They may also be proofed on a bed of coarse wheat meal on top of a proofing board, if you have a mill to make the meal. A thin piece of metal may then be slipped under each loaf when it is fully proofed, and used to transfer that loaf to the peel. Proofing on a board produces a slightly flatter loaf than proofing in a basket or colander. Yet another alternative, if you only make a few loaves at a time to bake on a baking stone in a kitchen oven, is to proof loaves on a bed of wheat or corn meal on the same peel you use to load them. If you don't have enough peels, you can proof individual loaves on baking parchment (sprinkled with meal) and use the peel to transfer the parchment and the loaf to the oven. I use colanders because they are perforated, like baskets, but cheap. They cost a dollar each at the discount store and I have twenty-four of them. The perforations allow the cloth to wick away a little of the crust's moisture, which makes it easier to slash and helps the crust to retract, like the petals of a flower, while it is baking. That retraction makes for a nice controlled "burst" or "bloom" of the loaf. A nice burst pattern is one sign of a well-formed, proofed, and baked loaf.

Back to the oven!

BAKING

At the end of the "burn" the thermocouple (thermometer) buried one inch deep (from the inner surface) in the masonry of the oven dome reads about 700–750 degrees Fahrenheit. The reading will stay close to that when I restrict the draft (partially close off the doorway) to allow the coals to finish burning down, which takes about half an hour. During this period, heat will continue to flow deeper into the masonry of the oven, to be available as I bake. The restricted draft will prevent an excess flow of air that would cool the oven.

When most of the coals are dead, I clean out the ashes and remaining coals with a scraper and close the oven for an hour. With the ashes gone there is nothing to shield the hearth from the dome's heat or vice versa. The interior surface temperatures will even out everywhere in the oven and drop a little as heat flows deeper into the masonry. For most naturally fermented wheat or wheat/ rye breads I want a surface temperature of about 600 degrees when I start to brush out the hearth with a bronze-bristle brush on a long wooden handle. After brushing I wipe it clean with a damp cloth on the end of a stick—kind of a mop. This cools the entire oven a little because the door is open. Ideally the surface temperature of the dome will be 550 to 570 degrees when I put the loaves in, with an air temperature of about 460 degrees Fahrenheit. The oven air is a bit cooler than the masonry heating it, after the hearth has been cleaned off with the door open.

Alan Scott is a master of rounding and forming his loaves, and I have seen the 100% whole wheat loaves he has shaped rise half again as high as the ones shaped by his students.

The hearth also should be cooler than the dome. Sometimes the oven floor is too hot for the bread to sit on it for the thirty-five to fifty minutes that it takes the bread to bake. Check for an overheated hearth by throwing a handful of white flour on the oven floor. It should take fifteen to twenty seconds to brown substantially in the heat. If it starts to smoke and go brown in five to ten seconds the hearth would be fine for pizza but is too hot for hearth bread. One more light swabbing will cool it down. Too much water might crack the bricks of the hearth.

When the hearth and oven are at the correct temperature I load in the bread. If the loaves had been raised in baskets I sprinkle the tops with meal so I don't need to put meal on the bread peel between loaves. The blade of my peel is just as wide as a large loaf, but a little over twice as long (I have a wider one for pizza). It holds two loaves at once, one behind the other. After slashing them with a sharp knife, I can flick them both off at once or I can slide each one carefully into place. The peel's narrow blade and rounded corners help me to avoid hitting the loaves I have already loaded.

I work quickly as I load, since shutting the door between loaves would allow the first loaves loaded to start baking before the oven humidity is raised to the proper range. When all the loaves are in, I use a hand-pumped tank-type garden sprayer (used only for water, never for garden chemicals) to spray just over and beyond the top of the loaves, before the door has closed. I spray until I start to see condensed vapor pouring out of the oven (about five seconds), then close the door. I start my timer. I check my masonry temperature, hoping for about 525 degrees in the dome. This figure will drop a little during the first part of the bake, then rebound in the later part of the bake when the loaves have been thoroughly heated, have formed a crust, and are not boiling off further moisture. I leave the door closed until I smell that "baked bread" smell, usually at least thirty-five minutes later. I check the loaves then, though they usually bake about forty-five minutes. If I start to smell "baked bread" sooner (fifteen to twenty minutes) I know that the oven is too hot and I have to take out those loaves that are baking too quickly and hold them out of the oven for a few minutes. If it is freezing outside I may just move them next to the door. In either case, simply opening the oven door to move the overheated loaves will cool the oven a little.

Loaves are most likely to bake too quickly when I bake two full loads in an oven that has only been heated for one day and is not fully saturated with heat. I put the loaves in when the oven is a little hot so that there will be enough heat for the second load. If I am thinking straight, I can avoid this problem by baking the first load as *baguettes*, which are supposed to bake quickly, or by making the second load rye bread, which does best when it bakes more slowly. Or, of course, I can jockey the loaves, shifting their positions to even out how quickly they bake.

If I have any doubt about whether the loaves are fully baked (because they baked too quickly, or too slowly, or didn't brown well, or they sound a little dull when tapped on the base), I check the internal temperature of a few loaves with an instant-read electronic thermometer with a stainless steel stem. Loaves have to be at least 195 degrees Fahrenheit, all the way through (and should be less than 205 degrees). I use a metal-bladed peel to remove loaves from the oven because it slides so easily under them. I cool the loaves on a wire rack, elevated far enough above the surface of a table to be sure air is circulating well around them.

How Alan Scott Makes Desem Bread

Alan Scott is my partner in this book. Although Alan travels around the country building brick ovens, consulting to bakeries and restaurants, and giving workshops, he has tried to organize these activities so he can be home on a ranch in Marin County, California, on Thursday night and Friday. Those days he's a baker and a teacher. Out behind the large old Victorian house where he lives he has a medium-sized oven that he fires with eucalyptus logs gathered on the ranch. He preheats his oven with a moderate fire on Friday, so it will be saturated with heat and he will be able to bake at least four loads after he heats it again on Saturday.

On Friday Alan uses a ball of Desem, a natural starter leaven, to inoculate a mixture of water and organic whole wheat flour that he has just milled, transforming that mixture in turn into Desem sponge. Alan uses a stiff storage leaven, the consistency of dough, saved from the week before. French bakers call a piece of dough like this a *chef*. (Most American bakers who know about Desem learned of it from Laurel Robertson and her colleagues in *The Laurel's Kitchen Bread Book*. Alan is a neighbor of Laurel's, and forged the metal parts for Laurel's masonry oven fifteen years ago.) Almost always there are a few visitors to watch Alan's baking process from beginning to end—bakery interns, people who are thinking of building an oven but want to see one in use first, visiting bakers from larger operations who just want to see how bread was made in the old days.

Here is how Alan describes his process of making a dozen two-pound loaves of Desem bread with 6 pounds of ripe leaven, 10 pounds of freshly ground organic flour, 16 cups of non-chlorinated water, and 3 ounces of sea salt:

"I keep a 1-pound ball of stiff storage leaven in the refrigerator, buried in freshly ground flour in a small container. This I triple in size on Friday morning after breakfast to make 3 pounds, which I leave out of the fridge, covered and in a cool place. By supper time it is ready to be tripled again, but I only need 7 pounds, so that is what I aim for. This I leave out again, covered in a cool place.

"Next I grind the flour I need for the morning, 10 pounds of fine flour from a blend of organic (or better) hard white and red wheats for the dough, and a little more for the starter. Also a little coarse flour for the peel. This is the time to set a small pre-heat fire in the oven and let it burn down.

"At 4 A.M. I take out a pound of the leaven and stiffen it with a little flour, bury it in more flour, and put it in a container in the refrigerator until next week. Now I disperse the remaining 6 pounds of intermediate leaven in 16 cups (1 gallon) of non-chlorinated water, add the 3 ounces of sea salt, and then the 10 pounds of flour. After a brief mixing the 24-pound lump of dough is dumped onto the table for kneading. Kneading is continued for 15 minutes by the clock, a rhythmic action of pressing, stretching, and folding, making sure that the whole lump is worked over systematically. At the end, the dough is placed in a lidded container and put out on the porch in the cool morning air. Now is the time to set the main fire in the oven with long logs that reach to the back wall. The fire is lit and allowed to burn its way slowly back wit or without the draft door, depending on the wood and the wind.

"Around 8 A.M. the dough should have just started to 'move' or rise. I check the fire to make sure it has burned well back into the oven, and switch on the proofing cabinet to 95 degrees and 100 percent humidity. Then it is time to place the dough on the table and measure it out into 2-pound pieces. Each piece is carefully shaped into a round, first as it is cut from the dough and again fifteen

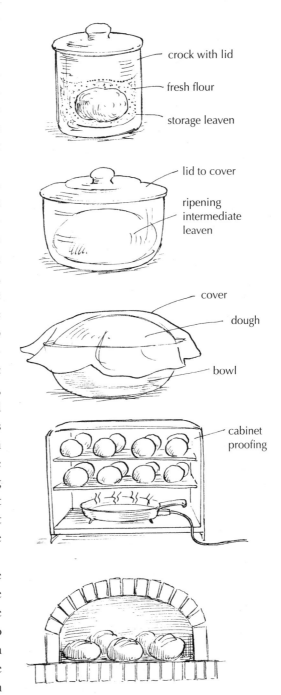

crock with lid

fresh flour

storage leaven

lid to cover

ripening intermediate leaven

cover

dough

bowl

cabinet proofing

Alan Scott buries his storage leaven in flour and refrigerates it from week to week.

minutes later before placing it in a cast iron bread pan, or in a basket lined with a well-dusted cloth that is removable for washing, or on a well-floured (with coarse flour) board. All shaped loaves are put into the proofer,* and this usually happens well before 9 A.M. The fire is knocked down to coals which are spread evenly across the oven hearth and left to burn down to ash.

*A proofer is a heated humidified box.

"Around 10:30 the loaves should be close to their maximum proof, so the ashes are raked from the oven and the hearth mopped with a damp towel. When the loaves are ready, those in pans are loaded first into the oven, next the loaves proofed in baskets are turned out onto the peel, slashed, and loaded, and then the loaves on boards are slid onto the peel and also loaded. The door is sealed with a damp cloth with perhaps a brief spray of moisture from a hose fitted with a misting nozzle. I note the time that the door goes on.

"Thirty minutes later I remove the cloth and check the bread. Another few minutes and the loaves are removed onto a rack covered with a thick cloth, ready for delivery: $5 of ingredients and fuel, transformed into $50 worth of bread.

"My favorite time to eat a slice is late afternoon when the loaf is still perceptibly warm but the crumb is set. An unbeatable treat is fresh bread with homemade jam and on top (instead of butter underneath) thick 'clotted' cream from our Jersey cow."

Alan carefully places the hot loaves on stacking plastic bread trays lined with paper from the empty grain sacks, and covers the whole stack with a blanket. This keeps the bread hot for hours so everyone on his delivery route gets a warm loaf. Also, the gradual cooling that does take place leaves the crusts softer than they would otherwise be. They are, he says, "user friendly" but still plenty chewy.

After lunch (bread, of course, and usually steamed or stir-fried greens and a side of black beans, with homemade ginger beer), Alan heads off for the coastal towns where his customers live. Stopping at certain doors, yards, and shops, he sells or trades his loaves not only for money, but also for whatever household items, fruit, and out-of-season vegetables he will need in the coming week. At almost every stop, Alan gets to visit awhile with his customers, their families, their friends—enough social life, business life, and networking to fill a week gets crammed into an afternoon. He revels in this contact, seeing his role in the community affirmed anew, setting the perspective for his dealings with the larger world. Alan could have given up the baking a long time ago, and focused on his oven-building business. He hasn't, because baking and delivering bread gives him something his other business doesn't always provide—continuity and a sense of role and place. Actually, that kind of connection is one great reason for anyone to start a baking business with a wood-burning oven.

When asked about general trends in baking, Alan says that bread is a hot topic today because many people in developed countries are returning to rustic hearth loaves produced in "artisan" bakeries. "The one-dimensional pungency of 'foreign' commercial yeasts in factory breads is being replaced by the more complex and interesting aromas that arise from natural leavens and their interaction with bread dough and oven heat. Folks can taste and feel the difference, and they are willing to pay for it. Baking schools, books, and associations (such as the Bread Baker's Guild of America, of which Alan is a commercial member) are appearing to help people produce 'real' bread that provides better flavor and better nutrition." According to Alan, hunger for better bread and a better diet is still outpacing the supply of good bread. He points out that the movement to better food is gaining momentum as facts emerge about the beneficial health effects of whole grains and unprocessed foods, the beneficial environmental effects of organic farming, and the sound economic effects of small-scale private enterprise.

Alan's bread is made of freshly ground, naturally fermented whole grain because he feels fermented whole grain is a nurturing food par excellence. Therefore, naturally fermented bread made from or incorporating mostly fresh whole grain is the heart and soul of baking.

Desem bread and rye Vollkornbrot are two examples of the delicious whole grain breads Alan bakes each week. The whole grain country bread called Desem was developed at the Lima Bakery in Belgium after World War II, based on an ancient type of European bread. Its recipe and the process of making it (and making a Desem starter) is described in *The Laurel's Kitchen Bread Book*. The Desem leaven is begun by cool fermentation of fresh whole wheat flour. Cool fermentation encourages the growth of wild yeasts and bacteria, while it discourages the growth of many types of bacteria that could cause a leaven to spoil. Desem bread itself is made of fresh whole wheat flour, water, salt, and the cool-fermented leaven. This bread, once Alan experienced it (baked in a brick oven, of course) was the inspiration for his research and his subsequent development of the ovens in this book. After fifteen years of baking, eating, teaching about, and selling this bread he has not found anything to rival it "in elegance, flavor, satisfaction, economy, and above all, in nutrition." To him, "any other bread seems simply a variation on this basic, unsurpassable standard, which in its turn relies on the fact that the whole grain is itself close to a perfectly balanced food package."

Equally basic is rye Vollkornbrot, made from coarsely ground or cracked organic grain, known in the milling trade as "rye chops." The meal is so coarse that, according to an old adage, "for every two grains ground you get three pieces of meal out." Actually that may be exaggerating a little. This bread doesn't contain flour in the conventional sense of the word: the cracked grain is mixed with salt, water, and a natural rye starter that allows just enough sour fermentation to make the grain digestible and to create small spaces between grains so teeth and saliva can break it up, releasing its deep flavor and moisture. Dense and moist, Vollkornbrot keeps for days and days and is in fact better when it is allowed to rest for a day or so before it is eaten. It is wonderful with simple foods—butter, cheese, fresh cooked vegetables, and soup.

UPLAND BAKERS

Marshfield, Vermont

ALTHOUGH I HAD VISITED MANY BAKERIES before I visited the Upland Bakery, I hadn't seen any that I thought could have been *my* bakery—an efficient, informal operation somewhere between my home kitchen and a full commercial effort, and organized to provide both a sustainable pace of work and an adequate income. Come to think of it, the Upland Bakery was the *only* place I saw that did that!

Helen and Jules Rabin live on a hilltop about twenty miles from my house in Vermont and operate a two-person business in a small building behind their house: Upland Bakery. They first saw an operating masonry oven during a 1971 visit to a commune in south-central France that followed a diet similar to the peasant diet of France in the 1800s. At the Ark (for so the commune was called) big loaves of *pain de compagne* were baked once or twice a week as the main calorie source for 120 communards.

Forced to find alternative employment when Jules's college teaching job was eliminated in the mid-1970s, the Rabins began selling naturally fermented European-style hearth bread from their own wood-fired oven. It is a little difficult, from today's perspective, to look back twenty-five years at the state of breadmaking, here or in Europe. There were just a few voices crying in the wilderness about good bread, and the Rabins sought out anyone here or abroad who they thought could help them establish an honest bakery.

They built a small bakery building and bought an old vertical-axis mixer (which weighs 1,500 pounds). They did not run any plumbing out to the bakery because the earth covering the underlying bedrock was so shallow. Eventually they were licensed by the health department as a "small bakery," which is the same designation that would have applied to a school or a summer camp. They built their own oven after a one-day orientation to masonry work by a neighbor. Helen did the more technical part of the construction and Jules was essentially a laborer.

Traces of this pattern have carried forward to the present—Jules cuts the wood, does some of the firing, runs the oven during the bakes, and is the resident rustic philosopher and delivery man; he is the "vice-president for marketing." Helen makes most of the dough, occasionally fires the oven, and keeps the accounts. On baking days they are together in the bakery most of the time, where they tend to finish each others tasks, sentences, and stories.

They are so familiar with the job they share that nods and single words are all they need to communicate.

Helen and Jules estimate that they work a forty-hour week (shared between the two of them) mixing, firing, baking, delivering, doing the bookkeeping; Jules works a few more hours than Helen, who on the other hand takes responsibility for more than half of the domestic chores they share. The forty-hour week is partly the result of a political/philosophical decision, like that of Helen and Scott Nearing: to do manual work, but to do it for a certain sustainable amount of time each day, week, or year. The Rabins have other things they want to do, baking is strenuous, and they are making a living appropriate to their needs. Helen is a painter, and Jules is writing a book on labor history, focusing on the central economic and nutritional role of bread for eighteenth-century English farm laborers.

They bake on Wednesday and Thursday and their bread is distributed and sold on Thursday and Friday at stores and food co-ops. They make about 350 pounds of bread each baking day, about 250 loaves, and experience has taught them how many will sell at each store. On Thursday Jules takes bread to Plainfield, while neighbors commuting down off the hill take the rest of it to Montpelier; on Friday Jules goes to Montpelier himself to deliver bread, stroll around, do the shopping, and schmooze with old friends—it is a part of his social life.

The Rabins still transport water to the bakery for making dough; because they don't use perishable materials in their bread (eggs, milk, fat) they can clean the work surfaces of the bakery by scraping. Woodcutting is simplified, as they realized long ago that the cheapest and easiest source is sawmill slabs. These are an inexpensive, convenient, and ecologically appropriate waste product of local industry. The slabs are delivered in bundles, and Jules knows how to safely gang-cut them to five-foot lengths with a chainsaw. The slabs are flat on one side and rounded on the other, generally two to three inches thick and eight or ten inches wide—ideal for firing the oven.

The Rabins' oven is built of salvaged firebrick and is round in plan. The oven they had seen in France was round, so they built theirs that way. The oven measures about twenty-six square feet on the hearth. Although they knew that the oven should be flatter in section than a hemispherical dome, they

The forty-hour week is partly the result of a political/ philosophical decision, like that of Helen and Scott Nearing: to do manual work, but to do it for a certain sustainable amount of time each day, week, or year.

≈

UPLAND BAKERS

The storage or heat delivery seems to be greater from the dome than from the hearth, so the oven needs to be carefully managed to control this imbalance, especially for the last bakes of the day.

~

didn't at that time know how to achieve that flat shape. They used a trammel stick, which is essentially a rotating template, to form the circular arch. In the years since they built the oven, the Rabins have raised its hearth significantly with more firebrick, so its current shape is less than hemispherical.

The oven has two flues: such a high, round oven might be difficult to fire with only an external flue, and the Rabins had not seen any traditional ovens on the Roman plan in their travels. One of the flues rises from the center of the dome, and because of persistent heat leaks, it is now sealed with two masonry dampers (in series) when firing is complete and baking is underway. The other flue is in a recess just above and outside the oven door, in the conventional location. The oven has high thermal mass, with about a foot of sand outside the dome. The sand is covered with vermiculite inside a fieldstone enclosure; there is a similar thickness of masonry under the hearth. However, that represents a bit of a problem. The several layers of firebrick in the hearth are not as dense as the sand outside the dome, so the hearth retains less heat than the dome. The storage or heat delivery seems to be greater from the dome than from the hearth, so the oven needs to be carefully managed to control this imbalance, especially for the last bakes of the day.

The oven door is made of insulated metal, hinged on its left-hand side. This works because (like some European ovens) there is no outer hearth—instead the stonework is cut away to form a recess or niche that runs from the floor up to the arch that conceals and forms the flue above the oven door. Operations that some bakers perform on the outer hearth, Jules performs on a bench or counter that juts out to the right of the oven—just beyond the peels that stand on end next to the door. This bench has an extension rest on it for the peel that is being loaded, a magnet for his razor, and a bowl of coarsely ground flour for coating the peel. It also has room for a plywood tray from the proofer, from which loaves can be transferred to the peel. Since he sprays the oven with a modified fruit tree sprayer (a stainless steel tank model from Sears, with a long wand) which he keeps by his feet in front of the door, Jules has everything he needs for slashing, loading, and unloading within reach. He tosses finished loaves into metal baskets on the floor to the left of the oven.

The Upland oven gets a preheat firing on Tuesday, and another long firing Wednesday morning and Thursday morning. On those days the fire is lit at

5:30 A.M. and refired at about one-hour intervals with a couple of armloads of slabs, giving a series of hot, bright burns. The last load of wood burns out at 9:30 A.M.; the heat is allowed to soak through the masonry and equalize until Jules comes in to rake out the oven at 1:30 P.M.; baking begins at about 2:30 P.M. Helen judges oven temperature by the amount of time required for soot to burn off the dome (which happens at 700 to 800 degrees Fahrenheit), since the oven doesn't have any thermocouple sensors. The oven is usually a little too hot when baking begins, but the central draft can be opened a little to spill some of the oven air. Jules also uses his twenty-five years of experience to move the loaves around in the oven as necessary to get everything to come out right. At first he is only baking ten loaves at a time, but later in the day (by 8 P.M., supper time) he can bake forty at once.

Most of their bread is based on a moderately high-protein unbleached white bread flour, King Arthur Special. Some of the breads contain an appreciable percentage of home-milled rye or wheat flour, but only the 100 percent whole wheat bread is whole grain and fully organic. All of the dough is naturally leavened: a small volume of *chef* is expanded twice the day before baking to make a fresh *levain*. Each batch of dough is made up in the morning, and Helen tries to take the temperatures of the air and flour into account when adding tempered water, to maintain consistent process times and products.

The mixer bowls rest in a wheeled trolley that allows Helen to move them away from the mixer by herself. The bowl and the dough are heavy, so she uses a long ironwood sapling suspended from the ceiling by a metal cable when she needs to lift a bowl of finished dough. The short end of the lever has two cables that end in metal hooks that grab the rim, so she can place the bowl on the counter to scoop the dough into a pail for fermentation. These rolling pails (each on a little cart) make it easy to move the fermented dough around. When it is time to dump the dough out for scaling, Jules is in the bakery, and they do it together.

Jules had a friend weld up a little rack which he uses to load long loaves into canvas *couches* more easily. On one side of the rack is a rectangular ring of round rod (about $^1/_8$ or $^5/_{32}$ inch in diameter) about 24 x 2$^1/_2$ inches. Welded to this ring are a series of hoops that go out from the ring at right angles about 20 inches, then turn down and come back to the other half of the hoop. To

UPLAND BAKERS

use it, Jules puts down a proofing tray, puts the rack on it, and lays a linen *couche* cloth on top. He then pokes the cloth down between the side hoops of the rack, and it stays in place as he quickly fills the cavities with loaves that Helen has just formed. When the tray is full, he pulls the rack out sideways, leaving the *couche* and its loaves on the tray. After the loaves are proofed he carries them over to the oven bench.

The Rabins aren't sure how long they are going to continue baking. Jules is certainly of retirement age and Helen is in a branch of the Women's International League for Peace and Freedom that is called the "Raging Grannies." They think about having more time to paint and write, but they know that the hard work is helping to keep them both physically and intellectually fit, and they will probably continue to work as long as it feels right. Then Jules hopes to find someone who will buy their good will, processes, and knowledge, and continue to provide good bread to their community. Helen and Jules often agree to disagree, and this is one of those areas. Although she developed many of the techniques they use, she doesn't feel proprietary about them, and would rather disseminate than sell them.

The greatest gift I carried away from my visit to the Upland Bakery is my appreciation of the extent to which the Rabins' consciousness has determined their baking and their lives. They made a conscious decision to support themselves by baking only as much as they could gracefully manage, and they have stuck consciously to their principles for twenty-five years. They have created a life that is congruent with their needs and natures, and have not let the market demand for their product (always more than they can supply) lead them astray. Like the Webers (see chapter 10), they don't pay rent and don't sell at retail. One advantage that the Rabins have, though, is that they sell to stores and co-ops that have adjusted to deliveries two days a week. The Webers sell to restaurants that are open six nights a week, so they have to bake and deliver six days a week, half as much each day as the Rabins. The Webers eventually will have to figure out how to take a vacation, while "everyone knows" that the Upland Bakery is closed for a few weeks a year. Also, almost half of the deliveries going out from the Rabins are carried into town by their commuting neighbors. The time saved by not delivering their bread is time that the Rabins spend consciously.

CHAPTER TWO

BREAD GRAINS

and FLOURS

I wish I could just tell you what kind of flour to buy to bake bread, but I can't. Not because I'm in the hip pocket of a flour company, but because I don't know enough about you. I don't know:

- where you live—the local all-purpose flour in New England will make good bread but not good biscuits, while the local all-purpose flour in Alabama will make good biscuits but not good bread.
- what kind of bread you like—hearth bread, pan bread, white bread, dark bread
- whether you only eat organic foods
- whether you have a grain mill
- whether you will hand-knead your dough
- whether you use natural leavens (sourdoughs)

I would need to know the answers to these questions, and others, before I could recommend a flour. "Wheat" is many varieties of grain, each lot of grain is different even within one variety, and a miller can make many types of flour from one lot of wheat. This chapter will give you enough of a background about wheat to enable you to ask the questions you need to ask to get the flour you need for the baking you want to do. Let's start at the beginning—the beginnings of agriculture.

Where Grain Came from Originally

The best current guess is that grains were first domesticated ten to twelve thousand years ago in the northern part of the Fertile Crescent, along what is now the border between Syria and southwestern Turkey. Fields of wild einkorn wheat grow there still, probably much like those that drew hunter-gatherers thousands of years ago at harvest time. There are wild wheat stands dense enough

*Baking
fermented
grain,
making
bread:* this
*is the way to
make grain
palatable and
nutritionally
available.*

~

to be harvested by hand, and experiments have shown that a few weeks of work could have supplied a family with enough grain for a year. In that bounty of wheat there are a few strains or types that are genetically and physically similar to strains of einkorn still cultivated today in some remote areas. Relatively few differences exist between some of the wild and cultivated stocks.

Archaeologists and agricultural researchers are now exploring how harvesting wild grain may have led to the evolution of the cultivated varieties. Characteristics such as sturdier stems to hold the kernel on the plant longer and thicker kernels with fragile spikes and loose husks may have been selected— inadvertently at first—that permitted the rapid (for so it seems to have been) development of agriculture. The cultivation of grain was soon followed by the domestication of animals and the development of early civilizations. Whether the first grain cultivated was einkorn wheat, emmer wheat, or barley isn't known—these were all domesticated over a fairly short span, and in the Fertile Crescent. What is clear is that the attainment of such a reliable source of food was the major technological breakthrough in human history. Rye was first cultivated later than wheat, and probably in a more northern area with cooler, wetter weather. Rye grass, the precursor and relative of cultivated rye, is widely distributed.

Eating raw grain would have been a real chore, though: people don't have the teeth, the belly, or the gustatory appreciation for it. Plain cooked grains are better but they won't keep long without refrigeration, and the taste is bland. Sprouting the grain first is a good way to make nutrients more available, but the sprouted grain must be eaten when it is ready, or drunk when the beer is sound. Baking fermented grain, though, making bread: *this* is the way to make grain palatable and nutritionally available. We have been doing it for thousands of years with a variety of grains, ferments, and baking techniques across cultures, continents, and centuries.

Throughout this history, almost everyone was involved with, or at least aware of, the process of making some kind of bread. Baking day has always been a bit of a holiday in rural settings, with most of the village involved. In the cities, citizens visited the baker every day of the week. The Vermont baker/writer Jules Rabin tells a wonderful story about meeting an elderly baker in New York's Little Italy. He had been visiting with the old man, asking about the big coal-fired oven in the tenement basement where he worked, when the baker asked him to come upstairs to the sidewalk. The baker pointed down the street, indicating about every fourth six-story tenement. "There was a baker there, and there, and there, and there. They are all gone, now, but me." Each group of tenements had been a little village, each with a baker. Each group of tenements probably held five hundred people, and that is the size of the community that a family of bakers can supply. According to Christian Petersen, an English bakery of the middle of the last century used about two hundred and eighty pounds of flour a day to make three hundred and fifty pounds of bread. This served a community of four to six hundred people; village bakeries throughout Europe were the same size, and interestingly, that is the same amount of bread Jules and his wife Helen make today.

We have, for the most part, lost our village bakers and the knowledge they carried in their heads and hands, and most of us are no longer closely involved with the process of making bread. We need to spend some time getting reacquainted with wheat—and to a lesser extent rye—as they are the great bread grains, and will provide the structure of the bread you bake, even when it contains other ingredients. I will discuss wheat and rye first as grains, then discuss the process of milling them into flour and the properties of the flours themselves, properties that affect doughs made from them; the next two chapters are devoted to dough and its properties. Suffice it to say here that bread rises because gas (produced by microorganisms) is trapped in the dough, and wheat and rye doughs are unique in their ability to trap gas. In wheat dough the matrix that does the trapping is formed of protein (gluten) sheets, sealed with vegetable gums present in the wheat. The formation and maturation of that gluten network is dependent on the quantity of gluten-forming proteins in the grain and on the performance of that gluten in the dough.* In rye doughs the protein network is less developed, but there are more gums available to trap the gas.

Varieties and Characteristics of Bread Wheat

Wheat is a domesticated grass, altered by long selection to permit the gathering and cleaning of its seeds. From the paleolithic domestication of wheat to our times there have been many refinements in this grain. For example, an ancient cross (hybridization) of wild emmer and another wild wheat

Wheat plant.

produced the main species of wheat cultivated in prehistoric and early historic times. Whether that cross was intentional, no one knows. Recent refinements, however, are clearly intentional: short stature, high yields when heavily fertilized, and resistance to specific diseases have been bred into modern wheats. Many other properties are selected or eliminated in particular strains as they are developed, but characteristics desired in mechanized farming may be disadvantages for organic growers or non-mechanized growers. There is some concern that with wheat, as for many crops, genetic diversity (thousands of strains are known) is being lost in the pursuit of yield.

Genetically, all wheats fall into three groups according to the number of chromo-

*Gluten is a gummy, stretchy protein formed by the linking of precursor proteins, glutenin and gliadin. The amount and the workability of the gluten in a dough depends on the total amount of these proteins (and the ratio between them) in the flour used to make it.

To define wheat one must state hard or soft, red or white, spring or winter, as in hard red spring wheat.

~

somes each cell carries. Einkorn wheats have two sets of seven chromosomes and are called diploid. Einkorn wheat is not widely grown, though it is historically important. Emmer wheats (the most common modern version is durum wheat) have four sets of seven chromosomes and are called tetraploid. The hexaploid wheats have six sets of seven chromosomes—common or bread wheat, spelt wheat, and club wheat are all representatives of this group. Of these genetically grouped wheats, it is common wheat that is of primary interest to the baker, and it represents more than 90 percent of American wheat production. The remainder is almost entirely durum wheat, grown for the manufacture of pasta and related products, and club wheat, grown in the Northwest and made into pastry and cake flour. Good bread can be made of durum wheat and its large-grain near-relative, Kamut, but it accounts for a tiny percentage of bread production.

These genetic distinctions are important to breeders, but the most important functional distinctions in wheat are not drawn along the genetic lines, but according to the way wheat is grown and the characteristics of the grain itself. For example, the distinction between winter and spring wheat is one of the most common distinctions a baker will draw, and it relates to how wheat is grown. Winter wheat is planted in the fall and stays in the field all winter. Its distribution is limited by climate, as it can be damaged by excessive freezing of the soil. In North America winter wheat is grown mostly on the Great Plains. Spring wheat is planted in the spring in harsher climates such as the Northern Plains and parts of Canada. The time of year wheat

is planted does not absolutely define any of the characteristics of the grain, though—you need to know more than its planting time to know whether a batch of wheat will be good for bread.

How about hard wheat and soft wheat? Their differences result from genetics and the interaction of genetics and growing conditions. Hard wheat kernels show a feature that is not as well developed in soft wheat: a layer of protein around each microscopic starch granule that turns to gluten as dough is mixed. Hard wheat has a high protein content and flour made from it (strong flour) develops more gluten when kneaded and thus makes lighter bread. North American hard wheat is prized by the world's bakers for the strong flours it produces.

Soft wheat, however, tends to have richer flavor, and it is best to use the softest wheat (weak flour) that will achieve your goals. For example, quick-rise, chemically leavened breads like soda bread don't need (and are the worse for) high-protein wheat flour, while bread raised by "yeast" (commercial yeast and natural leavens) requires at least a moderate protein percentage. If you think that these distinctions might not have practical applications, think again. The protein content of the flour sold as "all-purpose" flour in different parts of the United States varies greatly, and you *cannot* make good yeasted bread with some of them, especially those milled for the Southern market, where most flour has historically been used for biscuits, pie crusts, and cobblers. You can get the flavor of soft wheat into bread, though, by cracking the kernels and adding them to a dough made from hard wheat flour.

Since protein content varies from strain

to strain, even within the hard wheat group, and because growing conditions have a large effect on protein content, millers and volume bakers test grain and flour constantly. The protein content of a strain of wheat may vary by more than 100 percent, depending on climate and soil conditions. Because climate and soil conditions in most of Western Europe do not permit growing the highest-protein common wheat, traditional baking techniques there do not require or benefit from the highest possible protein content.

There is one more great division in wheat nomenclature, the division into red wheat and white wheat. Red wheat has a bran pigment that makes it darker in color than white wheat, but this pigment gives the bran a slightly bitter flavor, similar to the tannins in tea. White wheat does not have this pigment, and this difference is genetic. There is no necessary and direct relationship between the presence or absence of the pigment and other characteristics of the wheat, such as protein content.

To define wheat one must state hard or soft, red or white, spring or winter, as in *hard red spring wheat*. The following generalizations are useful, but not always apt, since wheat quality is always dependent on soil and climate conditions:

- Hard wheat will make more gluten than soft wheat
- Spring wheat will make more gluten than winter wheat of the same variety
- Winter wheat is generally higher in minerals
- Red wheat will make more gluten than white wheat, with some notable exceptions.

THE BASIC CLASSES *of* WHEAT *in the* UNITED STATES

Differences

Growing Season	*Winter wheat* is planted in the fall and harvested in late spring or early summer (75 percent of production) *Spring wheat* is planted in the spring and harvested in early fall
Color	*Red wheat* contains a slightly bitter tasting pigment *White wheat* does not contain the pigment
Hardness	*Hard wheat* contains more protein *Soft wheat* contains less protein

Hard Red Winter Wheat—Moderate protein content, accounts for more production than any other class, mostly grown west of the Mississippi and east of the Rockies, used for bread, rolls, all-purpose flour.

Hard Red Spring Wheat—The highest-protein bread wheats, grown from Minnesota to Montana, made into bread flour.

Soft Red Winter Wheat—Low-protein wheat grown mostly east of the Mississippi, used for cakes, pastries, flatbreads, and crackers.

Hard White Wheat—Similar to Hard Red Winter Wheat, but with pigment production bred out, used to make milder-tasting whole wheat products such as bread, rolls, bulgur, and tortillas.

Durum Wheat—Very hard high-protein wheat grown from Minnesota to Montana (especially in North Dakota), used to make semolina flour for pasta.

ORGANIC WHEAT

Although organic wheat is prized for health or nutritional benefits, there is no evidence that organic flour "performs" better in baking. The smaller available stocks of organic grain make it more difficult for millers to maintain uniform baking characteristics in organic flours, whether whole wheat or white, leading to higher prices for organic flour. On the other hand, the demand for organic grains is increasing communication between farmers and bakers as they work on ensuring the quality of the grain. Their discussions are likely to lead to the production of organic wheat that is better suited to bakers' needs, as bakers encourage farmers to plant the varieties suited to artisan baking.

Characteristics of Rye

Rye is second to wheat as a bread grain and is dominant in some regions where it is easily grown and wheat is not, especially wetter and colder areas of Northern and Central Europe.* It was grown in those areas in prehistoric times, and was carried to Britain by the Saxons after the decline of Rome. Wheat didn't get a foothold in Northern Europe until its cultivation was encouraged in the medieval monasteries, as the Church reached north from its base in wheat-growing Italy and Mediterranean France.

Rye kernels are thinner than wheat kernels and gluten-forming proteins are not the main structural and gas-trapping constituent in rye—the ratio of soluble and insoluble proteins is just not right for their formation. The critical gas-trapping gum in rye is a viscous solution of pentosans, which are polysaccharides (chains of sugars) that are structurally similar to starches and to cellulose. Though they are present in rye at more than twice their percentage in wheat, the ultimate gas-trapping capacity of rye dough is less than that of wheat dough. The hygroscopic (water-loving) pentosans also help rye bread stay moist and fresh longer than wheat bread. Rye has about 50 percent more fat than wheat, and there are some critical differences in the properties of their enzymes which I will discuss in a later section of this chapter (see p. 34). Chemistry aside, the flavor of rye is distinctive and wonderful, whether in bread or whiskey!**

In this era of easy bulk transportation of grain and fertilizer, the area planted to rye, worldwide, has dropped since World War II, though it is now on the rise again. This drop in plantings has had two causes: wheat has supplanted the rye that predominated in some traditional diets, and the per-acre yield of rye has increased dramatically.

While there are many varieties of rye, most whole grain suppliers for home and small commercial bakers don't carry a selection of strains. Most of us will have to buy what is available, choosing grain that looks healthy and will therefore have consistent enzyme levels and no ergot (which changes the appearance of the kernels). The situation is different for rye flour—most suppliers carry several types.

Wheat Flour Production: Threshing and Milling

The first and greatest determinant of the nature of flour is the nature of the grain it is milled from. When the stalks reach the right

*Rye is usually about eighth in world cereal production, behind wheat, rice, corn, barley, oats, millet, and sorghum

**Although rye grows well in its habitat, certain growing conditions favor the growth of ergot, a fungus that grows on rye and produces a large number of compounds, including the parent compound of the drug LSD. Poisoning by ergot was common in medieval times, and has occurred in modern times on occasion. Pharmaceutical companies now buy ergot from milling companies to manufacture drugs for headache.

moisture content they are cut and the seed kernels are beaten off the stalk, or threshed. Threshing also knocks off the seed husk (which is then called chaff) in most strains of wheat. Modern cutting and threshing are a combined operation and the machine that does it is called a combine. Standing wheat is mowed down and a stream of grain free of chaff pours out. These wheat kernels are made into flour in mills where they are mechanically broken down to powder. Mill machinery may be as basic as a mortar and pestle, or as complicated as the flour factories of the American Midwest.

The second greatest determinant of the nature of flour is milling. The first step at a mill is to clean the grain using gravity, magnets, and blasts of air to remove solid foreign matter. Disk separators (indented rotating metal plates that pick up kernels but leave larger material), screens, and centrifuges reject objects of the wrong size and density, such as bad wheat kernels, insect egg cases, weed seeds, and stray seeds of other grains. Clean, uniform kernels mill more predictably and allow mill tolerances to be closer. Commercially available wheat flour is stone ground, hammer milled, or roller milled.

STONE AND HAMMER MILLING

Stone milling is a cool process, assuming the stones are kept well dressed. The grain is sheared and pulverized between rotating stones, producing a flour that retains all the components of the grain. The patterns of grooves and pits in the face of a millstone not only move the grist outward, but do the shearing and cutting, even as the lands (the flat areas) do the crushing.

This process creates whole wheat flour, which can then be bolted (sifted) to become stone-ground white flour: the finer the sieve, the whiter the product. The wheat germ, the oily part of the seed that would have become the growing plant, is pulverized in stone milling. Even if it is later separated out by sifting, enough will remain to leave little golden spots of germ in the white flour that results. Thus stone-ground white flour is more perishable than the more common roller-milled white flour, because oxidizing germ oil becomes rancid and bitter.

Long ago, wheat was run through the millstones once. With the development of strains of harder wheat, it was no longer possible to make good flour in one pass through the mill. High-milling, previously uncommon, became the norm. In this process, grain is run through once to make a coarse grist, then run through another set of stones set closer together. Stone grinding is simple

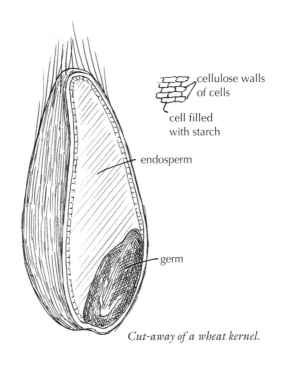

cellulose walls of cells

cell filled with starch

endosperm

germ

Cut-away of a wheat kernel.

conceptually, but it requires a skilled attendant at the mill, and regular maintenance by a millstone dresser. Whole wheat flour is an intrinsic product or intermediate product in all stone mills, but not in modern roller mills. Large milling companies do make whole wheat flour, but it is usually produced by adding back to white flour the constituents that were removed along the way in a roller-milling operation.

Hammer mills flail grain with metal links until the flour is fine enough to fit through a screen and escape the knife. The product is similar to stone-ground flour, but the degree of coarseness may be varied by changing screens and the process does not require a skilled attendant or a stone dresser.

RIGHT: Alan Scott grinding flour with a hand-cranked mill (photo: Dina DuBois).

ROLLER MILLING

Roller milling has been the dominant technique for over a hundred years and is especially suited to making white flours, as there are many opportunities to separate the constituent parts of the grain. For roller milling the grain is tempered—stored until its moisture content is ideal for milling—so the kernels will break up in a predictable way. The first pass through the rollers is called the break, and the process of removing germ and bran starts here. Rollers squeeze the wheat germ into a little plug or flake which is then separated out.* Splinters of **bran** (the woody outer layer of the kernel) that are free of endosperm (the part of the kernel containing starch and most of the protein) are also separated out.

The grist passes on to a further series of rollers, now smooth, called reduction rolls. One roller in each pair is spinning at about two and a half times faster than its counter-

*Fresh, this separated germ is delicious: it is as sweet and buttery as a cookie. Unfortunately, it becomes rancid very quickly, starting in about three days if it is not refrigerated or vacuum packed.

part, but the mating surfaces are moving in the same direction. This shears and crushes the grain in a way similar to the action of a stone mill. The powdered endosperm is separated out in a series of bolting stages. Flour is produced at nearly every point in the process, but the properties of the flour from different stages differ in ways that can affect its eventual use. Although historically roller milling used to overheat the flour, inactivating the vitamins it contains, most modern milling machinery incorporates systems to avoid excessive flour heating.

White flour has for years been enriched with niacin, thiamin, riboflavin, and iron, and folic acid is now added to the list to reduce the incidence of neural tube birth defects in developing human embryos. (Folic acid and B vitamins have also been shown to reduce the risk of heart attack, at least in women.) Most roller-milled white flour also gets some added barley malt flour for

its amylase, a necessary enzyme for baking yeast-raised bread. Ironically, the mill feed (everything that is not flour or germ) left after milling has a higher percentage of protein and better-quality protein (higher lysine) than the flour does. It is sold as animal feed.

In all, about 72 percent of the original kernel is left in most of the white flour produced in the United States. That is called an extraction rate of 72 percent. Most American mills hold to that figure because that is the highest extraction that leaves essentially no bran or germ in the flour. In Europe, flours with higher extraction (containing more bran and germ) are commonly available; the most common French bread flour has an extraction rate of 75 to 78 percent, and has a creamier color than American unbleached flour. The protein content of the French bread flour is about 2 percent lower than American bread flour.

Flour Processing

Millers and bakers have long known that fresh flour is harder to work than aged flour. Fresh flour tends to make a dough that is "bucky"—too springy and elastic to knead and shape, and reluctant to rise. Several methods are used to change this and other characteristics of wheat flour. Some of these are "natural" and some involve chemical treatments.

WHITE FLOUR

I am going to explain a little about flour oxidation, a subject of some contention. Freshly milled flour has unoxidized flour protein, and commercial white flour (bleached or unbleached), when it is ready to use, has protein that is at least partially oxidized. (If it were completely oxidized, it would be burnt up—that's what burning is, oxidation.) Oxidation reduces the number of thiol groups on flour

ABOVE LEFT: *A parade of American stone mills, from small to enormous (photo: courtesy of Jansen Mills and Oven-crafters).*

ABOVE RIGHT: *An old stone mill in North Carolina. The grain falls from the square wooden chute into a hopper from which it is steadily shaken into the center of the upper stones (photo: Nancy Iott).*

proteins, very sticky areas that would otherwise interact adversely with the gluten-forming proteins, leading to bucky dough. These chemical groups can short-circuit the process that causes gluten to pull back into shape when it has been stretched. An excess of thiols can decrease wheat dough's great advantage over other kinds of dough—elasticity with extensibility — though the importance of this decrease is much less pronounced when dough is hand kneaded and slowly fermented.

Flour is intentionally oxidized to decrease the number of thiol groups present. Partial oxidation of flour can be either a natural process or the result of chemical bleaching and oxidizing. Flour proteins oxidize passively as flour is stored, which is how unbleached flour gets oxidized enough to be "good" for baking lofty loaves of bread. Commercially milled unbleached flour is therefore usually stored for three to eight weeks before it is used. This storage process is called sweating. Unfortunately, fats in the flour are oxidized at the same time—they become rancid. This isn't a problem for roller-milled white flour because it has a relatively low fat content. Roller-milled unbleached white flour is therefore quite stable when stored at room temperature and moderate humidity. Rancidity is a major problem for whole wheat flour and, to a lesser extent, for stone-ground white flour.

Big mills eliminate the storage phase for white flour by bleaching it at the mill or by adding latent oxidizers to oxidize it during kneading or even during baking. Mechanized bakeries can also oxidize doughs with vigorous mechanical kneading, which incorporates more air in the dough (hence more oxygen). This mechanical mixing is sometimes done to oxidize and condition dough to the point that it does not "need" to have a first rise (or fermentation) stage, which costs time and money for factory bakers. (Of course, lovers of tasty breads realize that fermentation is *good,* and that trying to reduce the time devoted to it is *bad*). All of the methods that oxidize flour proteins also oxidize the fats in the flour, which may have an adverse effect on flavor and even on health. Bleached white flour may also contain traces of many agents used to whiten and oxidize the grain. While some ingredients or residues may be listed on the label, most are not. Most home bakers prefer to avoid such flours altogether, and they should be avoided for making naturally leavened breads, as the bleach may affect the balance of the yeast and bacterial populations.*

WHOLE WHEAT FLOUR

For aged whole wheat flour there is a delicate balance between (favorable) oxidation of the gluten and excess (unfavorable) oxidation of wheat germ oils, or rancidity. This can only be partly controlled by refrigerating the flour, and that is one reason why it is often more convenient to grind this type of flour at home. Milled whole rye and whole corn meal are even more perishable than milled wheat because of their higher fat content.

While it is commonly known that whole wheat bread is usually not as light (does not rise as high) as white flour bread, this phenomenon is not perfectly understood. Some believe that sharp fragments of the hard, high-fiber bran puncture the gas cells of the rising dough, and this may be so. However,

*There are many bakers who do not feel as strongly about chemical treatment of flour as I do. For instance, you can read a defense of bleaching and oxidizing on page 56 of Shirley Corriher's book, *Cookwise*. She also gives separate descriptions of bleaches, dough oxidizers, and bromate dough conditioners. But you don't need them to make good bread, so why use them at all?

recent research indicates it is more likely that gas cells are pierced or deformed by tiny hairs on the surface of the bran particles, not by the bran particles themselves. For certain wheat strains, removing the bran fractions that contained these little barbs increased loaf volume by about 7 percent. When various bran fractions were added to sample doughs, the outermost bran layer (the outer pericarp, containing the silicon-rich epicarp hairs) had the most profound effect. Thus, pearling—or abrading—certain strains of wheat kernels before they are milled might produce a flour that has the same nutritional content of whole wheat flour but without an adverse effect on raising a dough. More research is under way.

RYE FLOUR

Most rye is roller milled, though stone milling on the industrial scale was utilized for rye longer than for wheat, into the 1920s in some countries. Because rye is so hygroscopic (prone toward taking on and holding water), the grain requires less tempering before it is milled. It does require testing of its enzyme content, as its baking quality is related to constituents that vary widely in different lots of grain; one of these is the starch-breaking enzyme, amylase. Other important constituents, pentosan and pentosanase (the enzyme that breaks down pentosans), also vary significantly from one sample of rye flour to another because of variations in growing conditions. Millers must test the chemical and mechanical characteristics of samples of rye before they are milled, and reject those that will not make good bread. Unsuitable grain is diverted to other uses, including animal feeds and al-

cohol production—the whiskey makers are not so choosy.

Rye flour is commercially ground to a range of colors and particle sizes, and the nomenclature is confusing. Commercial rye flour is generally not a whole-grain product: white-rye flour is from the center of the endosperm; cream- or light-rye flour includes the next layer; and dark-rye flour includes the outside of the endosperm. Milled rye is available as these types of flour, or as meal, which is coarser (fine, medium, coarse meal) and is ground from the whole kernel. The coarse grade of rye meal is often called pumpernickel flour. An even coarser grind (used for rye Vollkornbrot) is called rye chops or rye grits. Large mills use air separation techniques to vary the chemical makeup of rye flours as they are produced, by selecting out particles with different densities and sizes at particular stages of the milling process. This can affect the ash content of the flour markedly, which affects the vigor of natural fermentation as the flour is made into sourdough bread.

THE IMPORTANCE OF NATURAL FERMENTATION IN BAKING WITH RYE FLOUR

Many American amateur bakers have had trouble making satisfactory rye bread. The loaves either don't rise well or don't seem to hold their shape while baking. The structure of a cooled loaf of baked bread comes from its gelatinized **starch**, whether the bread is made from wheat, from rye, or from a mixture of the two. This gel forms when starch is heated to a critical temperature in the presence of water: at the **gelatinization** point the starch uncoils from its crystal structure, breaks out of its granule, and traps water in its "arms." Gelled starch is essentially dissolved in the water it has trapped, and is thus susceptible to attack by amylases—the enzymes that break down starch. Before gelatinization, only the starch damaged by milling can be attacked by amylase.

The reason that a sturdy structure of gelatinized starch can form and then stay intact until *wheat* bread has cooled is that most of the amylase in wheat dough is denatured (inactivated) by heat before the starch gelatinizes. *Wheat* amylases are not "heat-stable." *Rye* amylase, however, resists inactivation by heat to a much greater extent. It is so heat-stable that it is still active when the gelatinization temperature of rye starch is reached in the oven. This gelatinized starch is accessible to amylase, so continued enzyme action could have disastrous consequences for the structure of breads with a high rye flour percentage. The starch could be broken down to sugar and the loaf would flatten out.

Fortunately, the activity of rye amylase is strongly inhibited by the acid in naturally fermented doughs. That is why all traditional rye breads are made from sour doughs—the low pH of the dough protects the starch gels until the amylase is permanently denatured as the bread continues to bake to higher temperatures. The degree of amylase inhibition is somewhat dependent on the salt content of the dough. The degree of inhibition achieved at pH 4.0 in a salt-free dough is achieved at pH 4.4 in dough with 1.5 percent salt (these percentages are according to the baker's percentage system described in chapter 1; 1.5 to 2 percent salt is typical in home and commercially baked bread).

It is interesting that some of Europe's best bakers put a small percentage of rye flour in their sourdough country-style wheat breads. Although this is usually done for flavor, it is possible that the amylase in rye flour provides something of a fermentation boost to the wheat dough (by liberating more sugar), as long as the pH does not drop too low. This increases not only fermentation, but also crust browning if there is some increase in the sugar content of the dough as it is baked. European tests indicate that bread with a little rye in it has more volume and keeps better than a similar 100 percent wheat bread. This is in part because small amounts of added pentosans increase the effective strength of wheat flour, and may interfere with the process by which bread becomes stale.

Successful baking of wheat breads represents a balance between dough viscosity and dough elasticity. (Viscosity is technically "resistance to flow.") In rye dough, only the viscosity is of great importance, determining the structural strength of the risen loaf and the size of the loaf. However, there is an ideal viscosity: if viscosity is too low, the dough may be light but not be stable to handling. If it is too high, the dough may be stable, but the bread dense and the loaf volume low. Viscosity is sensitive to mechanical mixing, pH, temperature, and salt percentage. In practice, the ideal combination of these factors is achieved by trial and error. Certainly rye doughs should be kneaded less than wheat doughs.

ORGANIC FLOUR

Certified organic loaves are not only made of certified organic flour, but as Thom Leonard points out in the *Bread Baker's Guild Newsletter,* any other ingredients added and the premises where the loaves are made must meet certification criteria, which are subject to inspection. Certification comes from several "third party certifiers" who judge a food's qualification as organic. This involves approved insect and rodent control measures and record keeping to be sure that noncertified ingredients don't wander into the organic foods. For flour, no synthetic fertilizers or pesticides can be used, not only on that crop, but on the field in which it was grown for a specified number of prior years, and a soil improvement plan must be in place to maintain soil fertility. Subsequent storage and transportation also must meet criteria (to avoid contamination with residues from other lots of grain). The cost of keeping all these records is inevitably passed on in the price of the flour.

There are significant differences between bread that is *certified organic bread, bread made with organic ingredients,* or *bread made with organic flour and nonorganic ingredients.* The meaning of organic certification may change if the federal government gets more involved. The initial federal proposals would have meant a slackening of the "organic" definition.

American Flours and Their Counterparts

European authors frequently mention the differences between American and European flours, and the effects those differences have on baking techniques and on the breads produced. What are these differences?

BRAN AND MINERALS

Raymond Calvel points out several differences between North American bread flours and their European counterparts. One difference is a higher bran percentage in French flour, which gives the bread crumb a slightly creamy or bran-flecked appearance. Another is the slightly higher ash content (mineral content) of the European flour. Calvel says this small difference stimulates the growth of natural leaven cultures significantly, and can be recreated by adding some whole wheat flour to white flour leavens.

PROTEIN CONTENT AND BEHAVIOR

Another major difference is in the protein content. This is about 11.5 percent in French bread flour ("type 55"), and nearly 14 percent in American high-protein spring wheat bread flour. Such high-protein flour has a rising potential that is only fully realized with mechanical mixing, commercial yeast, and pan baking. The low ash content of American bread flour (which results in less vigorous fermentation) and high mechanical strength of the gluten make typical American bread flours less suitable for the long-fermentation techniques and hearth baking that make for better taste and texture. This is not because of a difference in flour "quality," but because of its "qualities," such as gluten extensibility, dough tolerance, and so forth.

North American wheat growers and millers have for years primarily tried to meet the requirements of bakers of pan bread and soft hearth breads with similar characteristics to those of pan breads (like supermarket "Italian loaves"): fine crumb, thin flexible crust, no bursting of the loaf. These breads benefit from strong gluten, high protein content, and high water absorption. These characteristics do not make for good European-style open crumb, crusty breads.

Another area where French and American flours often differ is in gluten behavior. You know that gluten is formed by the union of glutenin and gliadin, its precursors, and that the relative amounts of these proteins can vary in strains and lots of wheat. Laboratory research has shown that glutenin and gliadin are responsible for different aspects of gluten's behavior, with variations in their relative proportions affecting gluten significantly. Gluten exhibits viscoelastic behavior in part because gliadin imparts viscosity and extensibility, while glutenin imparts elasticity and strength. Some French flours have a glutenin:gliadin ratio that makes for especially good thin-film extensibility (stretch without rupture).

DAMAGED STARCH CONTENT

Some of a grain kernel's starch granules are damaged (ripped open) during milling, making the starch inside available to wetting and therefore to amylase digestion. This is fortunate, as amylase digestion of this damaged starch provides sugar for fermentation. As starch is cleaved, however, the action of amylase also produces dextrins, a class of polysaccharides that are quite hygroscopic—they attract and hold on to water. All flour contains damaged starch but durum flours and American bread flours have a great deal. Although this high damaged-starch content has some real advantages (providing food for fermentation), the dextrins from that damaged starch also make it difficult to achieve the really crisp, thin crusts preferred, for in-

stance, in Latin American baking. I lived in Brazil as a child, and I have found it hard to make the typical Brazilian breakfast roll of my youth with American flour.

Differences in protein levels and qualities and differences in damaged starch content are two challenges that American mills (working with wheat breeders and growers) must face in attempting to make flours that will perform better in the varied uses to which flour is put internationally. Adequate hydration of the high protein in American bread flour requires more water in the dough (baker's percentage over 70 percent, while French dough is typically 60 to 65 percent and Latin American dough is about 58 percent). Raymond Calvel cautions that high water content may lead to a ". . . somewhat mediocre bread, with a thin and softer crust, with a tendency to soften. The crust may be rubbery to the touch and the teeth, leading to a lessening of the flavor (quality) of the bread" (see bibliography). In actuality, many people *like* bread with those characteristics, which are typical of some types of well-made Italian bread. But it can be frustrating to try to make a great loaf of hearth bread with a flour that is not suited to it.

Gas Production

Gas *production* in yeasted dough is about the same for wheat and rye, a little less for rye. The significant difference in rising potential for these two kinds of flour (in pure wheat or pure rye doughs) is due to wheat gluten's gas *retention* quality. Pure rye doughs retain gas fairly well in the first half of proofing, less well in the second half. They lose much of the rest of it early in the baking cycle (at 95

SPEAKING *for* WHOLE GRAINS

Although refined flours have been subjected to a phenomenal amount of research on behalf of the baking industry, and have been popularized by over a century of promotion by both individual bakers and the industry, the skillful baker who produces delicious, light whole-grain loaves offers his customers a wonderful gift: a pleasant way to better health.

With its full compliment of vitamins, minerals, soluble and insoluble fiber, antioxidants and other beneficial phytochemicals, the whole-grain bread naturally provides nutrients that, day-to-day, protect against diseases that have become chronic in modern society: diabetes, several cancers, diverticular disease, and cardiovascular problems.

Bread made from whole wheat provides significant amounts of essential minerals—iron, zinc, magnesium, manganese, selenium, and some calcium. In the past there have been concerns that the presence of bran acids in unrefined wheat could make minerals less available. Recent research shows that dough fermentation unlocks minerals from acid bonds. Moreover, it seems likely that phytic acid actually offers its own protection against certain cancers, and, in addition, helps to stabilize insulin levels.

Over the years, government authorities have acknowledged diseases caused by the deficiencies of white flour, and have required one and then another vitamin—now up to four, and one mineral—to be added back. To make enriched flour, manufacturers spray white flour with replicas of these four vitamins and iron. (Even there, because of the poor baking quality of bleached flour, artisan bakers tend to prefer unbleached flours and these may not be enriched even in so small a way.) Bleached or unbleached, however, enriched or not, white flour is mostly starch. There is a little protein, it's quality impoverished by the removal of the potent germ. Gluten flour is white flour one step more refined. Touted for high protein content, gluten is so deficient in the essential amino acid lysine that its protein usability score is only 28 percent.

—*Alan Scott*

degrees Fahrenheit, 35 degrees Celsius), so oven spring does not occur. This loss of gas doesn't happen with well-made wheat dough until it is about half-baked (dough temperature 125 to 165 degrees Fahrenheit, 50 to 75 Celsius). By that time oven spring is complete. (Oven spring is a relatively sudden increase in the size of a loaf of bread as it is baking. More about that in chapter 5.)

Nutritional Characteristics of Flours

Though whole wheat flour contains more vitamins than unenriched white flour, the availability of those vitamins is affected by the way dough is prepared. Bran increases bowel transit speed, and some of the vitamins will be locked in insoluble, indigestible bran unless they have been extracted by long fermentation.

A normal constituent of wheat bran is phytic acid (also called phytate or phytin), a kind of storage molecule for phosphorus in plants, which can interfere with calcium absorption under some circumstances: diets deficient in calcium and high in whole wheat products made with commercial yeast have led to epidemics of rickets when other sources of calcium were lacking, as in wartime. Because both wheat and yeast have an enzyme that breaks down phytate (the enzyme is called phytase), and because that enzyme is most active in dough between pH 4.3 and 4.6, prolonged fermentation with mixed cultures (an acid medium) frees calcium and phosphorus from the storage molecule and makes them available. According to one study, fast fermentation by commercial yeast left 90 percent of phytate intact, while all phytate was removed by the end of natural fermentation.

Although it has been stated widely that the phytate effect on calcium absorption is offset by using coarsely ground whole wheat flour when baking with commercial yeast the opposite is true. Fine ground flour has smaller bran particles, the phytate is in the bran, and it is therefore more accessible to fermentation organisms when the particles are small. Rye flour also contains phytate, and again it is completely broken down by natural fermentation.

The color compounds that are in red wheat but not in white wheat (and which have recently been bred out of some high-protein hard red wheats, producing grain now widely available as Kansas hard white winter wheat) are not the same as phytic acid. These color compounds are more complicated in structure. If they have any dietary effect, it is to compound with wheat proteins and make them slightly less absorbable.

The chief nutritional benefits of whole grains are their fiber content (three times greater than white flour), mineral content, and oil content (including antioxidants). Since the fiber in bran is partially insoluble (which promotes bowel health by decreasing transit time and nourishing beneficial microbes), it should be supplemented by sources higher in soluble fiber (which helps reduce cholesterol absorption and controls the rate of sugar absorption after a meal), such as legumes and fruits.

A mix of naturally fermented bread and other grain foods, beans, fruit, and vegetables will guarantee a full spectrum of amino acids in the diet, even without protein from animal sources. Fermented foods are an important source of vitamin B12 and biotin in a vegetarian diet.

What Kind of Flour to Buy

Despite my warning earlier in the chapter that I wasn't going to tell you what kind of flour to buy, I think you now have enough information to make your own informed decisions. I want to give you some idea where to start, though, based on what you know.

WHITE ALL-PURPOSE FLOUR

You don't want to make naturally fermented bread out of bleached flour (because bleach may inhibit dough bacteria, and because unbleached flour works as well or better), so if you are going to use white flour it should be marked "unbleached." Most "unbleached all-purpose flour" will work fine for hearth bread, if you use a fairly low hydration rate (baker's percentage of water) of 62 to 66 percent. Some national brands of unbleached flour often say something like "Better for Bread" on the bag, and have a protein percentage of approximately 12. Most regional unbleached all-purpose flours (such as King Arthur or Old Mill) are about the same. For example, King Arthur is 11.7 percent protein. By avoiding bleached flour altogether, you will avoid the Southern all-purpose flours, all bleached, that only have about 9 percent protein—they won't make good bread.*

WHITE BREAD FLOUR

Any white flour labled "bread flour" will have 12 to 13 percent protein. Bread flour is usually unchlorinated, but it may contain other bleaching or oxidizing agents—you may have to ask by calling or writing the mill. If you can't find out from your mill, you may want to buy organic bread flour from Giusto's (see 41) or a local mill (through a health food store), or unbleached, unbromated (but not organic) bread flour from a supplier such as King Arthur (King Arthur Special).

Bread flour is stronger than you need for hand-kneaded hearth breads. You may want to use it together with all-purpose flour, though, if you knead by machine. It also makes sense to use it with rye flour, so the pentosans in the rye can supplement those in the wheat and the extra wheat gluten will partly correct for the lack of gluten in the rye. Adding bread flour (or **vital wheat gluten**, a manufactured product made by drying and grinding gluten that is water-extracted from wheat flour, or **high-gluten flour**, which is a high-protein fractionated flour produced in roller mills) to whole wheat recipes does not work quite as well as it does for rye recipes. Lack of gluten (because some of the volume of the flour is taken up by bran that does not contribute to gluten formation) is not the only reason whole wheat bread does not rise as high as white bread. Adding high protein white flour will make whole wheat breads lighter, but not necessarily *light*.

WHOLE WHEAT FLOUR AND RYE FLOUR

For bread, you want your whole wheat flour to be made from hard winter or spring wheat, either red or one of the new hard white varieties. Because you want whole wheat flour to be fresh (not rancid) you want

*Many people don't realize that almost all health food/whole food stores either carry or will order organic white all-purpose flour (with or without restored germ) from regional mills. All organic flours cost more (usually twice as much). Store personnel can ask the mill what the protein content of the flour is. Regional mills also make organic white "bread" flour, with a protein content of about 13 percent.

to buy a local brand, and buy it where they sell a lot of it—preferably where it is kept refrigerated. That usually means buying it at a health food/whole food store—this is not an item to buy at the supermarket, unless there are plenty of bakers in your neighborhood. That is true for all whole grain flours—rye flour, fresh whole corn meal, and the like. Refrigerate any whole grain flour you keep longer than a few days.

MILLING YOUR OWN

Making your own flour is a great way to be sure of fresh flour. Many home mills may be adjusted to make flour, meal, or chops of any consistency, from any grain. For instance, I grind half of the rye in my bread fine, and make the rest very coarse. I add this coarsely ground grain to my sponge before I mix my dough, so it has plenty of time to take on water to become chewy and nutty when baked. I often make bread that has predominently unbleached white all-purpose flour, a moderate amount of King Arthur white whole wheat flour (because I like its flavor), and plenty of fresh cracked wheat berries that I make in my mill; I have a heavy-duty mixer with a mill attachment, but small, free-standing mills are widely available as well.

GIUSTO'S SPECIALTY FOODS

South San Francisco, California

They see the baking industry from the baker's perspective

∼

GIUSTO'S IS A MECCA for bakers in the Western states, so of course I wanted to visit. Not only do they manufacture and/or stock every kind of ingredient a baker might need, but they will create special flours to suit the requirements of their customers. They see the baking industry from the baker's perspective because this family company grew out of a bakery and retail health food business started in 1940 in San Francisco. There is even a painting on Al Giusto's wall of his grandmother baking in an outdoor brick oven at the old family place in Stockton around the turn of the century. Eventually, the whole grain bakery operation became a relatively small part of the company, important mainly as a test lab for their grain products. Although for some time they have done custom packaging of baking mixes under a variety of brand names, Giusto's is now in the start-up phase of a new business in mail-order sales and wholesaling of smaller quantities (five- and ten-pound bags) of specialty flours and other products under the Giusto's Vita-Grain label.

Giusto's contracts directly with farmers in several Western states for the production of organic and Number 1 commercial grains, which are delivered to contract mills in Utah, Oregon, and California in addition to their mill, warehouse, distribution center, and packaging operation in South San Francisco. Samples of every lot are kept and tested, and lab testing includes not only protein, ash, and farinograph, but also "functionalities": how each particular strain of wheat or batch of flour performs in bread production. Considerable risk is involved for both the farmer and the miller in pursuing such high-quality grains, especially organic ones. Changes in the weather and other factors may make the wheat crop poor in tonnage or in quality. Since the Giustos will only mill Number 1 grain, this may mean that the crop will need to go to another market or product at a lower price.

From the San Francisco warehouse, trucks go in all directions with organic and commercial-grade flours, grains, prepared grain mixes, seeds, dried peas and beans, spices, salt, sweeteners, oils, and dried fruit. The price list is twenty-seven pages long, and Giusto's offers sixteen choices of unbleached white wheat flour alone, plus custom flours. Included are flours with extraction rates, protein content, and ash content similar to French bread flours. All these flours are from their own or contracted

GIUSTO'S
SPECIALTY FOODS

*No flours stay
in Giusto's
warehouses more
than twenty
days*

~

mills and are delivered fresh, after a two-week aging or sweating period. Most of this is roller-milled, but the company has air-cooling equipment in all mills, so the typical temperature of just-milled flour is only about 90 degrees Fahrenheit (32 degrees Celsius). Some products are stone ground or hammer milled. No flours stay in Giusto's warehouses more than twenty days, and most is sold in fifty-pound bags on pallets. None of the grain or flour is fumigated—instead, a centrifugal fan machine is used to smash the insect eggs that are always present in grain products. The grain is blown with air at every step to remove dust, and the collected dust is sold as hog feed.

Giusto's also maintains a bakery. Although Keith Giusto's preference is for crusty breads, both Keith and Al are proud of a very sour nine-grain bread from their bakery. This is produced from grain that is first sprouted in water for forty-eight hours, then loosely ground in a sausage or coffee mill to make a coarse paste that is made into dough with flour and a sour culture. The ingredients are similar to the Austrian sunflower bread at Café Beaujolais, made with seeds and grain soaked overnight. Giusto's bread is something that would make a great sandwich, while the bread from Café Beaujolais is almost a chewy meal in itself. (You can read more about Café Beaujolais in chapter 8.)

What is unusual about Giusto's? The range of products they sell, the concentration on organic grains, and the attention that is paid, at every step, to make sure that grains and flours are shipped in peak condition. I can only hope that in the future a similar range of products will be easily available in all parts of the country.

CHAPTER THREE

LEAVENS *and* DOUGHS

Most kinds of bread are meant to rise: the structure of dough is intended to trap gas that is generated in it, and it is gas that makes dough rise. **Leavens** are the ingredients that make the gas. Pancakes, muffins, and quick breads use **chemical leavens**, such as baking powder or soda, while loaf breads and some raised flatbreads, like pizza, use living leavens, all of which contain some type of yeast. The most basic and original form of leaven is a "**natural leaven**," which contains only native yeasts—I am going to talk about natural leavens first and in detail. The more common methods of leavening (with commercial yeast) will come at the end of the chapter, for comparison.

Yeasts

Yeasts are single-celled fungi, part of the Eukarya (algae, fungi, and protozoa), organisms that have true nuclei containing DNA or-ganized into chromosomes. Once thought to be simplified plants without chlorophyll, fungi are now thought to be more closely related to simple animals. Yeasts are widely distributed in nature,* but certain strains of yeast are also grown industrially. Those I will call "commercial yeast," to differentiate them from wild or native yeasts. Commercial bread yeasts are derived from the yeast used to make ale.

The basic metabolism in yeast cells is useful to bakers: these cells convert carbohydrates into equal amounts of carbon dioxide and alcohol, making other organic molecules as byproducts. This conversion of carbohydrates is called fermentation. Yeasts are self-replicating and prolific. Given the right conditions and enough time the cells will double in number and keep on doubling until their waste products (alcohol and acids, predominantly) begin to poison them, or they run out of food. Bakers manipulate dough in order to encourage this fecundity.

Saccharomyces exiguus—also called *Torulopsis holmii* and *Candida holmii*—is a common yeast in natural leavens, but has also been found in cucumber brine, soil, sauerkraut, grape must, buttermilk, and the gut of insect larvae.

43

Natural Leavens and Their Differences from Commercial Yeast

Natural leavens are stable combinations of a native yeast and one or more strains of beneficial bacteria. They go by many names: starter, sourdough, barm, ferment, *levain* (French), *biga* (Italian), *lievito naturale* (Italian), *desem* (Flemish) and others. The term "natural leaven" is slightly misleading, because the process of fermentation is always essentially natural when it is performed by living yeasts and bacteria. I chose to write "natural leaven" because it is less awkward than "mixed ferment cultured from the environment and sustained with repeated inoculation." The term differentiates these continuously propagated leavens from commercial yeast, which is what I want to do. For our purposes here it also avoids the more specific connotations of sourdough, *levain,* and other common terms that are associated with particular styles of bread.

Although using a natural leaven has the reputation of a being a time-intensive process, the actual *work* is only modestly greater. It is the time span in which that work is done that is increased. The dough-making process is slowed down so that sometimes one is thinking of days and hours instead of the hours and minutes that define baking with commercial yeast. Natural fermentation is more gradual, and the results are distinctive and (to my taste, anyway) superior. The higher acid content and more complete fermentation of naturally raised bread bestows other benefits, beyond flavor. The most important of these are the nutritional advantages that fermenting yields in whole grain breads, better resistance to mold or bacterial spoilage without additives, stronger crust and crumb structure (crumb is the cellular inner part of the bread), and rich crust color.

"Natural leavens" are not identical. For one thing, they can contain a variety of strains of yeast and bacteria. For another thing, bakers use a number of terms for the various stages of natural leavens. For instance, there is a leaven that we keep from one baking to the next. In France that is a piece of today's batch of dough that is used to start tomorrow's bread, and it is called the *chef*. Here, it is more typical for a home baker to maintain a leaven culture for weeks, months, or years by putting it in the refrigerator between uses. Though most of us refer to that carry-over leaven as the starter, that word is also used for a leaven that is in the process of development, as in "I began a new starter last week from organic rye flour," and "starter" is also used by many to describe the leaven that is to be incorporated into a dough, as in "My country wheat bread contains 48 percent starter."

There has been a spirited debate about natural leaven terminology in rec.food.sourdough (the Usenet newsgroup) with no clear resolution. The lack of resolution has several causes:

- Any ripe leaven or starter is essentially the same as any other ripe leaven that contains the same leaven culture, regardless of the baker's intent in making them. The hydration may be a little different, but if they are both ripe, the bacterial and yeast populations in them are at peak and perfectly capable of either

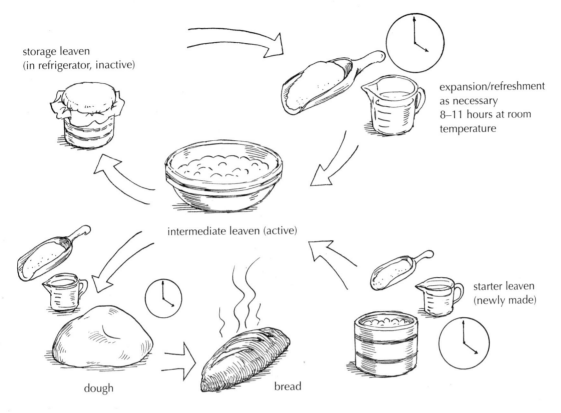

storage leaven
(in refrigerator, inactive)

expansion/refreshment
as necessary
8–11 hours at room
temperature

intermediate leaven (active)

starter leaven
(newly made)

dough

bread

Natural ferments are continuously re-inoculated in the leaven cycle.

raising a dough or inoculating another leaven or starter.

- The difference between two such leavens is thus in the mind of the baker: "What did I plan to do with the leaven when I made it?"
- Bakers tend to use the terminology they got from the person or books that taught them to bake, and every book seems to use these terms differently.
- Bakers are as inclined to quibble as any other group of technicians.

I am therefore going to try to be internally consistent in terminology: In *this* book I will refer to a "storage leaven" when speaking of a leaven that is saved from one bake to the next, and to "leaven sponge" when I mean an intermediate leaven—that is, a mixture of flour and water, inoculated with a leaven culture, incubated to ripeness, and destined either to be expanded into an even greater volume of leaven sponge by stages or to be incorporated directly into a dough. These are not universal, accepted terms—I am just using them for clarity in this book. On the other hand, "sponge" is an accepted term in baking, and refers to a fermented slurry of flour and water, something that is thinner than a dough, but full of gas.

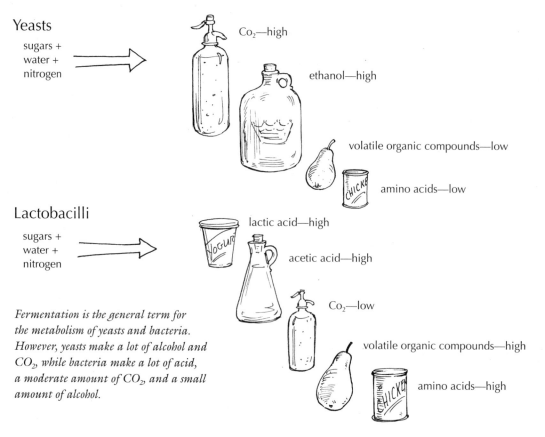

Yeasts

sugars +
water +
nitrogen

→

CO_2—high

ethanol—high

volatile organic compounds—low

amino acids—low

Lactobacilli

sugars +
water +
nitrogen

→

lactic acid—high

acetic acid—high

CO_2—low

volatile organic compounds—high

amino acids—high

Fermentation is the general term for the metabolism of yeasts and bacteria. However, yeasts make a lot of alcohol and CO_2, while bacteria make a lot of acid, a moderate amount of CO_2, and a small amount of alcohol.

*Brewing combines yeast with hops, which have antibacterial properties. Bakers one hundred and fifty years ago used to propagate their yeast cultures (derived from ale yeasts) in hop water to avoid sour flavor in delicate doughs.

All natural leavens are mixtures of wild yeast and acid-producing, acid-tolerant bacteria (similar to but not the same as the ones in yogurt) that are preserved from one dough to the next by feeding them a mixture of flour and water. Lush bacterial cultures take part in fermentation, breaking down sugars from the flour and converting them to acetic acid (vinegar), lactic acid, and other flavor compounds that are present in much lower amounts in bread made with commercial yeast and its very low levels of bacteria. Commercial yeast is grown in the near absence of bacteria, on a diet of molasses. It is descended from brewery yeast, passed through thousands of generations of controlled selection. This selection

leaves it specialized for a narrow range of fermentation characteristics that favor rapid gas production over flavor production or other possibly desirable qualities (resistance to bread spoilage, for instance). Although a wide range of properties are available in yeast sold to commercial bakers for specific applications, only a few different types of yeast are available in retail outlets such as grocery stores.*

A small population of bacteria is present in most packages of commercial yeast (unavoidably), but not enough to produce much acid in the short fermentation times that yeasted bread methods allow. Another difference between commercial yeast and natural leavens, aside from the lower bacterial count in com-

DON'T ADD SUGAR!

Most bakers know that natural leavens do not require and can in fact be inhibited by added sugar, but few people know that it is not necessary to add sugar to doughs leavened with commercial yeast. The supposed need for sugar in yeasted bread is a legacy of the faster-is-better fallacy of breadmaking. All easily available flours have enough amylase and enough damaged starch for either natural leavens or commercial yeasts to do their work. Because excess sugar dehydrates yeast cells, there are some situations where omitting or reducing sugar will improve the performance of commercial yeast. This is why recipes for sweet yeasted doughs call for more yeast than one would otherwise expect to use.

mercial yeast, is the concentration of the yeast cells. The concentration of yeast cells in commercial cake or dried yeast is much higher per volume or per weight than it is in any natural leaven. That is the biggest reason that a small cube or envelope of commercial yeast will raise the same two loaves of bread that will be raised by more than a pound of ripe leaven sponge. Does this mean that the individual cells in the leaven are weak or lazy? No.

Later in this chapter I am going to explain how to start and maintain a leaven culture. The yeast and bacteria in natural leavens are considered native or wild because the cultures soon become dominated by organisms from the environment. These leaven organisms are not refined in a microbiology laboratory or a giant food factory. Instead, you nourish them in your kitchen—the same place the culture will be used to raise bread. A new natural leaven can be made whenever needed, although that process takes about a week, requiring a few minutes of work every few days. Some bakers maintain natural leavens in

a relatively liquid state, while others maintain a doughy leaven with a high flour content. Once the microbiological makeup of a leaven is well established, it doesn't matter much (in terms of the bread produced) which you do, although it does change the process you use and the timing of the various stages of production.

Because the mineral content of whole grain flours is higher than that of refined flours, many bakers maintain leavens used every day with whole grain flour, even if another type of flour (unbleached white, for example) is added to make up the dough. The higher vitamin and mineral content of whole grain flour has been shown to make a more vigorous leaven. Rye flour is especially useful in guaranteeing a strong leaven, and improves the flavor of many breads. The natural microflora on rye berries and flours is quite diverse, and rye flour generally has a high ash (mineral) content. This leaven vigor is a drawback for those who only bake occasionally, as the storage leaven become overripe more quickly, even when refrigerated. That can be corrected by making the storage leaven stiffer (more flour) or by using white flour in the storage leaven, adding whole grain flour as leaven sponges are made.

The conditions under which a culture is developed and then maintained can select out strains of yeast and bacteria that have special characteristics, and the typical yeasts present in different locations also vary somewhat in their properties and their interactions with lactobacilli. This kind of co-evolution makes some natural leavens remarkably stable when regularly maintained. The more regular and consistent the maintenance, the more predictable the rising power, microbiological composition, acid balance (acetic/lactic), and acid production will be.

Representative Natural Leaven Breads

Since many people new to natural leavens would like to bake San Francisco sourdough, Desem bread, or German rye bread, let's look at some of their characteristics, as determined by their leavens, ingredients, and processes.

SAN FRANCISCO SOURDOUGH

Because San Francisco sourdough bread has a worldwide reputation, plenty of research has been done on the leaven cultures and baking techniques that are used to make it. Of course, research can't (and probably won't!) dispel the belief that it cannot be made anywhere else. I say belief, because it is hard to prove or disprove the uniqueness of San Francisco sourdough—the yeast species and bacte-

rial species that make up this culture are found all over the world and are in fact commonly found together, so that part of the process, anyway, is not unique. Who is to say what San Francisco sourdough even is? In 1997, a bread from the La Brea Bakery in Los Angeles was judged to be the best bread sold in San Francisco, narrowly beating out the bread from the Acme Baking Company for the first time (for a profile of Acme, see p. 89). To the extent that there is a recognizable San Francisco sourdough, all I feel safe stating is that it is a very-low-pH hearth bread (quite acid) made with white high-protein flour, in San Francisco!

Because of its metabolic preferences, the yeast strain that dominates most San Francisco sourdough cultures (*Candida milleri*) cannot fully utilize all of the sugars in the dough. It is, however, much more tolerant of acetic acid (which is a natural "antibiotic") than other yeasts. (Most yeasts are tolerant of moderately acid environments, but remain sensitive to acetic acid.) Meanwhile, the bacterial strain in that leaven prefers a type of sugar that the *C. milleri* does *not* use, maltose; it actively transports maltose into the cell and excretes glucose, which is then used by the yeast. The presence of so much glucose in the sponge actually inhibits the ability of competing bacterial species to utilize maltose, favoring the growth of *Lactobacillus sanfranciscensis,* the San Francisco bacterium. *L. sanfranciscensis* is a prolific acetic acid producer, and since *C. milleri* is more acetic-acid tolerant than other yeasts, *C. milleri* and *L. sanfranciscensis* thrive together.

The rising power of the San Francisco culture is less than that of commercial yeast, and less than that of some other natural leavens, but bakers compensate for this characteristic by increasing fermentation time and proof time. San Francisco sourdough bread is usually made of high-protein (strong) wheat and the modest rising power of the culture has a hard time overcoming the power of this gluten. The long time required for the dough to rise encourages acid production, so the finished bread has a pH of 3.9 (very acid). It contains a great deal of lactic acid and about twenty times as much acetic acid as conventional yeasted bread, which has a pH of nearly 6 (a pH of 7 is neutral).

DESEM BREAD

Desem is a Flemish word for a natural leaven—apparently a slang or cant term only used by bakers and thus not in Flemish or Dutch dictionaries. Regardless of its origins, Desem became the name of a superb kind of naturally fermented whole wheat bread produced for many years at the Lima bakery in Belgium. Two Americans, Hy Lerner and Paul Petrofsky, went there to learn how to make it, brought the technique back to Massachusetts, and started The Baldwin Hill Bakery. Since then, under the influence of the *Laurel's Kitchen Bread Book*, the Desem process has spread across the country, producing a whole grain bread with mild acidity, great flavor, and great keeping qualities.

Desem bread is as distinctive as San Francisco sourdough. The yeast strains that predominate in Desem cultures have large and active cells. Their growth is favored over competing yeast and bacterial strains by maintenance of a stiff starter in cool but vigorous fermentation, which also keeps acid production relatively low. Desem cultures are always started from fresh organic wheat flour. Thus, Desem is a type of natural leaven that maintains a close connection between the farm, the grain, and the finished loaf. The Desem dough itself is also made with fresh whole wheat flour, which by its nature will not be as mechanically strong as white flour or aged whole wheat flour, regardless of its protein content.

Desem dough is fermented slowly at a low temperature, then proofed at an elevated temperature (95 degrees Fahrenheit, 35 degrees Celsius). This produces a bread pH of about 4.2, much more acidic than commercially yeasted dough but without a pronounced acid flavor in the finished bread. The flavor is nutty and sweet, but not cloying. The rapid proof also prevents the loaves from going flat, even though the gluten in fresh flour is weak. Winter wheat flours of intermediate protein content, which are often richer in flavor than higher-protein wheat (and more like the wheat historically grown in Europe) are adequate for whole wheat bread dough. For reasons discussed in chapter 1, bread made from fresh flour will never rise as much as bread made from aged flour, and bread made from whole wheat flour will not rise as far as bread made from white flour. That said, what difference does lightness in bread finally make? Supermarket bread is as light as a feather and insipid, while great whole wheat bread is more dense but wonderful. Leavens are a tool to raise bread, but it is important to define the goals of your work before you start!

RYE BREAD

My mother's mother's mother was the daughter of a German baker in New Jersey. I

CHARACTERISTICS *of* SOME
NATURALLY LEAVENED BREAD PROCESSES

San Francisco Sourdough

1. All wheat
2. Low bran content, high-gluten white flour
3. Long leaven stages, short dough fermentation stage, very long proof (up to 8 hours)
4. High acid content, low pH, strong sour flavor

Desem

1. All wheat
2. Moderate gluten whole wheat flour, preferably fresh
3. Long, cool fermentation stage, short warm proof stage (1–1¹/₂ hours)
4. Moderate acid content, moderate pH, moderate sour flavor, strong wheat flavor

Pain au levain

1. All wheat
2. High bran, moderate gluten white flour
3. Moderate duration leaven stages, short dough fermentation, long proof stage (4 hours)
4. Moderate acid content, moderate sour flavor

Sourdough rye

1. Usually 30–70% rye, 70–30% wheat content
2. Contains dark or light rye flour; the structure of the dough comes from the viscosity of rye pentosans as well as any gluten contained in the wheat flour that is added
3. Moderate duration leaven, fermentation, and proof stages
4. Moderate acid content, moderate pH, moderate sour flavor, moderate rye flavor

Rye Vollkornbrot

1. All rye
2. Made of whole rye flour or coarse rye meal
3. Long leaven and fermentation stages
4. High acid content, low pH, strong sour flavor, strong rye flavor

think that is the right number of generations. That half of my ancestry is entirely German, that's for sure. I know that some of them were bakers, some were machinists, and most of them could sing. It's fun for me to sit here at my laptop computer and think about my ancestors who made great rye bread (for I am sure they did) before Louis Pasteur explained the process they had followed for generations. Atavism is "the reappearance of a characteristic in an organism after several generations of absence . . ." (*American Heritage Dictionary*), and that certainly is the word that applies to me. I like nothing better than to spend a day in my metalshop, taking breaks when I mix up a batch of bread or feed the fire in my oven. Maybe the singing just skipped a few more generations.

German and other Central European and Scandinavian bakers draw a distinction between their sourdough processes for wheat and for rye breads, even when the same organisms are present in the starters. Perhaps a brief review of the last chapter will help: wheat has strong and plentiful gluten that traps gas well over a broad range of pH and holds it until the baking dough reaches 150 degrees Fahrenheit/65 degrees Celsius in the oven. The lightness of wheat bread (white, whole wheat, or with less than 20 percent rye) is thus dependent on gluten and the gas-producing power of the leaven used. The acid content of wheat bread affects its flavor more than it affects its baking qualities. Rye flour does not have strong or abundant gluten, and dough containing more than 20 percent rye flour relies on the viscosity of starches and pentosans for most of its gas trapping and structure. Because

of rye's low gelatinization temperature, rye dough's structure begins to be lost at a lower temperature during baking, and remains weak longer into cooling, so loaves may collapse. Rye flour contains a lot of amylase that could break starches down as the bread is baked, leaving the dough sticky and too weak to support the loaf; this rye amylase is inactivated at any pH below 4.5. Naturally fermented rye dough is thus protected against starch degradation in the oven. Naturally fermented high-percentage rye bread is lighter, more mold-resistant and flavorful, and has better crumb elasticity (better starch swelling) than high-percentage rye bread raised with commercial yeast and no added acid.

Most German rye bread has at least 30 percent rye (sometimes 100 percent rye) and is thus dependent on acidification of the dough by a sourdough addition to control amylase activity and preserve dough structure. In most German bakeries, a fairly high proportion of the total weight of rye flour used (up to 60 percent) is involved in the acidic pre-fermentation (leaven sponge) stages leading to the fabrication of a final dough. Although German bakers often do make "sourdough" wheat bread, it typically contains only 1 to 5 percent of a very acid starter, for flavor, and is raised with commercial yeast.

It is interesting that in many German and Russian bakeries, up to 30 percent of the flour used in pre-fermentation is added in the form of ground up stale bread. Aside from the potential for recycling a waste product, this makes it possible to intensify dough acidity as needed.

The Biology of Fermentation

I don't want to overwhelm you with science, nor do I want to frustrate any interest you have in understanding basic processes by glossing over them. What I am going to try to do, therefore, is give you a reasonable review of the science of natural ferments, and no more. I will let the bibliography point the way to resources for further exploration, for those inclined in that direction. Those with a technical bent should also read the conversation with Michael Gänzle in the "Baker's Resource" in the back of the book.

MICROBIAL HEALTH AND REPRODUCTION

Controlled natural fermentation is achieved by inoculating dough with a large dose of organisms so that competing organisms cannot catch up under the prevailing conditions (temperature, osmotic strength, pH, salinity, etc.). For example, a San Francisco sourdough starter studied by Sugihara and Kline went from 3 million yeast cells and 86 million bacteria per gram to 18 million yeast cells and 1,650 million bacterial cells in seven hours. The key general principle is the same for both yeast and bacteria: the development of a ripe leaven is dependent much more on time and temperature than on the size of the inoculation. When a new leaven is inoculated with an established, inactive leaven, there is a period of no growth (the lag phase) followed by a period of exponential growth (the logarithmic phase). If the size of the inoculation is decreased by one half (say, from 40 percent of the final weight to 20 percent), the time from inoculation to full populations of bacterial and yeast cells (the static

*The amount of CO_2 produced by sourdough bacteria is significant: satisfactory leavened bread can be made without yeast—any yeast, wild or commercial—if fermentation conditions are carefully controlled to encourage bacterial gas production.

phase) is increased by one generation time. For sourdough bacteria under optimal conditions, this is a delay of about one hour, as the generation time of these bacteria is about one hour. For sourdough yeasts, the delay caused by halving the inoculation is about two hours—two hours is a typical generation time for yeasts under bakery conditions with temperatures in the mid-70s Fahrenheit. Contrast that with the effect of a change of only 8 degrees Fahrenheit (4 degrees Celsius) as a culture is overheated. Changing dough temperature from 82 to 90 degrees Fahrenheit (28 to 32 degrees Celsius) will double the time for achieving a static population of yeasts.

Some leavens contain one yeast species and one or two bacterial species, while others have more than one yeast and more than one bacterial strain. (A German rye-based culture contained four yeast and fourteen bacterial species, thirteen of them lactobacilli!) In general, the number of bacterial species in a leaven will decrease as it is continuously maintained over time. When cultures are fermented at higher temperatures, nonpathogenic acid-tolerant contaminants can intrude and dominate, affecting taste. This can spoil an improperly stored leaven, but it will not happen in a dough in the brief time that dough is in fermentation. At a symposium on natural leavens, Dr. Sugihara, who participated in the characterization of the flora of San Francisco sourdough and several other cultures, was asked whether natural sourdough cultures could be contaminated with commercial yeast. His reply was no, not if you have a stable culture that is continuously maintained with the same conditions and ingredients.*

THE BREAD BUILDERS

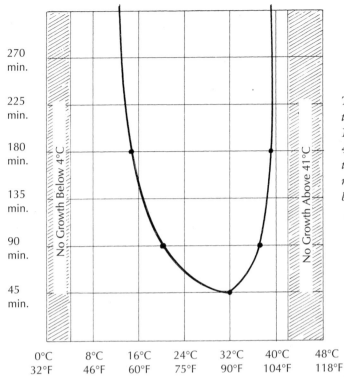

This chart shows the relationship between temperature and growth for L. san-franciscensis. *Note that the shortest possible doubling time is 45 minutes at 90° F (32° C). The optimum temperature for fermentation (as opposed to reproduction) is slightly higher (93° F or 34° C) but the curve is the same.*

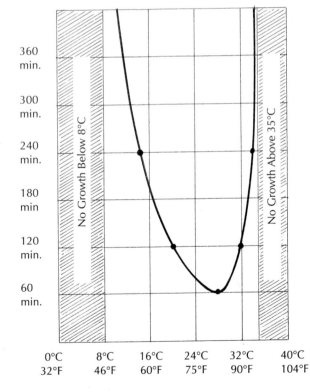

This chart shows the relationship between temperature and growth for C. milleri. *Note that the shortest possible doubling time is 60 minutes at 82° F (28° C). Again, the point of fastest fermentation (and gas production) is slightly higher (about 86° F or 30° C).*

ACID TYPES AND ACID PRODUCTION

Bakers are interested in the acids produced by leaven microbes because much of the distinctive flavor of naturally fermented bread comes in the form of organic acids that are products of fermentation. Yeast and bacteria ferment because they need energy to grow and divide. Yeast fermentation may be aerobic, producing CO_2, water, and a lot of energy, or anaerobic (as is typical in dough since the oxygen is used up quickly), producing CO_2, ethanol, and less energy. Bacterial fermentation produces energy and organic acids (lactic, acetic, proprionic, and others), CO_2 and ethanol. The spectrum of products depends on the organism and the environment. The proportion of lactic acid produced (relative to acetic acid) is increased in more liquid sponges, starters, and doughs, compared to stiffer ones. Lactic acid production also increases as dough temperatures rise, while acetic acid production stays about the same as the temperature of the fermentation medium increases. Therefore, a piece of dough fermented or proofed at a higher temperature will have a higher lactic acid level than a similar piece of dough fermented at a lower temperature. When dough is inoculated with yeast-free bacterial cultures, bacterial acid production is about 15 percent slower, and less acetic acid is made than would be made by the same number of the same type of bacteria if yeast had also been added.

The sour taste of especially sour naturally leavened bread comes more from the total amount of acid in the bread than from the pH of the bread. Flours with a high ash (mineral) content tend to buffer the acid produced, while the mineral content also encourages vigorous bacterial growth. Thus, increasing the ash content of the flour is one way to increase the sourness of bread—the acid *content* gives the sour flavor at the same acidity *level*. One way to increase ash content is to add some rye flour or whole wheat flour, if you have been working with a white flour dough previously. This effect is increased when a higher proportion of leaven sponge is used to make up the final dough, when the sponge is relatively stiff—for the same pH—and when the starter refreshment time is increased to between 12 and 24 hours, nearly the point where yeast activity would begin to decrease.

Because acetic acid is more volatile than lactic acid, the relatively small proportion of it in a naturally leavened bread may be quite important in rendering the bread flavorful, and even sour. The German expert Gottfried Spicher, in his *Handbuch Sauerteig,* says a ratio of 20 percent acetate and 80 percent lactate is best, and this ratio is commonly achieved in typical natural leaven processes. Acetic acid is a more potent inhibitor of spoilage than lactic acid is.

There is much variation in the size and shape of yeast cells from different species, and there is enough cell-to-cell variation in size and shape within species that biochemical differences such as the spectrum of acids they produce and the sugars they can metabolize are used to tell them apart—in fact, the names of many yeast species have been changed several times in recent years, creating taxonomic confusion for the layperson.

IMPLICATIONS FOR LEAVEN PROPAGATION AND STORAGE

Home bakers often have trouble maintaining a stable, active leaven culture because they don't understand the proper methods or they forget to use them. The most common problems are death of a leaven, change in the apparent character of a leaven, or unreliability in the rising power of a leaven which works well sometimes but not all the time. It is my belief that these problems are *usually* caused by storing a leaven that is too ripe, by failing to adequately refresh a leaven that has been stored, by using a leaven that is not yet ripe enough to start a dough, by using a leaven that is too ripe to start a dough, or by failure to propagate the leaven in an appropriate temperature range.

Natural leavens should be actively fermenting and reproducing when they are incorporated into a dough. A relatively thin leaven (100 percent hydration) should be bubbly and frothy. A thicker leaven should be spongy, gassy, and tenacious when stirred. It should look elastic and lively. For the yeast this means they have to have food available, that the pH is not too low, and that there are enough of them alive. Yeast activity drops as starters become too acid and anaerobic. The bacterial population in a culture falls substantially when there is too much oxygen or too much acid; 90 percent of bacterial cells are dead in a week in a warm culture. The bacterial death rate is only about 20 percent when that same culture is stored in a refrigerator for a week. Yeasts are more sensitive to acid when they are in a cold medium, so only relatively immature cultures should be put away in the refrigerator for long periods; im-mature cultures are less acid and more yeast cells will survive. Once out of the refrigerator, the storage leaven must be refreshed to help the populations recover.*

Some people have reported success drying out their storage leaven on wax paper, then using a bit of the dried matter to restart the culture later. I haven't done it.

The more accepted and consistently successful way to store a culture for a month or so is to make a fresh and very stiff storage leaven, put it in a well-covered vessel (the classic plastic yogurt container), and place it immediately in the refrigerator—labeled well so someone doesn't try to make a smoothie out of it, or think it is old, infected cottage cheese to be thrown out. When it is time to reactivate the storage leaven, mix it with water and fresh flour and take it through a few cycles of expansion at room temperature to allow the culture to come into balance. When it is active, you have your old culture back! The stiffness of such a storage leaven guarantees that it will be three to six months before the medium becomes acid enough to kill the culture.

Some bakers have been known to add a little commercial yeast to their culture occasionally in an attempt to revive it, but this is not effective. Adding some yeast to a *dough* that has been inoculated with a natural leaven is more accepted. Unfortunately, the addition of commercial yeast to a natural leaven has a mildly depressing effect on the reproduction and activity of both the wild-type yeast and the wild-type bacteria in the leaven (at least for the San Francisco strains). The survival of the added commercial yeast is also reduced: half of a .5 percent addition will die in seven hours, probably because it is in-

*When yeast and bacteria do die in large numbers they autolyze as they are digested by their own enzymes. This produces the terrible smell of an old culture that has gone bad from lack of maintenance and needs to be thrown away.

ROUTINE CARE *of a* LEAVEN

- Allow your leaven refreshments to ferment at 70 to 75 degrees Fahrenheit (21 to 24 degrees Celsius) so that neither yeasts nor bacteria are favored.
- Only store a leaven that is active enough that you know it would be ripe and bubbly in eight hours or less at room temperature, if it were not refrigerated. If the leaven is not that active, continue to refresh/expand it at room temperature until it is.
- If you will use a leaven the next day, let it ferment for five or six hours (after it is refreshed with water and flour) before you put it away in the refrigerator.
- If you will use a leaven in three days, let it ferment for three hours before you put it away.
- If you will use it in a week, let it ferment for only an hour before you put it away.
- Refresh leavens before they become soupy. Gluten softens at pH 3.7; *L. sanfranciscensis* dies at pH 3.6

Many bakers try to preserve their leavens for longer periods by freezing them. Some leaven yeast strains will not survive freezing at all, and for most strains only one in two thousand yeast cells in a mature culture will survive frozen storage for four days, while 60 to 80 percent of bacterial cells will. Yeast survival improves by about 6 percent if a young culture with pH 4.5 or above is frozen. This means that if you want to freeze a leaven, do it when you have just refreshed it. The discrepancy in freeze hardiness between yeasts and bacteria is not as unfortunate as it might seem, though, since bacteria are more responsible than yeasts for the distinctive flavor of particular starters. On the other hand, yeasts seem to be more hardy than bacteria when cultures are refrigerated.

hibited by acetic acid excreted by the bacteria. It is better to maintain your culture regularly to keep it active.

Obtaining or Creating a Natural Leaven

It is my belief that amateur bakers spend too much time talking about starting a natural leaven and too little time taking care of the ones they have. There is little reason to start a culture if you have a friend who has a good one, or if you can afford to buy one from Sourdoughs International or King Arthur. Even famous bakeries have been known to give samples of their leavens away when asked nicely, and members of the sourdough news group are willing to share cultures, too. The main reason many bakers are not jealous of their leavens is that the use and maintenance of a leaven is as important as its microbiology in determining the characteristics of the bread made from it.

Still, there may be someone out there who does need to start a leaven because of some terrible misfortune—recently cast away on an island in the Caspian Sea, maybe, with fields of ripe wild wheat and no leaven. So for that person (or for you, if you just like to do things for yourself) here is a system that works for me. It is a slight adaptation of the one given in *The Laurel's Kitchen Bread Book*—that recipe makes a classic and fairly stiff Desem leaven, stiffer than I think is necessary. I use a 100 percent hydration leaven mixture and theirs works out to about 50 percent hydration. They also keep the starter at a temperature of less than 65 degrees during its whole evolution, and I feel this is only desirable for the first few days, when the culture is susceptible to contamination and when it is desirable to favor yeast growth over bacterial growth. After the first few days, the young culture is robust enough to grow at room temperature, the same temperature it will experience when I start to use it. As a result, the intervals in the later stages of my method become about half as long as those in the *Bread Book*. It usually takes me less than a week to get a vigorous leaven.

Another book that is popularizing natural ferments is Nancy Silverton's otherwise excellent book, *Breads from the La Brea Bakery*. Her directions are so complicated and so prolonged (more than two weeks and feeding three times a day) that people become intimidated and feel that they will mess up if they forget one feeding. Also, her culture is based on fresh organic grapes—these are certainly not available year-round in most of this country, and there is absolutely no evidence known to me that cultures nourished by grapes are superior to those nourished by grain. My biggest disagreement with her, though, is about the amount of material one should use in a starter. You don't need to work with large quantities of flour to encourage microbes that can only be seen with a microscope.

Therefore, let me state a few things I hold to be true about this arcane topic. I am not going to cite chapter and verse, but I am not going to lead you astray, either.

Here are six principles: First, the organisms you want are not likely to come out of the air. The yeast you want may come from grain or fruit, but the bacteria are more likely to come from you. Experiments that have attempted to culture *L. Sanfranciscensis* from the air (or from grain) have been uniformly

A ripe leaven sponge (100 percent hydration) has been poured out of the bowl, then allowed to fall back. See how gassy it is?

unsuccessful. In academic microbiology circles there is a rumor that the only place (aside from leaven cultures) that *L. Sanfranciscensis* has been found is in dental plaque! So it is more likely that the bacteria in your sourdough will come from you than from the air. The yeast you want may be on organic grain, though.

Second, I hold that a flour/water sponge is a better place to propagate the organisms you want than an infusion of grapes, though it is true that grapes will work. People have used grapes for years—but I think flour is better. For one thing, it is available anywhere (by mail if necessary) any time of year. For another, the environment of a grain-based sponge is the same one in which these organisms will live when they are working for you, raising dough.

Third, I recommend you use a mixture of wheat and rye flour for your initial sponge. Wheat because that is what most bread is made of, and rye because it has a greater mineral content, which favors microbial growth. Using just rye flour or just wheat flour will work, though.

Fourth, it is not a good idea to use sugar, yogurt, sour milk, potato water, boiled hops, commercial yeast, or anything but organic grain (possibly fruit) and water when you are starting a leaven culture. You want the environment to be nearly the same in your starter sponge, your leaven sponges, and your dough.

Fifth, you have a life to live, and you should not be too obsessive about this process—the anxious postings on the sourdough news group from people trying to follow some of the complicated directions that have been published are pitiful.

Sixth, you can always throw the stuff out if it does not smell healthy or if it never starts to "work." You reduce your chance of having to do this if your hands, tools, and vessels are clean before you start, and are clean each of the first few times you refresh the culture. After that it doesn't matter.

Directions: Get some fresh organic whole wheat flour and an equal quantity of fresh organic whole rye flour, ground in a cool mill. Even a few tablespoons is enough to start a culture, and you can make that much in a mortar and pestle or a stone or steel-burr mill, run slowly. If you have a mill, it should be cleaned before the grain is ground, to prevent contaminating the flour with mold. You are going to be watching this thing and tending it, and it is worth starting with the correct ingredients. Don't start with roller-milled flour or chlorinated water.

Day One: In a clean jar mix 60 grams (two ounces weight) of the rye flour and 60 grams (two ounces weight) of wheat flour with about 120 grams (four ounces weight) of non-chlorinated water. If you are connected to a municipal water supply, use charcoal filtered water or bottled spring water instead. When the water/flour mixture is thoroughly mixed, cover the jar with plastic wrap and leave at 60 to 65 degrees Fahrenheit for about forty-eight hours. The idea of the 60 to 65 degree temperature is to discourage spoilage organisms. The forty-eight hours is a good figure because it will take that long for the very low populations of organisms on the flour to reach anything like an equilibrium population, and 48 hours is not long enough for them to become inhibited by lack of food or by excess acid.

Day Three: You now have 240 grams of a new but inactive leaven culture. Throw away half of it, then add 60 grams of the wheat/rye flour mix, if you have more of it (if not, you can just start using an unbleached white flour or whole wheat flour—the culture you want has already started to grow, though you can't see it) and 60 grams of non-chlorinated water. You will have 240 grams of starter leaven again. Put it back in the jar at room temperature, but only for a day.

Day Four: Do the same thing as on Day Three.

> *Label your storage leaven well so that someone doesn't try to make a smoothie out of it, or think it is old, infected cottage cheese to be thrown out.*
>
> ∼

Day Five: By now, your leaven will be somewhat active, with bubbles in it that can easily be seen with the naked eye before you refresh it. Over the next two or three days the leaven will get more and more active, until it is as light, airy, slimy, fragrant, and tenacious in eight to twelve hours as it originally was in twenty-four hours. When it gets to that point, you are ready to expand it for baking bread, keeping some back to mix a storage leaven. The activity of your leaven

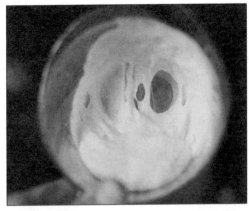

A cup of ripe leaven is turned on its side. See how tenacious it is?

A ripe leaven being poured from a cup to a bowl: tenacious and gassy.

will improve over a period of weeks as you use it, then stabilize. It is then fully mature, and you should treasure it (and share it freely, if it is good).

Using a Natural Leaven: Baking without Commercial Yeast

The classic Alaskan sourdough technique was to have a jar of the culture (it was usually called the starter) sitting around the cabin somewhere, brewing. When you wanted to make some flapjacks or soda bread you dished some out and used it to mix up baking soda batter. The acid from the sourdough hit the baking soda, releasing CO_2 and creating light, tangy pancakes. You then tossed some water and flour in with the remaining starter and stirred it up to keep it going. Even if you used it every day, this starter stayed overripe and full of acid, because it was so long between refreshments at room temperature. There was no need for the yeast in the sourdough to be active, as most of the leavening gas did not come from the yeast, but from the acid/soda reaction. Sourdough starters were thought to be too sour and too inactive for making bread, except with soda.

American commercial bakers of the nineteenth century (before the discovery of the microbial basis of fermentation in the late 1860s) prepared their own new supply of "head-yeast" each week, instead of using a continuously propagated leaven. They used this head-yeast to prepare a "stock yeast" to raise each day's bread. Head-yeast was made by boiling hops, then pouring the boiling hop-water over flour to make a paste which was then cooled to 90 degrees, when ground malt was added. The malt not only contained amylase, but was the "ferment," carrying yeast cells that reproduced rapidly in the rich, sterilized paste. At the same time, bacteria were inhibited by the mild antimicrobial effect of the hops. The head-yeast took thirty-six hours to work, at which point the day's stock yeast was made up in a sequence similar to that for head-yeast, but with no hops added, and with head-yeast as the inoculant instead of malt. This process was ideal for encouraging the growth of yeast at a rate faster than that of any accompanying bacteria, to make a bread without significant acidity. This is a wonderful example of a stable, successful technology, practiced by adepts who had no idea what the underlying principles were for their process.

FRENCH LEAVEN BAKING

This book is supposed to be about making great hearth bread, not about the diet of soldiers in the Civil War. Well, what nation comes to mind when we talk about hearth breads? The French, of course! I am guessing you would like to know a little more about traditional French bakery processes.

The classic process for naturally fermented bread relies on a continuously propagated leaven, refreshed three times before it is used to make a dough. On the scale of a village bakery, this process—called *travail sur trois levains*, or three-leaven work—involves the preservation of a piece of the previous day's dough. It is called the "chief leaven" or *chef*. After the *chef* is allowed to ferment for eight to ten hours (typically at 75 degrees Fahrenheit or 24 degrees Celsius) it is worked with water and flour until its mass is increased by a factor of three (or more), becoming the "first

leaven," which is allowed to work two to three hours before it is expanded by three (or more), becoming the "second leaven." After eight hours this is tripled to become a complete, or final, leaven, *levain à tout point*, which becomes one quarter (to as much as a half, if the bakery temperature is low, as in the winter) of the volume of the final dough being mixed. One kilogram of chief leaven has grown to over 100 kilograms of dough at this point, which is fermented an hour, divided and rounded, rested half an hour, shaped into loaves, and proofed for four hours before baking.

In rural villages with a communal oven but no bakery the *chef* used to pass from one family to another to keep it fresh. Families baked once a week, but on different days. When it was your time to start bread next week, the *chef* would come back to you.

AMERICAN HOME LEAVEN BAKING

In chapter 1 I describe my baking sequence. Let's review that sequence now to see how an American home baker (me) can create a storage leaven using the refrigerator.

If the newly made storage leaven is to be used the next day, I allow it to work about five hours at room temperature before I refrigerate it. If it will be used in three days, I allow it to work three hours before refrigerating. If it will not be used for a week, I put it away one hour after it is mixed, so it will not be too ripe when it is needed. When it is brought out, it is treated like a *chef* to make a leaven (except that in my case the storage leaven is not as stiff as the traditional *chef*). Since I weigh all my ingredients on an electronic scale and bake once a week, I generally remove half of my storage leaven to go into

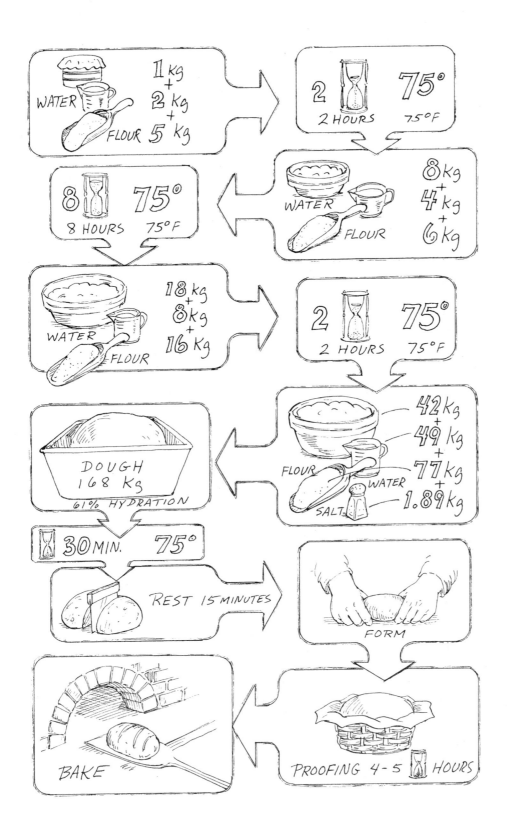

WATER
1 kg
+
2 kg
+
FLOUR 5 kg

→

2
2 HOURS
75°
75°F

8
8 HOURS
75°
75°F

←

WATER
FLOUR
8 kg
+
4 kg
+
6 kg

↓

WATER
FLOUR
18 kg
+
8 kg
+
16 kg

→

2
2 HOURS
75°
75°F

DOUGH
168 Kg
61% HYDRATION

←

FLOUR
WATER
SALT
42 kg
+
49 kg
+
77 kg
+
1.89 kg

↓

30 MIN.
75°

REST 15 MINUTES

→

FORM

↓

PROOFING 4-5 HOURS

←

BAKE

The traditional French three-leaven process (after J.C. Groscher, data from Calvel). This converts 1 kilogram of active intermediate leaven into 168 kilograms of dough. The celsius equivalent of 75°F is 24°C.

my first leaven sponge. I replace that half with equal weights of water and flour and mix it all up before I put the storage leaven jar back in the refrigerator. Done. No chance of forgetting to save starter by baking it all off accidentally. I then increase the volume of the storage leaven I have taken out of the jar, creating a leaven sponge. I make a series of leaven sponges (usually two—one made from the storage leaven, and a final one made from that one), fermenting each one for eight to twelve hours until I have enough leaven sponge to equal 20 to 40 percent of the weight of dough I need. Less in hot weather, more in cold weather. Although I could increase the storage leaven to a ripe, final leaven sponge in one step, experience has taught me that the final leaven sponge that I add to my dough will be more active if there is at least one additional refreshment between storage leaven and the final leaven sponge.

RETARDING FERMENTATION

If you are intimidated by the need for about eight hours from first mixing and kneading of dough to the point you take bread from the oven, you should use retardation of fermentation or of proofing. This will break the eight-hour block up into smaller blocks of time, and it can improve the appearance and flavor of your loaves, as well. Another use of retardation is to allow you to bake bread in the late morning (for a special lunch) without getting up at 3 A.M. You can get up at 7 A.M. instead.

The easiest way to retard is to proceed through kneading, fermentation, loaf shaping, and the first hour of proofing, all on the day before you bake. This will take three-quarters of an hour (measure, mix, knead), three hours, (fermentation), forty-five minutes (divide, round, rest, shape), and one hour (of proofing). That will mean five and one-half hours in one block of time, the first day. After the dough sits at room temperature in its *banettons* or *couches* for an hour, put it in the refrigerator, covered with cloth. (If your refrigerator air is unusually dry, cover the dough with cloth and cover the cloth with plastic.) You can let it sit for twelve to twenty-four hours. Remove the dough from the refrigerator three and three-quarter hours before you want it to come out of the oven. Let it proof at room temperature for three hours, then bake it.

Retarded dough may give you better looking loaves than usual because the cool gas in the loaf has more expansion potential, even though the oxygen in the gas cells is gone (metabolized by yeast) and the pressure in the cells is low because much of the CO_2 has dissolved into the dough. More CO_2 will develop as the loaf re-proofs, and the slight stiffness that cooler temperature brings to the dough seems to potentiate oven spring—you can get well-shaped loaves of bread from a slightly more hydrated dough. If you like the flavor better, it is probably due to more complete fermentation than you could usually use without making the dough too weak for easy handling. There will be one difference in the appearance of the loaves—small crust blisters caused by gas that escaped from the crust while it was in the refrigerator.

The Long-Term Health of Your Leaven

Certain lactobacilli found in leavens produce only lactic acid while others make both acetic acid and lactic acid. In either case, how much acetic acid is produced will depend upon environmental conditions and the bacterial strain present. Dough may begin to become slack as dough pH drops much below 4 and the gluten takes on excessive water. If leaven refreshment intervals are excessive—too infrequent for the leaven temperature, thus too acid—dough structure will be compromised, rising power (gas production) will drop off, yeast will become dormant, and flavor may become too strong for many tastes. Too frequent refreshment, on the other hand, will dilute the culture and lead to insufficient fermentation, gas production, and acid production, especially if the culture has been long dormant in the refrigerator and cell populations are low. Such a leaven needs serial refreshment at longer intervals, to revive and rebalance it. Final doughs should be made up with a similarly active starter to give optimal gluten tolerance with full but controlled flavor.

If you and your leaven get out of synchronization because you haven't used it in a while, the universal treatment is to throw out all but about 20 percent of it (to remove its acid load), then replenish it to its original volume and wait until it is full of bubbles again. Then refresh it by tripling it each time it gets really bubbly or triples in volume. When the culture can again get to this point in six to eight hours at a temperature of about 75 degrees Fahrenheit (24 degrees Celsius), it has recovered completely from storage and is ready to be used in a dough. Acidity and cell counts will have come into line and your fermentation results will again be predictable.

Refreshment schedules are always dependent on temperature (see the charts on p. 53). A culture that might be stable when refreshed once every few days at refrigerator temperature should be refreshed twice a day at 57 degrees Fahrenheit (14 degrees Celsius) and four times a day at 75 degrees Fahrenheit (24 degrees Celsius), as in the classic French three-leaven method. More or less active cultures might be refreshed at different intervals than these, but the intervals will still decrease proportionately as the temperature rises.

A healthy, active leaven will have a milder aroma than an old one that just came from the refrigerator, or one that has been at room temperature too long. Using a very active starter will mean that you use only 20 percent (summer) to 40 percent (winter) leaven sponge in your dough, and this will prevent excessive flattening of your loaves in proof (from slack gluten, due to excess acid).

Using Commercial Yeast

Dry commercial yeast goes through an initial period (about forty-five minutes) of adjustment or shock after being mixed with water and nutrients, as the cells become rehydrated. There is a fairly high proportion of dead cells in a package of yeast—fewer in instant yeast—and even more cells will die as the yeast is rehydrated. The proportion of dying cells is lowered if the water in which the yeast is reconstituted is at ideal temperature (105 to 115 degrees Fahrenheit, 41 to

46 degrees Celsius).* Dead yeast cells release glutathione and proteases—chemicals that can interfere with the linking of gluten and thus with the quality of the bread.

The maximum rate of fermentation for commercial yeast occurs at two to three hours after mixing. This is affected by temperature and the chemical environment in the sponge or dough: excess alcohol, excess acid, and high sugar or salt levels (both of which dehydrate the cells) inhibit yeast, while available nitrogen, phosphorus, magnesium, potassium, and sulfur increase activity. Factory bakers often use *yeast foods* to control this chemical milieu because they are trying to shorten the process.

Adding Commercial Yeast to a Naturally-Leavened Dough

Those who want some of the flavor, keeping qualities, and crust color of naturally leavened bread but feel they cannot wait for the natural leavens to act sometimes add both a natural leaven and commercial yeast to the dough mixture. Research in the U.S. and France suggests that small quantities of commercial yeast (up to 0.2 percent of the weight of the flour used, or about one-seventh the usual amount used for yeasted bread) will increase the rate of rising with relatively little effect on other qualities. The pH of the resulting bread is about 4.6. The commercial yeast will live long enough to boost gas production before it is out-competed by more acetic acid–tolerant yeasts.

Although this technique has its own logic (especially if you don't *really* believe in your starter), it is hard to justify maintaining a natural leaven if you are going to mix it with

commercial yeast every time you use it. In order to take full advantage of the natural leaven, you need to learn to time your naturally leavened bread production to your lifestyle and schedule, and to retard your dough as necessary in the refrigerator while you are away or busy.

Recently I heard about a Saturday cook-in and open house for all members of the rec. food.cooking newsgroup who could get to San Francisco. I was visiting in Berkeley, so I thought I would go. I had plans for part of Saturday morning and I didn't want to get up at dawn, either. So I made a naturally leavened dough (with no yeast addition) on Friday morning and allowed it to proof for only an hour that afternoon before putting it in the refrigerator. I went to the movies. I took the dough out in the morning, let it proof for three more hours, baked it in a cloche, and it was beautiful—well received in a discerning company. That is how you can adjust natural fermentation to your lifestyle.

ADDING PRE-FERMENTED DOUGH: *PÂTE FERMENTÉE* OR THE OLD DOUGH METHOD

The addition of a yeasted dough that is three to twelve hours old to a new mixture of the same formula is an easy and controlled way to get some of the flavor (but little of the acid) of fermentation into volume-produced bread. The old dough method is a widely used technique in Europe, popular because it fits well into the schedule of commercial bakeries and because most of the *baguettes* and other hearth breads made this way are consumed immediately. The fact that they don't keep very well is not a concern in a country where bread is bought every day.

French bakers now seem to feel they have to have hot, fresh, and at least somewhat flavorful bread available for the first purchaser in the morning and the last one at night. Combining new and old dough is the easiest way to stretch production across the day.

The yeast percentage of both doughs used is 2 percent of the weight of the flour used to make the dough. The amount of old dough added to the final mix varies with the type of bread being made and the age of the old dough. For *baguettes* the amount of the first dough added is about 50 percent of the weight of the flour mixed into the final dough, while for larger round country loaves it is 150 to 175 percent. These figures are reduced if the old dough is a trifle ripe. If you are using 1 pound of flour in your new mixture, you add ½ pound of old dough for baguettes, or 1 to 1¾ pounds of old dough for country bread. If it is not convenient for you to mix two batches of dough in the same day, you may make the first dough a day or two ahead—not more—and allow it to stay at room temperature for an hour or two before refrigerating it until it is used. You will be retarding the old dough until you are ready for it.

This method of prefermented dough addition makes good bread, but the yeast percentage is high enough to affect the flavor unfavorably, and bread made with a low percentage of old dough doesn't keep particularly well. The sponge method described next may be more satisfactory for home bakers and produces similar results.

YEASTED SPONGE OR *POOLISH*

The French word *poolish* reflects the belief of bakers a hundred and fifty years ago that the sponge method came from Poland. Perhaps it did, but it seems to have travelled first to Austria, as it came to Paris from Vienna. Its arrival coincided with the arrival of commercial yeast and the elongated Vienna loaf (which became the *baguette*), which was usually made from a *poolish*.

Bakers used the sponge method for most of the bread made in the U.S. and Europe for a hundred years, from the introduction of commercial yeast in the mid-19th century to the early 1950s—although some bakers used the faster "straight dough" method by the 1920s. The sponge process was given up by many bakeries because the price of commercial yeast dropped as its production was perfected. (The straight dough method is faster but uses more yeast.) Sponge baking is slower overall than the straight yeasted dough method and is considered less convenient for bakeries than the old dough method. For home bakers, though, it is more convenient than old dough because there is only one complete kneading phase, with better results than straight dough.

In the sponge method all or most of the water called for in the recipe, a small amount of yeast (one-third to one-half of that used in faster methods), and part of the flour are allowed to pre-ferment for three to twelve hours as a sponge before the body of the dough is finally mixed. Making this mixture takes just a couple of minutes. The sponge is more liquid than a finished dough, encouraging rapid fermentation, although the low level of bacteria present will limit acid production to a level well below that of a naturally leavened bread.

During this time the yeasted sponge should collapse of its own weight at least

*Added sugar is
not a necessity for
yeasted bread—it
just makes the
process faster.

once. This collapse is called the **drop**. This drop serves the same purpose in gluten development that punching down does for straight dough: it conditions the gluten somewhat, and is a guide to the ripeness of the sponge and its readiness for mixing into a dough. The gluten is not over-stressed by this dropping process because the sponge—while its thickness can vary according to the time it will be left to ferment—is always softer and wetter than a dough. The bubbles coalesce and burst and the sponge gives way after the gluten has been conditioned but before it is injured.

The long, active pre-fermentation stage allows some appealing flavors and acid to develop without much danger of over-fermentation. Bread pH using a three-hour sponge method is between that of naturally leavened and straight dough bread, although the acetic acid level is only one-eighth that of the naturally leavened bread. This technique can make very good bread, and in fact, many people do not want bread that is more highly flavored than that produced by the sponge method.

Yeasted Straight Dough

Straight dough is made by mixing/kneading all the ingredients at once, with no sponge stage. It is held to be the simplest dough method, but it relies on the availability of refined commercial yeast, which is the product of an immense, complicated, energy intensive factory.

Commercial yeast is constitutionally ready to ferment the breakdown products of sucrose, glucose, and fructose. Although it is capable of fermenting maltose, it must

be induced to do so. This is one reason that most straight dough formulas include sucrose (sugar), since the goal of these processes is to create bread as soon as possible.* The rapid rate of fermentation means that minor errors in timing may have grave end results. This is more likely to affect the home baker than the commercial baker, who has more control over all aspects of the process—more time and temperature control, no crying baby in the next room.

Commercial yeast is used in dry or cake form, usually by dissolving the yeast before adding it to the other ingredients. Mixing is similar to the process for naturally leavened and sponge dough. The dough is then allowed to ferment until doubled in bulk (this step is omitted in the high-speed power mixing method now used in very large bakeries, in which the gluten is developed and conditioned mechanically, not through a rise during fermentation). The dough may be degassed (punched down) once during this fermentation to allow longer fermentation without injury to the dough structure. Straight dough must be closely watched to prevent over-fermentation, especially in recipes that contain higher yeast percentages and added sugar, which in low concentrations stimulates the yeast.

The main drawback of the short fermentation time of straight dough has to do with flavor development, or the lack of it. The fermentation time is too short for the dough to develop the acidity and complex flavors of great bread, and the percentage of yeast used may leave the bread with an unpleasant aftertaste. These effects are not noticeable in highly flavored breads (cinnamon raisin, cheese bread, whole wheat) but straight-dough white flour breads become bland or unpleasant when they cool. The flavor of straight-dough breads may be improved but not corrected by retarding (cooling) the dough to some degree to prolong fermentation, or by using a little less than the recommended percentage of yeast. This may also make the baking process fit more easily into

DOUGH ACIDITY

Acidity can be expressed as flavor (an acid flavor), as pH, or as total acidity. A solution's pH is only a measure of its acidity in the way a metal's temperature is a measure of its heat: a pound of aluminum at 400 degrees has less heat than a pound of steel at the same temperature. Real acidity (total titratable acidity) is tested by titrating with a measured amount of a base until the dough becomes neutral, just as the heat in a bar of metal is tested by seeing how much heat is lost as it is cooled. Two doughs may have the same pH without having the same amount of acid if the flour/water proportions of the doughs are different, or if one dough has a markedly different ash content. The intensity of sour flavor in sourdough bread is more dependent on acid content than on pH. Using a higher-ash flour and allowing a longer fermentation to the same pH is one way to make very sour bread.

In the German literature on rye sourdough production, the figures for dough pH and acidity are usually both given, along with the percentage hydration of the dough. These completely define the acid/base condition of the dough. In the clas-sical method of rye sourdough production the sourdough is thicker (equal parts rye flour and water by weight), while in continuous machine fermentation more water is used (125 parts water to 100 parts flour). At any given temperature the thinner starter will ferment faster and reach a lower pH, but will not contain as much acid. Therefore, a much greater proportion of thinner starter must be added to reach a desired level of acidification in the dough. The classical (thicker) starter reaches a pH of about 3.6 and an acid level of 20 to 30 units after a 48 to 72-hour fermentation, while the continuous process gives the same pH and an acid level of 10 to 15 units in 10 to 15 hours. Rye bakers need a lot of acid to inhibit the rye flour amylase, which would break down the starch that rye dough needs for its structure.

Rye bakers are not worried about pH-related inhibition of the yeast portion of the sourdough culture. Rye doughs never have the gas-trapping capacity of wheat doughs, so lower gas production is not much of a liability. Unfortunately, the people who want to (but can't seem to) create very acidic bread are probably baking with wheat, not rye, and are using a sourdough technique that has been developed to make light sourdough wheat bread without an intense acid flavor.

the baker's schedule. Since very fresh bread is almost always delicious, straight dough formulas are most appropriate for bread cooked for immediate use. The straight method *baguettes* sold in some French bakeries and markets are only palatable for about four hours.

Very Sour Bread

Lots of folks are attracted to really sour sourdough bread, like German sour ryes and San Francisco sourdough. Very sour (acid) bread can be hard to bake successfully, as its acidity can inhibit yeast and cause gluten to get swollen with water. Sometimes the result is a pungent brick. I have found that the easiest way to make good sour bread is to modify the "old dough" method, using natural leavens.

Start the dough process seventy-two hours before mixing the final dough, by using a storage leaven to mix a relatively firm leaven sponge (that will contain, say, 50 parts water to 100 parts flour by weight or 50 percent hydration by baker's percentage) which is allowed to sit at room temperature until the final dough is mixed three days later. The water in that stiff sponge should be calculated to be 30 percent of the total water needed in the whole dough recipe. Then, eight hours before the dough is mixed, make up another (separate) thinner sponge, at 100 percent hydration. This is inoculated with your usual storage leaven. The total water in this sec-

ond sponge should equal 20 percent of the planned total water in the dough. When it is time to make dough, combine both of these sponges with the remaining 50 percent of the water and with enough flour and salt to make the dough.

From the stiff, slow starter you will bring a big load of acid. From the fresher, thinner starter you will bring a big load of highly active yeast cells. The final bread will be both light and acid. If it isn't acid enough, you can increase the amount of the seventy-two-hour sponge in the bread. If it isn't light enough, increase the fresher sponge.

You must realize, in making a bread like this, that gluten strands begin to swell and become less elastic as the pH drops significantly below 4, to somewhere in the region of pH 3.8. You might consider baking this bread in a pan unless you are very proficient at forming loaves. The pan will help support the dough. Another possibility is to always use plenty of rye flour in your very sour bread. Since the structure of rye dough is dependent on pentosans and not on gluten, acidity will not weaken it appreciably.

Whew! That was pretty technical! Not just the last part, about the *sour* rye bread, but the whole chapter. I think you will forgive me, if you ever have trouble with your fermentation and seek out this book again. The technical stuff won't seem so bad if it turns out to help you solve the problem.

Let's get baking!

SANDS, TAYLOR, & WOOD
(KING ARTHUR FLOUR)

Norwich, Vermont

At the turn of the century, 80 percent of the flour sold in New England was used at home…Now, less than 4 percent is used at home and King Arthur is the only large brand pursuing the home market

～

KING ARTHUR is the most widely recognized name in American home baking. Not King Arthur the knight, but King Arthur the flour, catalog, and store. All these are parts of the Sands, Taylor, & Wood Company, which has had two hundred years in the "family flour" business in New England and one hundred years with the same logo: King Arthur on his horse, with lance and banner. King Arthur's troops have done more than any other group to make baking supplies, tools, and techniques available to home bakers, so I would have visited their operation even if they had not been just down the road a piece.

At the turn of the century, 80 percent of the flour sold in New England was used at home (known in the trade as "family flour"). Now, less than 4 percent is used at home and King Arthur is the only large brand pursuing the home market, in which it is successful despite "premium pricing." The company never permitted chemical treatments of its all-purpose, bread, and pastry flours, and marketing on this basis has allowed its flour business to grow while national home flour consumption has been shrinking by 1 to 2 percent per year, averaged over the past fifty years.

This has been a family business for generations, and remains one today. Frank Sands is most involved with the flour business, while his wife, Brinna, is more involved with the Baker's Store, Baker's Catalogue, and home baking research and education. Let's look first at the flour business, then at the catalog and store.

This company neither leases nor owns mills, but instead contracts its production requirements with the large companies that dominate the industry, as well as a number of smaller mills in Kansas, New York, and Vermont. The grain used is not purchased directly from farmers, but it has to meet certain specifications. Varieties and lots of grain must often be blended since grain characteristics vary from year to year. Every load of flour is tested at the mill and the results are reviewed on a daily basis in Vermont. If the mills don't meet the specifications (ash content, protein percentage, farinogram plot) the flour is not shipped. This ensures the level of consistency for which King Arthur flours are known, even though the flour is made at different mills. The only differences between the family and commercial flours are the brand names and the packaging. For example, commercial "King Arthur Special Flour" is a 12.7 percent protein,

SANDS, TAYLOR, & WOOD

(KING ARTHUR FLOUR)

0.48 ash, spring wheat bread flour, sold in fifty- and one-hundred-pound bags. When the same flour is sold in stores in consumer packages it is labeled as "King Arthur Special Flour for Bread Machines." The "King Arthur" all-purpose flour (11.7 percent protein, 0.50 ash, primarily hard red winter wheat with added hard red spring wheat as necessary to maintain specifications) is sold in fifty-pound bags as "Sir Galahad," for artisan bakers.

Brinna Sands has been the driving force behind a fifteen-year effort to make the tools, methods, and ingredients used by artisan and ethnic bakers available to home bakers around the world. This process begun in her home kitchen has now extended to the catalogue (1989), the cookbook (1990), the store, and a test kitchen with a staff of bakers who test recipes and equipment. They are prepared to answer questions raised by customers and food writers who call or write for information. For some technical questions, commercial accounts refer to Frank (who long ago took industry courses in baking, and who has been solving problems for his commercial customers for thirty years); if he is stumped, he calls in the food scientists in the laboratories of the milling companies. Brinna and the baking staff prepare a subscription newsletter *(The Baking Sheet),* which goes out to thousands of home bakers six times a year; this contains recipes and occasional reviews of baking topics. They have also translated the formulas and terms of European bakers for home use. Many of the people recruited by the company are themselves bakers. For example, Heather Leavitt of Barnard, Vermont, used to answer phones for the catalogue three days a week; now she runs her own workshops on baking in a clay oven. Keeping up with all of this takes Brinna up to eighty hours a week, but she cannot say how much of it is work, and how much is play.

What is the future direction of this company? They have recently built a large and impressive headquarters in a field behind what is now their store, and the store team is now planning a new store that will have room for a teaching kitchen and a baking library. Eventually King Arthur may have both indoor and outdoor masonry ovens, and perhaps a small bakery. Expanding their line of organic and/or whole grain products will depend in large part on an available supply of appropriate grain, and they are working to create a milling and marketing structure for grain grown locally in the Champlain

Valley. They are also arranging for more widespread distribution of their products, into the South and West.

Although my visit to King Arthur was not focused on technical information, I left loaded down with handouts and back issues of their newsletter. In those publications I found many useful technical points, and I insist on listing a few of them here so you can see what kinds of material (in addition to recipes) the newletters contain.

- Bread consists of approximately one part water and three parts flour, by volume—a handy ratio to remember. Very fresh flour (such as home-milled whole wheat flour) will take a little more water than this.

- Poor crumb (coarse, crumbly, dry) may be caused by excess flour (stiff dough), or may develop when bread is baked at too low a temperature. Another cause is inadequate primary fermentation, especially with yeasted recipes, if they are not punched down at least once. Lastly, inadequate kneading makes a coarse, lifeless crumb.

- Although bread stores well when frozen, self-defrosting freezer compartments actually cycle above freezing for some part of every day, to clear ice from the walls. This may have an adverse effect on frozen bread (not to mention ice cream). If you have that kind of freezer, be sure to wrap bread tightly, and don't expect to store it for a long time.

So—the King (Sands, Taylor, & Wood) has set his sights supplying every need of the home and small commercial baker. He is "doing well by doing good." The only criticism I have or hear (and I hear it a lot) relates to prices, not only for the flour, which is significantly more expensive than store-brand unbleached flour, but also for catalogue items, which (when they can be found) can be bought elsewhere for less. However, it is in that parenthesis that King Arthur is doing us a service, since many of the things he sells *cannot* be easily found elsewhere.

CHAPTER FOUR

DOUGH

DEVELOPMENT

Dough is developed in stages. First is the mixing of ingredients, leaving the dough slack, wet, and sticky. The second stage marks the start of gluten development; the dough has a wet, rough, clumpy appearance. In the third stage the dough is drier, more elastic, more cohesive, but still wet in spots. The final stage, called by commercial bakers the "development" stage, is marked by **clearing**. At this stage the outside of the dough mass becomes smooth and satiny and the dough can be stretched into a thin translucent membrane of uniform thickness. For artisan breads, it is best to stop mixing before this stage is reached.

The Sequence of Kneading

Kneading breaks down flour particles, wets flour proteins, dissolves sugars and broken starch, and wets the outer surface of the starch granules. The combined surface area of these granules is immense and the starch on their surfaces is tightly linked, so they are resistant to wetting. The mechanical action of kneading exposes them to water, but they do not become fully hydrated until the dough is baked and the starch undergoes gelatinization. Dough must contain enough water to hydrate proteins and vegetable gums, dissolve dextrins and sugars, wet starch granules, and eventually allow gelatinization.

Because the surface tension of dough is high, gas bubbles from fermentation would not easily form in it except for the persistence of microscopic nitrogen bubbles carried into the dough by flour particles, and the development of bubbles created in mixing and kneading. These tiny bubbles form a nidus, or focus, for the gas evolution that is to come. They become larger as gas diffuses out of the dough and into the bubbles, creating gas cells. An excess of bubbles, though, can lead to an excessively fine or closed crumb.

Measuring and Temperature

I recommend that you weigh ingredients and utilize the baker's percentage system in any calculations you do. Because flour and other dry ingredients tend to settle, weight is a better method than volume for measuring bread ingredients, and it is the technique used by professional bakers who are looking for consistent results. A good scale costs about fifty dollars, and I think you should buy one.

Bakers refer to the weight of all other ingredients in relation to the total weight of the flour used to make the dough. For instance, dough is considered to have "65 percent hydration" when it has 65 parts water to 100 parts flour. (The true water percentage in such a dough is a little less than 40 percent.) The "baker's percentage" of hydration makes it easy to compute and weigh out batches—especially in the metric system, as I showed (I hope!) in the first chapter (see pp. 7–9).

Dough temperature affects both fermentation and the mechanical properties of the dough. Dough temperature is affected by the temperature of the ingredients, by heat liberated as the dough is mixed and kneaded, and by the temperature of the environment in which the prepared dough is placed. In general, water temperatures of 90 to 95 degrees Fahrenheit (34 degrees Celsius) at home and 50 to 55 degrees Fahrenheit (12 degrees Celsius) in a mechanized bakery are appropriate. Machine mixing generates the rest of the heat that will raise the dough temperature to about 75 degrees Fahrenheit (24 degrees Celsius), a typical fermentation and proofing temperature. Fermentation also gives off heat, but not enough to be significant if the volume of the dough mass is small.

Water

Water is referred to as hard or soft. Hard water has higher levels of calcium and magnesium ions in solution than soft water, although both will usually have enough other trace minerals to adequately feed the yeast in the dough. If it takes a lot of shampoo to wash your hair, your water is probably hard. It may also be alkaline, but you would have to test it to be sure, since not all hard water is alkaline. If it is *very* alkaline, yeast may have a hard time getting started with fermentation, until enough fermentation products are formed to correct the alkalinity. If water is too soft, and not enough salt is added to correct it, the dough may be sticky and hard to handle, and poor at holding fermentation gases. It will act like bread made without any salt, or with very fresh flour. Although debate has raged for years about the importance of particular water supplies for making certain kinds of bread, most research on the subject doesn't bear out any other major differences.

What *is* important, however, is chlorine. If your tap water smells like the pool at the YMCA, there may be enough chlorine present to inhibit the bacteria, especially in breads made from a natural leaven. Water like that should run through a chlorine-removing filter before you bake with it.

The total amount of water you use will depend on the absorption characteristics of your flour (protein content and quality, amylase and damaged starch content, etc.) and the type of crumb and crust you want to achieve. French bakers speak of three consistencies of dough (soft, medium, and stiff, called *pâte douce*, *pâte bâtard*, and *pâte ferme*). Classic *baguettes* (made with *pâte bâtard*) get 60 to 63 percent water in France, with French flour, but 64 to 65 percent or more here, with American flour. In France, a *pâte ferme* typically has less than 60 percent hydration when the goal is to have a tight, uniform crumb and a dull crust, while in Italy the spongy, chewy *ciabatta* is hydrated at 80 percent of the flour weight, and is full of holes, like an English muffin. Latin American hearth breads are hydrated 58 percent to promote a more dramatic burst pattern at the slash.

A last warning about water content, though: it is hard to adequately develop or condition the gluten in a very wet dough. Flour particles don't break up well when they are floating around and avoiding other flour particles that could abrade them, and developed gluten can only form when there is plenty of friction in the dough when it is being worked and stretched. If you want to make a very soft dough, you have two choices. One is to really beat up the dough, stirring it very vigorously, then stretching it way out of your bowl. The other is to add less than the full amount of water, work the dough until it is smooth and stretchy, then add the rest of the water and work it in completely.

> *An extensible dough is tolerant of stretch without losing strength and elasticity. It is like a strong spring that does not fail or kink when it is stretched a long way. If you stretch a dough that is not extensible it will rip or develop thin spots.*
>
> ~

Salt (and Yeast, If You Use It)

The sequence of ingredient additions is not important, with the exceptions of commercial yeast (if you are mixing a straight yeasted dough) and salt: yeast because it has to activate, and salt because it changes the chemistry of the gluten. Active dry yeast gets to work sooner and releases less material that interferes with gluten formation when it is premixed with warm water. If you use commercial yeast, you should mix it with warm water (as it says on the package) in a separate bowl, then let it sit for a few minutes before you add it to the main mix. In the main bowl, the rest of the water and some of the flour are mixed to a smooth consistency before your leaven sponge (or yeast/water) and the rest of the flour are added. Salt may be added with the flour at the beginning of dough making (usually the case when bread will be hand mixed and kneaded), or it may be added when the dough is nearly worked; this late salt addition decreases the mechanical energy that must be expended during mixing/kneading and makes for a more extensible dough. An extensible dough is tolerant of stretch without losing strength and elasticity. It is like a strong spring that does not fail or kink when it is stretched a long way. If you stretch a dough that is not extensible it will rip or develop thin spots.

Most people find bread baked without salt unpalatable. If you have ever forgotten to put in the salt, you probably realized it with your first bite. Only a few types of bread are made without salt on purpose, although salt has only been generally added to bread for a few hundred years. The main flavor characteristic of salt in food beyond saltiness is its ability to intensify other flavors, including sweetness.

What is not commonly known is that salt has effects on dough chemistry, not just taste. Salt helps baking dough take on a golden color and helps create an open crumb texture. Too much salt makes the crumb texture tight and prevents full proofing and springing of the loaf. ,

Salt is available in a variety of forms (big grains, little grains, flakes) and two general types: mined or mineral salt and sea salt. Smaller salt grains and flakes dissolve more quickly than big grains, but big grains have a certain look and flavor punch when baked onto bread or pretzel crust that small-grained salt lacks. Also, the structure of a salt grain is a legacy of the technique used to form it, and this makes different kinds of salt dissolve at very different rates. Similarly, the same weight of two different forms of salt will have different volumes. (Another good reason for using weights, not volume measurement!)

Gourmet cooks tend to prefer sea salt but many people can't tell the difference. Most sea salt is now so refined that any difference in taste or effect is not worth pursuing, and only crude preparations have much of a difference in trace minerals. Use whatever kind

THE PARADOX *of* SALT

Salt has an unusual effect on the mechanical properties of gluten and dough. Salt makes properly conditioned gluten tighter and at the same time able to endure more stretch without injury. The gluten essentially becomes stronger. R.C. Hoseney sums up current thinking on the nature of salt's effect on gluten by explaining that some of the atoms in gluten are positively charged, and the positive charges repulse one another. When salt is added, chlorine ions from the salt bond with the gluten, cancelling the effect of the positive charges and allowing it to compact, tighten, and stiffen—the cohesive gluten becomes stronger.

When salt slows the rising of bread, then, it does so both because it slows fermentation (a minor effect) and because it makes the gluten tight. As a result of gluten tightening, salt increases kneading time markedly. Those who want to shorten kneading may consider adding salt after the bread is partially kneaded, at what commercial bakers call the "cleanup stage," or after *autolyse* if the dough is given an *autolyse* stage. The salt will strengthen the already developed gluten network, and there will be no difference in the effect on the fermentation or eventual flavor of the bread.

you prefer, but I find that inexpensive fine sea salt from my health food store is finer than commercial salt from the supermarket and dissolves more easily.

Bread dough typically incorporates $1/2$ to 2 percent salt by weight. Salt tends to slow down fermentation by slightly dehydrating the yeast and bacteria, making the yeast work harder to import the fermentable sugars it needs. Fermentation is slowed about 10 percent in a 1.5 percent salt dough. This allows the dough to develop a more complex flavor than it would otherwise have and reduces the risk of over-fermentation and over-proofing in yeasted doughs.

Salt inhibits lipoxygenase, reducing the fat-oxidizing and vitamin-reducing effect of oxygen that enters the dough during kneading. Salt markedly inhibits protein-breaking enzymes present in flour, too, and keeps dough from becoming too plastic as it ferments. It also tightens the gluten sheets, making dough less sticky and easier to handle while increasing its gas-trapping ability. Dough generally tolerates less kneading at low pH, and therefore may not develop full strength; salt corrects this tendency.*

The Autolyse Method

The **autolyse** is a modification of the mixing process—a rest in the middle of mixing—that helps make exceptionally extensible doughs. It has been championed by Professor Raymond Calvel, who led the rediscovery of traditional-process breads in France. He recommends it for doughs that will be used to form highly extended loaf forms such as *baguettes,* including naturally leavened doughs. *Autolyse* is a stage added after all of the water and flour in the dough (*usually without the leaven sponge, and without the salt*) are thoroughly mixed (five minutes in a commercial mixer, or perhaps ten minutes by hand). This unleavened dough is allowed to rest for twenty to thirty minutes before the leaven sponge and salt are added and mixing/kneading is completed. There are two reasons the leaven is added late: one is that it is already well hydrated and essentially digested by its long fermentation; the other is that one of the reasons for the *autolyse* is to allow the flour proteins and damaged starch plenty of time to completely hydrate *before* they are exposed to the acid of the leaven, or to salt.

The *autolyse* allows the flour time to hydrate and allows gluten tension to relax before final kneading. This increases the eventual extensibility of the dough without sacrificing its elastic qualities. It makes a strong, extensible, less-sticky dough that is easier to form into loaves. It gives bigger, lighter loaves (regardless of the type of flour) with strong, supple, open crumb and possibly better keeping qualities.

Practical experience shows that an *autolyse* step makes a dough easier to work to any desired degree of gluten conditioning and extensibility, especially in machine mixing. Hand kneading is so much slower that most of the tension in the dough is relieved at the rate it is created, so an *autolyse* may not give such dramatic results.

Most recipes involving a pre-fermented dough—an old dough—call for it to be added to the rest of the ingredients close to the end of kneading, cut into chunks to help it disperse. Adding it late prevents the gluten in this part of the dough (which is already fully

*Reduced tolerance to kneading is a theoretical risk with naturally leavened dough, because of its low pH. In practice, reduced tolerance to kneading is not a problem for several reasons. The chief one is that flour proteins and starch granules are so well hydrated during the pre-fermentation (sponge leaven) stage that naturally leavened doughs don't require as much kneading as straight doughs.

developed) from being over-mixed. Recipes that add a great deal of pre-fermented dough (equal or greater volumes) do not benefit from an *autolyse* stage.

Kneading: An Overview

The goal of kneading is to obtain a dough that is both elastic and extensible, that resists stretching but stretches without tearing. Kneading creates dough that is plastic enough to be worked, viscous enough to retain gas, and elastic enough to help the loaf hold its shape. It must have a viscoelastic balance, showing fluid and springy characteristics that will allow it to move, swell, and retain gas in rising, and that balance is something you can feel in your hands when the dough is adequately kneaded, or later when you are shaping your loaves.

The viscoelastic balance is reached when the gluten molecules are aligned in roughly parallel sheets, with the gluten strands linked, kinked, and stacked in layers and nets. Some of these links can be broken temporarily as the dough is stretched, to reform when the stretch is released. This pulls the dough back into shape and gives it its elastic quality. How many and what kind of links may form is dependent on:

- the level of flour oxidation (aging);
- the mechanical treatment of the dough;
- the fat content of the flour;
- the original quality and quantity of the flour proteins.

Even today, there are no chemical tests to perfectly predict this linking behavior, and flour is still tested for its functionality: how it behaves mechanically in simulated dough and in bread.

Good-quality wheat flour is slower to absorb water, forms fewer crosslinks (between polymer chains) than poor flour, and has a better viscoelastic balance than poor flour, possibly because poor-quality gluten interacts excessively with the starch granules trapped in it, making it flow poorly in the walls of the expanding gas cells (He and Hoseney). Hard wheat starch granules do

MIXING and OVERMIXING

R.C. Hoseney has explored the "mixing phenomena" in great detail. Mixing abrades flour particles, releasing starch granules and gluten precursor proteins into the water of the dough. When all the proteins and all the granule surfaces are wetted, the dough is fully developed: it reaches a peak of elastic strength, due to its highly linked gluten and the filler effect of the starch granules trapped in the gluten. If the dough is then allowed to relax, it will become viscous again, as weak chemical bonds between gluten molecules break and re-form, preserving but de-stressing the gluten network. If rapid mixing continues beyond full hydration, however, dough is "overmixed." Oxidative and mechanical stress make gluten progressively weaker: crucial bonds in the gluten are broken, the gluten net starts to break apart, and the dough becomes less elastic. The gas-trapping potential of the dough is lost. Hoseney has shown that the stability of dough (its resistance to overmixing) is significantly lower at a low dough pH—such as that in naturally leavened bread. That is one reason that artisan bakers have to be careful when selecting mixers and setting mixing times.

not interact as strongly with gluten as starch from soft wheat does, while hard wheat gluten also does not interact with starch (from any source) as strongly as starch from soft wheat does (Petrofsky and Hoseney). What this means to the baker is that good wheat gluten can stretch farther in the wall of a gas cell, leading to lighter bread.

Hand Kneading

Hand kneading is hard to overdo. Hand kneading is usually barely sufficient to utilize all of the capacity of hard wheat flour. Before he bought a gentle mechanical mixer, Chad Robertson, one of the best artisan bakers in the U.S., used to knead his breads by hand. So did the famous bakers in France with whom he apprenticed. His method was not as heroic as one might expect, though—it was slow, gentle, and moderate, since he made full use of *autolyse*. The breads he made were moist and fully risen, with superb texture, so the kneading he did was clearly sufficient for hearth breads. The crumb of Chad's bread was more open, variable, and interesting than that of mechanically kneaded breads, some of which are uniform to a fault.

Alan Scott has always hand kneaded his weekly production of Desem whole wheat breads (sometimes as many as 250 loaves). He feels that the few minutes saved and the slightly higher-risen bread from mechanical kneading are not worth allowing a noisy, costly machine to usurp what otherwise is a quiet, satisfying time in the tender hours of a new day. He divides each 100-pound batch of dough (enough for sixty loaves) into three manageable portions that are each kneaded for five minutes in turn by the clock until each has had fifteen minutes of kneading. This way each lump has ten minutes of rest, three times during the kneading. Kneading the whole 100 pounds of dough takes forty-five minutes in all, single-handed. With a helper the dough is divided into four lumps, each given five minutes of kneading with five minutes of *autolyse* three times, a total of thirty minutes. Alan likes hand kneading that is slow, gentle, and rhythmic, with the baker stretching, folding, and pressing in a pattern that keeps the whole lump active. A lump is too large to handle if you notice you are just working a part of it and not keeping the whole piece involved.

Some bakers today are having traditional wooden kneading troughs made up to suit their needs for working height and dough capacity. That can be expensive, but the troughs are beautiful. Others find it is simpler to use shallow square or round plastic tubs to mix, knead, and raise the doughs (as Chad does), with a sturdy table at the right height to hold the tub. Alan's table was purposely made low for kneading, but it is raised on chocks to be just as comfortable for scaling and shaping loaves.

Mechanical Kneading

Mechanical mixing has the potential to fully knead a dough, even to drive it over into failure, especially if the dough pH is low: lowering the pH from 5.8 to 4.2 decreases the time to ideal development by two-thirds and decreases the dough's tolerance to over-mixing (Harinder and Bains). Failure occurs when the gluten has been so pulled apart that it slips: each molecule loses its grip on its neighbor. This

Alan Scott making Desem dough in his ranch kitchen. He weighs fresh whole-wheat flour as he mixes dough (above, left). He dumps fermented dough on the counter (left), then divides the dough into lumps of consistent weight (above). Next he rounds the lumps to let them rest (top, far right).

The bakers at Della Fattoria make special
decorative breads for their restaurant
customers. Here a ring of loaves is slashed
in a helix (above). The knife (or lame) is a
single-bladed razor on a thin metal shaft.

At Bay Village Bakery, the counter and scale
are dusted with a mixture of rice and wheat
flour (left). This dough is "wet" and sticky.

Alan Scott firing, loading, and unloading masonry ovens (below and right). The oven to the right is at the home of Bernadette Burrell.

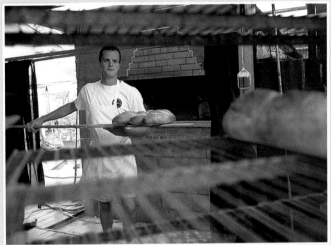

*Long days and
hard work yield
splendid results at
Della Fattoria,
in Petaluma,
California.*

Vermont oven built by Wood Masonry (left).

Commercial oven in Peru (right).

Fagots beside a French oven (far right). The board is used to carry risen loaves in baskets.

A beautifully preserved French communal oven building (below). The oven itself occupies the entire space from the chimney to the back wall.

DOUG WOOD

Oven at the Obester Vineyard, built by Ben Woolcombe, an apprentice of Alan Scott's (above).

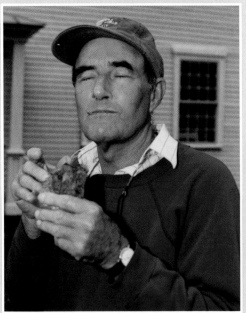

Bake bread with your eyes open. Eat it with your heart open and your eyes closed...

creates a worthless, watery dough with bits of gluten suspended in it. Well before that point is reached, however, over-mixed dough will suffer from over-oxidation and flavor changes. Dough that is over-mixed but not to the point of failure will also become hard to work after fermentation, although this can be corrected by remixing it. Bakers who hand-form their loaves find that mixing to a point just below full gluten development gives better workability and flavor, at the cost of a few percent in loaf volume.

Given that there is a total number of strokes (of the hands) or revolutions of the mixer beyond which bread quality begins to suffer, is there ever any justification for high-speed mixing? Well, perhaps: some artisan bakers use a fast mixing speed for a markedly shorter mixing time (and fewer revolutions of the mixer), or put a short burst of rapid mixing on the end of a shortened cycle of low-speed mixing (in French these techniques are called *petrissage ameliore*, or "improved kneading"). Bakers report that taste and color do not suffer, while gluten structure (extensibility, loaf volume) improves. If you try this, you will have to be careful to avoid over-mixing, driving the dough to an accumulation of gummy balls and watery soup.

Prolonged high-speed mixing (intensive mixing) can be used to replace primary fermentation of the dough (by stretching and mechanically conditioning the gluten, and by mixing in a volume of air), although this factory baking technique is done at the near complete expense of flavor, as the dough becomes over-oxidized.

In the two countries thought by many to have the worst commercial bread in the world, England and Australia, the process of mechanical mixing is extended to an art form. Most English bread is made by the Chorleywood process, in which mixing is done under a partial vacuum, fermentation is omitted, and dough goes directly to proof. In large Australian bakeries the need for both vacuum and fermentation are eliminated by the addition of high levels of chemical oxidants to supplement the already high level of oxidation achieved by vigorous mixing. The poor quality of some Australian bread is ironic, given the fame of Australian wheat. Much of Australia's wheat production is soft wheat, bred to thrive in an arid climate. However, some of Australia's current production is of white, hard wheats, which are being made into good hearth breads by artisan bakers. These strains have been bred to thrive in low-altitude, unirrigated areas with minimal rainfall.

The development of high-speed mixers is felt by some to have signalled the beginning of the end for good bread in France, at least until the bread renaissance of the past ten years. It was coupled with the use of fava and/or soy bean flour additives, which act as oxidizers as dough is mixed, increasing gluten strength, bleaching the crumb of the finished

> *In the two countries thought by many to have the worst commercial bread in the world, England and Australia, the process of mechanical mixing is extended to an art form.*

bread (and oxidizing its fats and vitamins), and shortening primary fermentation. Since none of these effects is desirable in good bread, both the bean flours and over-mixing are in disrepute. Also, a small percentage of people of Mediterranean ancestry develop a hematological disorder when exposed to fava beans.

Mixers

There are three types of mixers in common use in small bakeries: vertical axis (or planetary), oblique axis, and spiral mixers. Another kind, the diving-arm mixer, is used less often, though it reproduces the effect of hand-kneading. Horizontal-axis paddle mixers were once common but have been superseded, at least for artisan bakers: they rip the dough too

violently. If you are interested in mixers for small commercial bakeries, check out the sidebar on pages 82 and 83. There is also a useful home mixer that uses a roll-and-fold action not seen in commercial machines.

The most common heavy-duty home mixers in the United Stat es—such as the KitchenAid models—are essentially small vertical-axis mixers, producing enough dough for two one-and-one-half-pound loaves per batch. The dough is about three-quarters developed by the machine, and is often finished off by hand to develop enough dough structure for hearth breads.

Another heavy-duty mixer, the Kenwood, has a more powerful motor than the KitchenAid, but can only handle 3.25 pounds of dough (about 1.7 kg) and is not as strongly built overall than the KitchenAid.

LEFT: *Chad Robertson checks a batch of dough in his diving-arm mixer (photo: Alan Dep).*

RIGHT: *The planetary vertical mixer at the Cheese Board. The sacks of flour are piled on a pneumatic lifter. The oval shape in the upper right corner is the mouth of a duct that sucks airborne flour away from the baker as flour is poured into the mixer.*

The Magic Mill mixer, made by Electrolux in Sweden, is based on a model that has been in production for more that fifty-five years. It is capable of producing about three times as much dough as the KitchenAid, enough for six medium or three very large loaves. This mixer rotates a bowl around an indented plastic cone, after which the dough is flipped and folded by a separate fin. One loaf will be completely kneaded in about five minutes, a maximum load in ten to fifteen minutes. The action is in some ways similar to a spiral mixer (see the sidebar), and the Magic Mill mixer may be used with other attachments to make batters and whip liquids, which it does very well. There is also an optional steel-burr grain mill attachment. The company makes a metal dough hook to use instead of the roller in some situations, but this is not recommended by people who know the machines; the consensus is that it is better to use the plastic cone, and adjust mixing times as necessary to achieve the gluten development you want.

Punching Down and Forming

In a home kitchen or small bakery, dough is deflated (punched down) when primary fermentation is complete, then turned out onto a table and cut into pieces of appropriate size. Bakeries weigh these pieces to guarantee that loaves will meet weight specifications. This process is called dividing and scaling. About two ounces of additional dough per pound of finished bread allows for the anticipated weight loss in baking.

The pieces of dough are flattened, then rounded to produce a ball with a taut outer layer. The rounds are allowed to sit until the tension in the dough has relaxed and enough gas has been produced to soften the loaves and allow them to be reshaped. This *rest* after rounding is typically fifteen to twenty minutes for fully fermented bread, twenty to thirty minutes for a younger dough.

After the rest the round is rerolled with greater dough tension, this time in the shape of the desired loaf. This is called molding or shaping, and a variety of techniques are used to avoid trapping excess air in the dough, which would create a big bubble in the loaf. Shaping must stretch the gluten net of the dough in all directions, as it will be stretched by its growing gas cells. Seams on the dough roll must be sealed to prevent unrolling as the bread proofs and bakes, but the dough must be handled gently—a difficult balance to achieve.

CONDITIONING GLUTEN

An ideal loaf ready for baking is balanced between the gas volume in the gas cells and the gluten's ability to contain that gas. A dough that has just been mixed has tight gluten, which, like a tight hamstring muscle when you first start out to run, is prone to damage. If dough is not allowed to fully ferment, which gently stretches or conditions the gluten, this tightness will lead to shredding and other problems in the baking bread. This is true for both naturally leavened and commercially yeasted doughs. Most straight yeasted doughs and fully mixed (completed) yeasted sponge doughs can have their conditioning time extended by punching down. This step is not necessary for naturally leavened doughs, which have intrinsically long fermentation with little likelihood of over-rising during fermentation.

COMMERCIAL-SCALE MIXERS

Planetary Vertical-Axis Mixers

Planetary vertical-axis mixers are common in the United States and use a dough hook that follows a planetary path around a stationary bowl. They are not exclusively designed for kneading: they can be used for a wide variety of mixing and beating jobs as well. There are some trade-offs, however: dough mixing times are long; mixing can be uneven and unpredictable if the dough mass sticks on the hook; and a lot of heat is developed in the dough. Day in and day out use for kneading full batches of bread also puts a lot of strain on the small and middle-sized machines, and repairing their gear trains can be expensive. The leading manufacturer, Hobart, publishes a capacity chart that relates the capacity of the mixers to the percent AR (percent absorption ratio), defined as water weight divided by flour weight. A twenty-quart mixer, for instance (the smallest one rated for all types of bread dough), can handle twenty-five pounds of 60 percent AR dough, fifteen pounds of 55 percent dough, and ten pounds of 50 percent (high-protein) dough, and can only work that dough on first speed. At 60 percent hydration, a twenty-quart mixer will produce sixteen one-and-one-half-pound loaves

per batch. Larger mixers can of course handle much heavier loads, but never an amount that one might expect at first glance, because the bowl capacity in quarts is so much more than the dough capacity. Most people buy these mixers used: a new twenty-quart mixer lists for $3,250 and used ones are about half that. The heavy-duty KitchenAid home mixers are scaled down versions of the Hobart machines, but their capacity is limited.

Oblique-Axis Mixers

Oblique-axis mixers (fork mixers) were for years the most common type in Europe. They are gentle with the dough, develop it fully without heating it excessively, and are quicker than the vertical-axis mixers. Most are quite durable. Their drawback is a relatively narrow range of batch sizes: a fifty-pound mixer does best with a fifty-pound mix: they cannot handle less than 75 percent of capacity. They are not used to mix foods of thinner consistency (cake batter, for example) and they are expensive—$8,000 or more for a small commercial unit. Recently the Santos company (www.santos.fr) has made a home-size oblique-axis mixer, which may cost less than $2,000.

Spiral Mixers

Spiral mixers also have a vertical axis, but use a different spinning motion (the bowl moves around, instead of the mixing head) and a spinning spiral hook. They don't work the dough so hard (or heat it up), even though they knead it more quickly. They can be used with varying batch sizes and for many kitchen tasks, like vertical-axis planetary mixers. They are expensive—$8,000 or more—and you probably won't find one at an auction at a defunct pizzeria, as you might with a planetary vertical-axis mixer.

Diving-Arm Mixers

The diving-arm mixer is felt by its adherents to most closely reproduce the action of kneading hands. It can only be used for dough, but it will handle mixes as small as 30 to 40 percent of its capacity. Again, as with the others, these mixers tend to be very expensive.

PUNCHING DOWN YEASTED STRAIGHT DOUGH

Punching down is a misnomer, because excessive handling by punching or heavy kneading during fermentation does not contribute to good bread quality. Harsh handling of any kind after the bread has started fermentation will disturb the balance between elasticity and extensibility. In France, the action of de-gassing is called, literally, "giving a turn." This is more descriptive of how it should be done, especially with lean dough formulas (no added fat or emulsifiers): it is not necessary to fully de-gas the dough when it is punched down, and one should try not to overwork it. Instead, a fist is slowly pushed into the center of the bowl, creating a hole. The dough is then folded over the resultant hole several times, expelling most of the gas and helping to restructure the dough; refolding the dough reconstitutes the gluten webs. The nutrients in the dough and any areas of unequal dough temperature are redistributed by this practice, keeping fermentation active.

The best way to determine when a dough is ready for punching down is to check the dough by pressing on it. A new dough is quite plastic and will retain the shape of the hand when it is pulled away. When the dough is elastic and gassy and quickly fills the void, gas pressure is high enough for punching down. This is to some extent the opposite of what is desired in bread that is tested for proof before baking: in fermentation you want the dough to be well within its elastic limit; at the end of proofing you want it to be just about at its elastic limit, but not over it.

Primary fermentation of yeasted straight doughs should continue for an additional one-half the amount of time it took for the dough to be ready to punch down. If the dough took two hours to be ready for punching down, the dough should rise one additional hour or a little less before it is ready for rounding. Omission of punching down (in a yeasted straight-bread process) impairs both bread volume and flavor. If the bread fully ferments without punching down, gluten will be overstretched and some gas-trapping ability will be lost. Conversely, if the dough is not allowed to fully ferment, the gluten will be inadequately stressed and developed, and again the bread will suffer.

Proofing

Proofing is the stage where all your previous work comes together. Either you see a wonderful alchemical transformation as your loaves bloom, or you start to look for a place to hide.

METHODS OF PROOFING
HEARTH-BAKED BREADS
Hearth-baked bread loaves can be allowed to assume their own semi-flat shape while proofing on a thick bed of coarse meal spread on a wooden surface (so that the peel can be slid under them to transfer them to the oven) or they can be proofed in *bannetons* (baskets or colanders, lined or unlined) or *couches* (folded linen cloths) that preserve their moisture and their shapes. Again, the proofed loaves are transferred to a peel for loading into the oven.

Bannetons can be used in two basic ways. Most simply, the loaf can be formed to a round or oval shape, then floured by rolling it on the floured counter before it is placed in a basket of coiled wicker or woven straw or reed. These will leave their spiral mark or woven mark on the loaf. They are available in round and oval shapes to preserve the shape of round and oval loaves.

More typically, baskets or colanders are lined with linen cloth, in which case the loaf is not floured or is only very lightly floured before it is placed in the basket. Sometimes the cloth is basted onto the rim of the basket, and stays with the basket when the loaf is turned out. Alternatively, the loose square of cloth in the basket can receive the loaf, then be closed over it as it is proofing to keep the top of the doughball (which will be the bottom of the finished loaf) from drying out. The only drawback of this is that the cloth needs to be held onto the rim of the basket as the loaf is turned out. It takes two hands to turn out the loaf instead of one. Even when loaves are not purposely floured, raising in lined *bannetons* will leave a faint pattern on the loaf after it is baked, because some areas of the skin of the dough will dry more than others during proof, and those areas will appear lighter in color. There will be a slight imprint of the cloth, too, if the weave is open.

Home bakers often have trouble figuring out how to get risen loaves out of baskets and into the oven. They have bought a baking stone but not a peel, or they have a peel but don't know how to get the bread onto it. The answer for bread raised on a board heavily coated with corn meal or coarse wheat meal is to quickly slide the edge of a piece of metal (a flat cookie sheet is fine) under the loaf, then slide the loaf off of that and onto the oven peel. For loaves raised in baskets, just invert the basket over the oven peel after sprinkling the peel with meal, then slide the loaf off the peel and into the oven. Most masonry oven bakers load two or four loaves at a time onto a large peel, to keep their ovens open a shorter time.

Baguettes and most *batards* are proofed in linen *couches*. This means that a long strip of cloth wider than the length of the loaf is pulled into folds. Each fold holds one loaf and separates it from its neighbor, and the seam of each loaf (where it was healed up after it was shaped into its elongated shape) is facing the same way. That allows the baker to pull out the strip, rolling one loaf at a time onto a floured transfer peel. This is a long thin wooden batten that transfers the loaf to an oven peel, where it is placed seam down. Usually two loaves at a time will then be loaded into the oven.

There are two reasons for using linen to line *bannetons* and to form *couches*. One is that it does not carry small linty fibers, so the loaf is not likely to stick to it. The other is that it is absorbent, and wicks just enough water from the surface of the loaf to form the kind of thin skin that will help open the slash on hearth loaves, without drying the loaf to the point of losing crust color.

PROOFING TEMPERATURE

Commercial bakers want to proof formed loaves at 95 to 110 degrees Fahrenheit and a humidity of between 75 and 90 percent, until they reach a balance between their gas volume and the ability of the dough to contain that volume. At a temperature of 95 degrees Fahrenheit this typically takes an hour for yeasted bread and sometimes longer for sourdough breads. Industrial tests have

ABOVE: *After* bâtards *proof in folded linen* couches, *the linen can be pulled straight, rolling the loaf onto a transfer peel, from which it can be rolled onto an oven peel.*

Baskets are stored on shelves between uses, where the baker can reach them easily.

These loaves at the Brickery at Café Beaujolais are proofing in floured willow baskets or in wicker baskets lined with linen.

shown that a bread that is ideally proofed for sixty-three minutes will be under-proofed at forty-eight minutes, and over-proofed at seventy-two minutes—indicating the relatively narrow tolerances for rapidly proofing yeasted breads. Longer proofs lead to more flavor development, which may or may not be desirable. Proofing at higher or lower temperatures was, until recently, thought chiefly to affect the duration of proofing, but more careful recent research on white breads indicates that a cooler proof to the same proof volume results in a larger loaf.

What about naturally fermented loaves? There are those who always proof at elevated temperatures, and have a reason for doing it. In Alan Scott's case, the Desem dough is 100 percent whole wheat and his loaves might tend to be heavy if proofed at room temperature—gas would escape at a rate only a little slower than the rate at which it was produced. Instead, Alan finds that with the high-temperature proof his loaves pop up in proof and in the oven. During a lower-temperature proof, his round loaves would have more time to flow into a flattened shape—he proofs on boards, not in baskets, and there is nothing to hold the shape of the proofing loaves but their own integrity. Because whole wheat promotes vigorous fermentation, the loaves could also become too sour. Alan delivers his bread the day it is baked, and is able to leave home at 1 P.M., making good use of those two hours saved in proofing.

Most home and artisan bakers do not proof at elevated temperatures. Many artisan bakeries retard proofing loaves, actually refrigerating them, not warming them. For loaves that are not proofed at elevated temperatures or retarded, most bakers feel the correct *degree* of proofing is more important than the time or temperature of the proof. At typical temperatures of 70 to 75 degrees Fahrenheit, proofing naturally fermented loaves will take three to four hours, and if you have that much time available, creating a special environment for your loaves is probably not justified.

The most common test for full proofing is to touch the loaf with a wet or floured finger: it should leave a dent but spring back slightly; it should not collapse. This can be a hard judgment to make. Under-proofing slightly reduces final loaf volume, but over-proofing leads to pale crust, poor keeping qualities, and a crumb so open that it is disorganized, lifeless, and unsatisfactory. Over-proofed loaves look sad and downhearted, flat and wrinkled. It is best to err on the under-proofed side. You will know that your loaves are significantly under-proofed if they burst excessively at the slash, distorting the overall shape of the loaf until it looks like a pillow that has burst and is losing its stuffing. When you get to that point you should begin adding fifteen minutes to your proof each time you bake. When you get it right, you'll know.

PROOFING HUMIDITY

A relative humidity that is too low in your kitchen, bakery, or proofing box will have a detrimental effect on proofing dough. It can dry out the dough, reducing loaf volume, crust formation, and crust caramelization. Fortunately, loaves raised in a *couche* or *banneton* have most of their surface protected by the *couche* cloth or basket liner, which protects them somewhat, and it is desirable for the outer skin of the loaf to dry out a little if it is going to be slashed. Many artisan bakers making hearth breads want a bit of a semi-dry skin on a loaf to tighten it up and create a more dramatic slash and burst pattern. Naturally leavened breads tolerate this kind of treatment better than their straight-method cousins do. Even loaves retarded in a refrigerator seem to stay moist enough with just a cloth over them for up to twenty-four hours.

Loaves that are proofed on boards need a very high level of humidity to avoid excessive drying of the outside of the proofing loaf. Otherwise, the crust may be too restrictive and the loaves may be small or burst uncontrollably. One benefit of Alan's high temperature proof is that he achieves it by heating water (in electric skillets) at the base of his proofing cabinet—this gives him a little less than 100 percent humidity at 95 degrees Fahrenheit. The skin of his dough remains fully hydrated when it goes into the masonry oven. Such loaves may not need slashing, except for decoration. With a little added steam in the oven the loaves are resistant to bursting, and he feels this helps his whole wheat loaves achieve the maximum possible oven spring. It is important in creating this kind of a proofing box to avoid so much humidity that water will condense on the loaves in drops. Excess humidity during proofing may toughen the crust and make it leathery.

The upshot here? If you are going to raise your loaves in *couches* or lined or unlined baskets, don't worry about humidity unless you see signs of excessively dry loaves. Feel free to provide supplemental moisture in proofing when you proof on boards, especially if you live in a dry climate and are planning to make unslashed loaves.

Slashing

Slashing is the last step before loaves of bread not held in pans are placed in the oven. It must be done with a very sharp knife or razor blade. Double-edged blades are thinner and sharper than single-edged blades. They can be purchased mounted on a little stick of metal or plastic called a *lame*, and can be replaced on the *lame* when nicked or dull.

The cuts should be a quarter-inch to a half-inch deep, angled slightly to encourage the top edge of the cut surface to curl up a little in the oven, and sufficient in number and depth to relieve the crust stress that develops during oven spring. If the slashes are not placed frequently enough or made deep enough into the dough, the loaf will tear uncontrollably.

PROOFING IN LOAF PANS

Proofing bread in pans will affect the volume of the loaf and the volume of the air cells in the loaf. Loaves baked in pans have a slightly smaller overall volume and smaller gas cells in the crumb. The cell structure will be more regular, and the loaves will not require slashing to control break and shred during baking, assuming the volume of the pan is appropriate for the finished size of the loaf.

Ideal pan volume is six to seven cubic inches for each ounce of dough used (for yeasted white bread), with bigger pan volumes per ounce giving a more open crumb in the baked bread. Pans are coated with fat to prevent sticking: straight vegetable oil does not do a good job, and should be mixed with some melted butter or with lecithin. Commercial non-stick sprays are an alternative: they contain oil and lecithin.

Whole wheat breads made with spelt or durum wheat flour (such as Kamut flour) are best baked in pans because their dough structure is weak. Shaping is not so important for these doughs, as it will have less effect on loaf volume. Proofing times and temperatures remain important but, overall, pan breads are much more forgiving of minor errors that creep into baking processes when several batches of different doughs are being juggled in the same kitchen. Pan breads are more tolerant of over-proofing, overheated ovens, or lack of oven space. Alan Scott uses a smaller-than-usual pan made of cast iron, and places more than the usual weight of dough in each one to compensate for the reduced dough structure and risen volume of whole grain doughs.

So: artisan bakers are careful with their dough. They use good flour, they use good active leavens, they don't over-knead, they give plenty of time for fermentation, and they are careful when they form and proof their loaves.

Then they cast fate to the winds, and their dough into the oven.

ACME BAKING COMPANY

Berkeley, California

The biggest difference between Acme and other bakers is record-keeping. *As simple as that!*

≈

THE ACME BREAD COMPANY was one of the first commercial bakeries I visited when I started to work on this book. I went there at a time when I naively thought there was some essential "secret" that I must learn to be able to make the kind of bread I wanted. In a way, there was—but what I learned at Acme was not at all the kind of secret I imagined!

Acme is one of the best large artisan bakeries in the United States, and was founded by Steve Sullivan. He was working at Chez Panisse in Berkeley in the early 1980s and was asked by Alice Waters to see if he could bake better bread than she was buying. After a great deal of experimentation he found that he could, and he started the Acme Baking Company. Although it began as a wholesale operation selling to restaurants, this led to a general wholesale and then a retail operation. Now there is the original bakery (Division I), which sells retail and does some wholesale; Division II, which is a larger operation (wholesale) about a mile away; and the new Division III, on the San Francisco peninsula. I chose to visit Division II because I had heard it had a "brick oven" and I wondered how European-style breads could be turned out in a larger operation than any I had visited.

That brings me to the Acme "secret." Early in my visit I asked Doug Volkmer (the head of the operation at Division II) what it was, that magical factor that accounted for the excellence of their bread. He thought about it for several seconds, then said that the biggest difference between Acme and other bakers is *record-keeping*. As simple as that!

The people at Acme have learned that only by carefully keeping records of materials, temperatures, techniques, and times—and by correlating those data with results—have the variables in dough production and baking been recognized and then manipulated. One baker might be able to keep all that in his head, but many bakers working together have to rely on established procedures, and at Acme most of those procedures have been developed in-house over a period of years. Doug feels that this kind of attention to detail is especially important for naturally leavened breads, because there are so many variables in those processes and because the processes are so extended over time.

Most of Acme's breads are "sourdoughs" of one kind or another. Many are based on unbleached white flour with an 11.5 percent protein content, about the same as good all-purpose flour. All the doughs are

ACME BAKING COMPANY

retarded during primary fermentation or proofing—usually both. In addition to a large cooler (for bulk doughs and for some loaves) there is a tempering room (kept at 85 degrees Fahrenheit), a walk-through cooler/proofer (the temperature is changed depending on production needs) and a large walk-through proofer. Bakers are in the plant twenty-four hours a day: mixing goes on around the clock, loaves are shaped twenty-one hours per day, bread is baked about eighteen hours a day, and deliveries are made from 5 A.M. to 4 P.M.

Division II divides *baguettes* with a hydraulic divider, after which they are placed in a machine that gives them a rest before they are partially formed mechanically to a length of about sixteen inches. They are then rested again briefly before they are finished off by hand at 24 inches. They are proofed in linen *couches* on boards placed in racks that are rolled in and out of retarding and proofing rooms, while round and oval loaves are proofed in *bannetons*. Much of the dough is still cool when it is baked, which is one cause of the

The bakers at Acme let the machines do the heavy work. This batch of dough has just been dumped out for dividing. Just after I took this picture, the baker checked the temperature of the dough with an electronic thermometer and entered it on a clipboard.

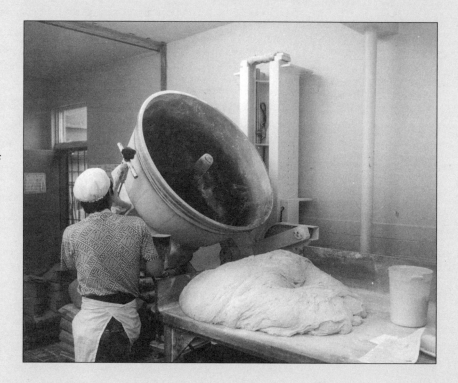

small crust blisters that are a mark of Acme bread. Another mark is a deeper crust color than most other American commercial bakers accept. Acme is one bakery that tries to get three distinct colors on each loaf.

Division II gets nearly equal production out of its two ovens. The gas-fired four-level deck oven has a refractory hearth surface and is heated with superheated water that is circulated under the hearths (hearth temperature 400 to 420 degrees Fahrenheit for various breads). It is quite a sight to see ten or twelve *foccacia* or eighteen Italian loaves going into or coming out of one chamber of the oven at one time! There is no steam injection—water is automatically dripped on cast iron plates and boils into the oven air in the first phase of baking.

The other oven is an externally fired wood-burning rotary oven, designed and partially constructed in Spain and erected in Berkeley. Only the outer facade and the hearth of this oven are masonry; the oven walls and the oven roof are steel. The hearth is a circular plate covered with refractory concrete and about twelve or fourteen feet across. It rotates around a central column when the baker turns a big metal wheel next to the oven door. The oven door itself is made of clear high-temperature material and is spring-loaded; it is pushed down by the peel, leaving a metal ridge on which the peel can be braced and slid. Almost no heat or steam is lost from the oven when it is loaded or unloaded, so no supplemental source of steam is necessary after the first batch is done. The high water percentage in the dough reduces the need for supplemental moisture in the oven, and the bread bakes beautifully.

I found that the people at Acme were very generous with their time. The simplicity of the "secret"—that record-keeping is their key to both innovation and consistency—just made me respect them more. They acknowledge that producing a consistent product remains a day-to-day struggle for them, even after years in the business. Not because of variability in the cultures or the flour alone, but because of the summation of all the factors that contribute to bread quality. This is especially important to a three-location, twenty-four-hour-a-day operation like Acme, where production workers probe dough frequently with digital thermometers and record temperatures to allow control of fermentation at various stages, where fermentation containers are limited to 50 pounds of dough for temperature control, and where almost all doughs are retarded during production.

ACME BAKING COMPANY

TECHNICAL POINTS:

- There are charts on Doug's wall for "Products and Price Levels" (details the volume price break points and price for all products) and for "Production Limits" (how much of each product the facility can turn out in a day—most of these limits are filled, and Acme cannot take on new accounts for them; sometimes there is available capacity for a similar product). Reference to these charts allows him to respond quickly to requests from wholesale customers, who tend to get frustrated if they, say, open a new grocery store and can't get the same stock as they carry in their other stores. Doug can also make judgments on firing accounts that are not paying invoices on time.

- The change-over to organic flour may eventually lead Acme farther down the supply chain, and give Acme more control over the characteristics of the flour as well. Currently, Acme has no in-house laboratory facilities—any testing must be sent out.

- The timer on the retarder/proofer unit allows a baker to cool dough in the evening, knowing that the timer will switch to proofing heat at 2:30 A.M. That way, say, the Danish pastry will be ready to bake at 5:30 when the baker comes in. In contrast, at 10:15 A.M. some walnut *levain* loaves have proofed for two and one-half hours (risen two-thirds of the way) and are going to be cooled for the rest of the day to be the first thing baked by the night shift.

CHAPTER FIVE

BAKING, OVENS,

and BREAD

I had no idea what bread was before I started to work on this book. I knew it was food made from grain—I had been baking for many years. I just had no idea what happened in the oven. Does the dough just dry out as it heats up? What causes it to pop up and burst out? How does it get brown? What makes the flavor? What makes it stiff, so you can slice it?

Now I have the answers to these questions, and many more, at least on a basic level. Understanding the baking process has changed the way I bake, and I am guessing that you will have the same experience. It turns out that dough does not become bread just by being dried in the oven. Drying is part of baking, but a smaller part than you might expect. In fact, dough only loses 12 percent of its weight as it is baked. What turns dough into bread is an amazing chain of physical events and chemical transformations, most of which involve shifts in water *within* the dough.

The Baking Process

Bread changes from a soft, pliable dough to the more solid, finished loaf of bread through heat-driven changes in which starches and proteins take on new forms. For starch, this change is the result of sudden hydration of the starch in the previously stable starch granules, to become a gel. For protein, the change is in part a result of a loss of water. The appropriation of water by starch dehydrates and alters dough proteins, which are also irreversibly changed in structure by heat.

GELATINIZATION OF STARCH

Gelatinization is the process in which starch takes on water and becomes a water-starch gel. In raw dough, most starch is present in a dry crystalline state, in the form of microscopic starch granules. These granules become wrapped in wet protein nets as the dough is kneaded and flour particles are broken up, but the starch inside unbroken granules is only slightly wetted. The dough is a stiff suspension of starch granules and yeast cells in water until the temperature of the dough rises to 130 to 135 degrees Fahrenheit (about 55 degrees Celsius). At that temperature the yeast dies and the dough softens considerably because the hot gluten becomes softer and more plastic.

At about the same temperature, the starch in the dough begins to gelatinize, and gelatinization continues as the dough temperature continues to rise. The crystalline granules break apart and starch chains uncoil, soaking up all the water they can attract and trapping it in gels. The extent of this process is limited by the availability of water in the dough and therefore does not run to completion inside baking bread—there isn't enough water available. Once gelled, starch becomes the major structural element in the dough, taking over that role from the gluten web and its gas cells. When the dough reaches a temperature of about 160 degrees Fahrenheit (71 degrees Celsius) it loses much of its ability to trap CO_2: many of the gas cell walls break as the water in them is taken up. The space in which gas is retained becomes more continuous than it was as many gas cells coalesce.

PROTEIN'S TRANSFORMATION

Dough proteins are not only softened by mild heat and dehydrated by gelatinization, they are eventually **denatured** (coagulated) starting at about 165 degrees Fahrenheit (74 degrees Celsius). This is the same process that occurs in an egg as it cooks and becomes hard-boiled. The physical properties of the denatured proteins (enzymes as well as gluten) change. They lose flexibility, extensibility, and solubility, but remain elastic. When the proteins are stiff enough, at about 200 degrees Fahrenheit (95 degrees Celsius), gas cell expansion halts and the final shape of the loaf is set.

OVEN SPRING

As the bread bakes, trapped gas is heated and expands. Enlarged gas cells (bubbles) hold some of this expanding gas, so the dough expands. These cells contain carbon dioxide that was in them before the baking process started. More carbon dioxide (previously dissolved) is driven out of the dough, most of it coming out by the time the dough reaches 130 degrees Fahrenheit (55 degrees Celsius). In addition to this carbon dioxide, there are many volatile organic compounds synthesized by the yeast (alcohol, aldehydes, esters, etc.) that are boiled into the cells at about 180 degrees Fahrenheit (82 degrees Celsius). Gas cell expansion at a time when the dough is still very soft produces the **oven spring** that is essential to the pleasing appearance of a loaf of bread.*

What effect does the temperature of an oven have on oven spring? Why are hearth breads baked at an oven air temperature of

> *Dough proteins are not only softened by mild heat and dehydrated by gelatinization, they are eventually denatured by oven heat. This is the same process that occurs in an egg as it cooks and becomes hard-boiled.*
>
> ∼

*About one-quarter of oven spring is due to expansion of carbon dioxide already in the cells; one-fifth is due to migration of existing carbon dioxide into the gas cells, and a little less than half is due to boiling of alcohol into cells. The rest comes from steam generated inside the loaf and from some additional carbon dioxide produced in baking bread before the yeast is killed. This last doesn't contribute much to oven spring because there isn't much time for it to occur.

Left: *Richard Freeman's loaf holds its shape well, and will spring rapidly on the hot hearth (photo: courtesy of Richard Freeman).*

Above: *This hearth loaf was proofed in a floured, linen-lined basket. Look at how much oven spring it shows.*

about 425 degrees Fahrenheit, on a hearth that is much hotter, while pan breads are usually baked at 350 to 375 degrees? Aside from the lack of excess residual sugar in hearth loaves (sugar that would burn at high temperatures), the reason is that hearth loaves are intrinsically frail until they are baked, as they get no support from a pan. The rate at which the pressure inside a loaf increases in the oven is much more critical for hearth loaves than for pan breads.

If an oven is too cool the gas won't boil out of the dough fast enough, water won't boil and turn to steam fast enough, and the pressure rise in the dough won't rise high enough to overcome the tendency for the loaf to sag and spread as it heats and thus gets softer. The loaf won't spring, and if you cut it open when it is baked you won't see the kind of elongation and streaming of gas cells that

are marks of good hearth-baked bread. As far as I am concerned, the ideal oven temperature is the one that will just get the crumb of the bread to full temperature before the outside of the loaf is burned. Thrust an instant-reading thermometer into the middle of a loaf when it looks done. It should be at least 195 degrees Fahrenheit, though 200 degrees is ideal. Bread baked to a higher temperature does not keep as well.

THE EVAPORATION OF WATER AND THE DEVELOPMENT OF FLAVOR AND COLOR

Let's look at this process in greater detail. You know that water lost from the loaf during baking boils and turns to steam. As it does, it absorbs heat, slowing the rate at which the temperature of the baking dough can increase. This evaporation limits the temperature of the interior of an overcooked loaf of bread to 210 degrees Fahrenheit, just below the boiling point of water, and just above the desired temperature in the middle of a fully cooked loaf.

The temperature of the crust of a loaf, though, can soar above the boiling point of water, since the crust dries out more than the crumb. At elevated temperatures some of the sugar in the crust will break down, become sticky, and participate in two types of chemical reactions:

- First, sugar combines with protein breakdown products (amino acids) in the so-called Maillard reactions. These start when the crust is still moist, at temperatures below the boiling point of water. At higher temperatures the Maillard reactions can produce a deep brown crust color and a variety of flavor molecules.

- The second reaction is caramelization, a reaction in which sugars and their breakdown products interact at somewhat higher temperatures (starting at 275 degrees Fahrenheit, or 135 degrees Celsius) to form complex polymers. This adds brown color and some bitter taste compounds, but caramelization is not as important as the Maillard reactions in the proper browning of bread.

Together, caramels and Maillard products are responsible for much of the flavor and aroma of fresh bread, although of the two, Maillard products are much more intensely aromatic. Only certain sugars—not including sucrose, but including sugars produced in doughs by yeast enzymes—can participate in Maillard reactions. These are reducing sugars, such as maltose and glucose. Sucrose (table sugar) is not a reducing sugar, and does not contribute to browning to the same degree, although enzymes in fermenting dough convert some of it to glucose and fructose, which both promote browning through the Maillard reactions. The aroma of Maillard products differentiates some yeasted products from their chemically leavened counterparts, raised with baking powder.

If an oven is never hot enough to dry and bake the crust sufficiently, bread will cook through without forming attractive crust color or flavor. Bread cooked experimentally in a microwave never undergoes these reactions and is devoid of *bread* flavor: it's cooked paste. Interestingly, though, steamed or boiled bread is more nutritious in one way: some of the amino acids (especially lysine) in baking bread are degraded by the high heat in the crust, but are not broken down to the same degree when dough is only boiled. The same phenomenon of amino acid loss occurs when bread is toasted. Some nutritive value is lost, but flavor is enhanced.

THE EFFECT OF MOISTURE ON THE CRUST

High moisture content in the dough and high humidity in the oven in the early phase of baking increase the chewiness and color of bread crust. The moisture allows for more complete gel formation in the crust, higher sugar levels, and more sugar reactions. (On the other hand, an excessively dry oven will produce a crust in which more of the starch remains in its original state.) After a starch gel forms in the crust, further heating and drying toughens it and makes for a strong crust. Heating is of course slower in the interior of the loaf and the crumb gels never get as dehydrated during baking as the crust. It is the push of the relatively liquid crumb, as it is heated, that thrusts apart the slash in the crust, forming the shred of the loaf and completing oven spring.

Because both gel formation (hydration) and gel drying (dehydration) form the crust, it is possible to make an especially crisp crust by either leaving the oven door open for the last few minutes of baking, or by spraying loaves lightly with water once or twice in the last phase of baking.

THE STRUCTURE OF A FULLY BAKED LOAF

Bread is said to be fully baked when the bottom of the loaf rings with a hollow sound when tapped. This is only a reliable test when bread is evenly baked from all directions. Pan-baked breads increase in internal temperature slowly during the first half of baking, rapidly for about three-eighths of the bake, then slowly again in the last eighth of the baking cycle. This slow-down is partially due to evaporation of water from the surface of the loaf, which cools it. Though I found no similar studies of hearth breads, it is likely that the initial delay in rising internal temperature is shorter due to the rapid transfer of heat from the hearth to the bottom of the loaf. The hollow sound heard from a fully cooked loaf is a sign that the dough has changed from a plastic paste to a semi-solid gel throughout the loaf. If many gas cells are still surrounded by dough in which the starch is not gelatinized, the sound is muffled, dead, and wooden; the bread is not yet baked. You know that overcooked crumb seems dry and flavorless (and becomes stale quickly); undercooked crumb is gummy and can rot.

Heating Processes: Conduction, Convection, and Radiation

Just how does heat get into the bread to cook it? There are three basic processes: conduction, convection, and radiation.

CONDUCTION

Conduction occurs when a hot object touches a colder object, or when heat is applied to one end of an object and flows to the other end. This is the way heat flows out of your hand and into a cold piece of metal that you take out of the freezer, or the way heat flows from one end of a metal bar to another. How much heat can flow by conduction in a specified unit of time is determined by the relative temperatures of the touching objects, the area of their contact, and the heat qualities of the objects. Different materials have different heat properties, just as they have different densities. A high specific heat material has a lot of heat to give up before its temperature falls very much, but it may or may not *conduct* heat quickly. For example, bricks store heat well, but don't conduct it quickly. Aluminum, on the other hand, can't store much heat; it is, however, a wonderful heat conductor. Iron and steel store a great deal of heat and also conduct it fairly well. Water stores heat well; air stores it poorly. Conduction between a hot object and a cold object is reduced by *insulation* between them, which slows down the flow of heat. When insulation is present, heat flow by conduction depends not only on the temperature difference between objects and on their surface area, but also on the effectiveness and thickness of the insulation between them.

CONVECTION

Convection occurs when some type of fluid (a liquid or a gas) takes on heat from a hot object and carries it to a cold one. The fluid is an intermediary in the heat flow, and it moves either as a result of changes in its density as it is heated and cooled, or as a result of some kind of pump, like the fan in a convection oven, which takes air that has been heated elsewhere and blows it around. Heat transfer by convection depends on the qualities of the fluid (especially its capacity to hold heat) and the rate at which it circulates. If the circulation rate is very low, films of fluid on the surfaces of objects can act as insulators, reducing heat flow. Also, at low convection

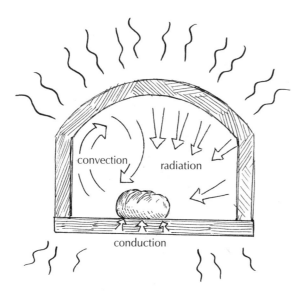

The three methods of heat transfer in a masonry oven: conduction, convection, and radiation.

rates all the available heat in the transfer fluid may be gone before it gets back to the heat source again, and this will reduce the rate of heat transfer to the cold object. For example, an egg in a pot of boiling water is receiving heat from the bottom of the pot, convected to the egg by the water. A rapidly boiling pot of water will be free of cold spots and the egg will cook quickly and evenly.

RADIATION

Radiation is a direct heat flow process and doesn't rely on physical contact or a transfer fluid. That is how the sun warms the earth and the inside of your car. How fast the heat flows depends on the difference in temperature between objects, the surface area and surface characteristics of the objects (color, texture), and the distance between objects. We can't see the process occurring, as the heat waves are predominantly in the infrared part of the light spectrum and can only be seen with special goggles, like the ones used by people on night military maneuvers. In spite of its mysterious invisibility, radiation can transfer a lot of heat in a hurry. Since radiant heating is so critical to masonry oven baking, it is probably worth considering this type of heating in that context.

RADIANT HEAT IN MASONRY OVENS

One of the conditions that could affect radiant heat transfer is the vessel within which the radiation occurs. Some people have postulated that the radiant heat from a masonry oven wall is qualitatively (not just quantitatively) so different from that of other ovens that the difference accounts for the particular nature of the crust of hearth-baked breads. This theory holds that the relatively cool temperature of the oven walls (compared to an electric heating element, say) would produce light waves that are longer than those of a hotter radiant source, and that these waves would be able to penetrate farther into the dough (making a thicker crust). Shorter rays (from a glowing electric heat element) would be absorbed or reflected on the surface, giving the crust a superficial sunburn.

Part of this is true. Masonry oven walls do make a high proportion of longer waves (in the near-infrared part of the spectrum). However, electric heating elements and the walls of metal-lined ovens do, too. Regardless of the source of these waves, none of them penetrate deeply into the dough for two reasons. First, the water molecules in the dough absorb most of the radiation. Second, deep penetration is unlikely because starch granules and pigments in the dough also scatter or absorb radiant energy waves.

The excellent crust formation in masonry oven baking has to do with the *quantity of radiation available*, and the high rate at which it is delivered in an environment that is initially moist and gradually drier through the bake. The quantity of radiant heat available is partly dependent on the surface temperature in the oven. In a masonry oven this is typically 100 Fahrenheit degrees (38 degrees Celsius) higher than the temperature of the oven air. The cooler oven air will have a higher relative humidity than hotter air containing the same amount of moisture. The crust *will form quickly because of the intense heating effect from radiation, but will not be dried out quickly, because of the high oven humidity*. In other ovens the oven air may be hotter than the oven walls.

Heating Processes in a Masonry Oven

All three heat flow processes are at work in a brick oven, *all at the same time*. That's why brick ovens work so well for cooking bread! There is a lot of conduction, for instance, from the bottom of the oven directly into the bread that sits on it, or into the bread pan and then into the bread. The great heat storage capacity of the masonry on the floor of the oven means that the floor doesn't cool too much as the bread cooks. It provides plenty of heat during the initial phase of cooking, when the crust is forming on the bottom of the loaf. In the case of a pizza or pita, the conducted heat just jumps through the flat, thin disc of bread, cooking it in a few minutes before the masonry cools. A larger loaf will cool the bottom of the oven somewhat, but more heat will flow up to the surface of the masonry from deeper down, replacing the heat lost by the oven floor and helping to maintain the heat flow into the bread at a rate that does not burn the crust.

Convection currents are stirred up when cool dough is put into a hot brick oven. Moving air carries heat from the oven walls to the loaf, where the air cools again, transferring heat to the bread before the cooled air is replaced by new, hotter air. Although the heat storage capacity of air is low, the fact that hot air is continually renewed in a masonry oven means that convection is an important part of the brick oven effect.

Heat transfer by radiation is what makes a big difference between a masonry heat-retention oven and other ovens. The interior surface of the oven will not cool much in a single bake, and a massive radiant heat flow into the dough will continue even after the temperature of the air in the oven drops because the door has been open and bread has been added. The amount of radiant heat reaching a loaf will vary little between a large oven and a small one, if the inner surfaces are equally hot. This is why a bread cloche will bake one loaf of bread as well as a masonry oven will bake ten or twelve.

The Cloche

"La Cloche" is the brand name of a pottery accessory (which I will refer to generically as a cloche) that can be placed in a conventional home oven, heated to full temperature, and then used to bake one round loaf at a time. Although the instructions don't actually say to use the cloche this way—by heating it to full temperature—I have discussed my way of using a cloche with its inventor, and he says it's fine. What it does is to reproduce most of the charcteristics of a retained-heat masonry oven. In fact, the inventor/manufacturer of the modern cloche, Steve Schwab, based his prototype on an ancient one-loaf pottery oven illustrated in Elizabeth David's book, *English Bread and Yeast Cooking.*

Here's how I use the cloche*: First, heat both pieces (top and bottom) to 425 degrees Fahrenheit. Carefully remove both pieces when you are ready to bake, and sprinkle some meal or bran into the hot bottom of the cloche. Flip the dough into it from a proofing basket. The loaf must be quickly slashed, the heated bell-shaped top replaced, and the cloche put back in the oven. Do not spray the top of the loaf with water—the cloche traps some of the moisture from the loaf as the bread bakes, and added moisture will not

help. Remove the top of the cloche after the loaf has been baking for ten to fifteen minutes.** Removing the top will allow the crust of the loaf to brown completely before it is taken from the oven, done, in about twenty-five more minutes. It is helpful to have a good electronic timer when baking with a cloche, so you don't forget a step—heating the pottery, taking off the top in fifteen minutes, taking the bread out.

Why bother with all of this? Because the results are *breathtaking*, if you have never baked in masonry before. If you haven't built your oven yet, baking one loaf at a time like this is a good way to work on your baking technique.

The story of Steve Schwab's trip to a gourmet cooking equipment show in San Francisco in the early 1980s with the only existing cloche prototype is pretty funny—the cabin attendant wanted him to check it, but he wouldn't even put it down. He held it on his lap all the way. At the show, Chuck Williams of Williams-Sonoma wanted to have it for a trial. Since it was the only one,

Cloche from Sasafrass Industries.

*The alternative method works well too: Either proof the loaf in a basket and flip it into the room-temperature cloche (lightly sprayed or greased, and sprinkled with meal) or let the loaf proof in the cloche. Then slash the loaf, recover it, and put it in a hot oven (500 degrees Fahrenheit).

**When you use the alternative method of baking with a cloche (cool cloche, hot oven) you leave the top on longer—at least thirty minutes. Then bake until the loaf is brown.

Steve had to say that he would send Williams another one when he got home—which he did. He had to have it made first. Then Williams had him make another one to send to James Beard, who wrote it up: suddenly people from all over were trying to buy cloches when, essentially, none existed.

Eventually Schwab got things straightened out, and he went on to buy the pottery factory in western Illinois that had made the prototype for him (by attaching a handle to the bottom of an unglazed bowl to create the top of the cloche, forming a lip on the rim so it would mate with a large pottery pie plate). Production of La Cloche has been steady work for the factory ever since. With the closure of many old-line American earthenware producers since World War II, Schwab's factory is now one of the few sources of things like bean pots and stoneware bowls, not to mention pizza stones, bread stones, and cloches. Schwab feels these natural pottery products have distinct advantages over similar products made of refractory cements, due to the ability of pottery to absorb some of the moisture in dough as it is baked.

Conventional Ovens

Conventional gas or electric ovens don't recover their heating effect as quickly as a masonry oven or a cloche and oven combination, and don't maintain high heat flows (or adequate moisture) when the crust is forming and the bread is springing. The metal on the wall of such an oven is too thin to deliver this kind of heat in the face of the radiant and convective drain of the cool dough. A commercial convection oven may keep up, but the air is very hot, and moving the air so quickly tends to dry out the surface of the dough just as it is supposed to be moist. These ovens have to be modified to employ water sprayers in their fan sections. Most ovens are hard-pressed to maintain their maximum cooking effect in the face of a quantity of cool, moist dough, both because of the thermal load of the cool dough and because of the continuing requirement for heat as water and volatile compounds are boiled out of the dough.

The usual way of baking hearth breads in a conventional oven (for those without a cloche) is with a baking stone or baking tiles. These are heated to 425 or 450 degrees Fahrenheit before the dough is flipped onto them from a *banneton* or a peel. The moisture required to form the crust is best supplied by heating a cast-iron pan on an oven rack below the baking stone. After you slash and place the loaf on the stone, pour a cup or so of water into the cast-iron pan. Spray the walls of the oven in two or three minutes if the crust is drying too quickly.

I have, on occasion, made wonderful bread in a large metal casserole pot with a lid, but the process is laborious, and I am only going to include it here at the direct request of my wife. Either she wants you to know how to do it if you need to, or she wants you to know what a fool I am. Here goes.

Baking with a cloche in a conventional oven has breathtaking results, if you have never baked in masonry before.

~

This technique involves preheating the pot on top of a cookie sheet in the oven until everything—oven, sheet, and pot—is hot: 450 degrees Fahrenheit. Next I take the hot pot out of the oven, put in a little corn meal, flip the dough in, slash it, replace the lid, and put the pot in the oven for twelve minutes. I then take the pot out, take the top off, and put the loaf and pot back in the oven to allow the crust to start to form. The loaf needs to be strong enough for me to handle before I can take it out of the pot, and it won't start to get a nice color until I do; it needs this second phase of baking to get strong. Generally twelve or fifteen minutes is long enough.

Then I take the pot out, and, holding it with one potholder, I rest it on the top of the stove and gently flip the loaf upside down onto a potholder in my other hand. The bottom of the loaf is likely to be nearly fully baked at this point, but the top of the loaf will be completely blond. If I were to put the loaf directly onto the cookie sheet the bottom of the loaf would burn before the rest of the crust was baked. So I do one more crazy thing: I put the loaf on an upside down metal pie plate, and then I put them both on the sheet. The airspace in the pie plate controls the flow of heat to the bottom of the loaf as the rest of the loaf bakes perfectly in about ten minutes.

Perfect Crust

Moisture and heat are two of the secrets to chewy and colorful crust—the kind of crust that is hard to produce in a metal kitchen oven. The degree to which starch in the dough will gelatinize depends on the pres-ence of adequate available moisture and the maintenance of temperature within a specific range. Because bread crust dries out in the later stages of baking, its temperature will far exceed the boiling point of water, while the crumb will not. This high temperature sets (dehydrates) the starch gel, but excessive drying will crack it and burn it.

One factor that the baker can manipulate is the availability of water during the early stage of baking, when the crust is between 120 and 140 degrees Fahrenheit, during gel formation. At least enough moisture must be present to allow gelatinization before the crust begins to dry out. The crust really gets cooked twice: once wet and once dry. Moisture keeps the developing crust flexible and plastic in the early stages of baking so it can accommodate the oven spring of the dough without ripping excessively or constricting the loaf. Moisture is necessary for the action of the enzymes that release sugar in baking, after the yeast is killed. This sugar is necessary to the Maillard reactions, and the Maillard reactions themselves require the presence of water.

An appropriate moisture level is necessary for the normal formation of starch gels. In an oven that is too cool and too humid the crust gel will be too deep, making a thick, excessively chewy pale crust with little flavor. A hot, dry oven will make a thin, crisp, dark crust with a poorly baked crumb, while crust flavor may be poor because the crust burned too fast for good development of flavors. An oven which is moist *and* hot at first, and dry and slightly cooler later, will produce a moderately thick, slightly chewy, and moderately crisp crust with full flavor: hearth bread.

Although each loaf of baking bread will release enough water to make about three cubic feet (cf) of steam, that moisture is released too late to allow proper conditions for the development of a good crust for that loaf—unless the oven is very small, like a cloche. Ideally the highest oven air moisture level is reached shortly after the oven is loaded and the door is in place. Humidified air has a higher heat content, and will start the baking process that much faster, driving heat into the interior of the loaf. In contrast, a crust which is sprayed directly with cold water will be cooled, delaying gelatinization. Although brick-oven bakers have historically tried to pre-saturate oven air as they swab ashes off the oven floor, most or all of that moisture is immediately lost out the mouth of the oven. Instead, it is probably better to spray into the oven with a three-head fogging nozzle on a garden hose wand (the nozzles are usually used in greenhouses and nurseries) just as the oven is closed. (Pump-up garden sprayers also work, but use one that has *never* held chemicals.) Direct the spray over, not directly on, the loaves. If more moisture is desired, a wet towel can be draped over the inside of the oven door before it is closed. This should be removed in ten or fifteen minutes, to allow the bread to dry and the crust to set. Don't leave the oven door off for a long time in the early part of baking, as the dough at that time is quite delicate, with softened protein and little gelatinization. A fully loaded and tightly sealed oven shouldn't need supplementary steam after the first few minutes.

If your crust color is poor, look at your fermentation as well as oven conditions. Maggie Glezer addressed this point in an article in the *Bread Bakers' Guild Newsletter*. The Maillard reactions are catalyzed by the organic acids released in fermentation, and utilize sugars and amino acids that yeast releases into the dough. Over-fermentation will remove these sugars, and starch digestion during baking may be insufficient to restore them.

Small crust blisters are a frequent feature of the crust of hearth breads baked from lean-formula dough (no added fat or emulsifiers), especially when the dough has been retarded (refrigerated) during proof. They are caused by escape of gas from the crust. Gas is lost more quickly in cool dough because cooling increases the solubility of carbon dioxide in water.*

Good Crumb

Like crust, which may be chewy or soft in different breads, the nature of the crumb—the bread inside the loaf—should be appropriate in texture to the bread being baked. A *baguette* or a hearth-baked country loaf should have an open, irregular crumb texture, with a mixture of air cells of all sizes and strong cell walls. A white sandwich loaf, on the other hand, should have a fine, even crumb pattern, with no big holes that carry through from one slice to the next (to let jam or mayonnaise drip on your lap).

The crumb pattern is determined both by ingredients and by technique. For example, lower-protein-content flours (such as all-purpose flours or the flours used by traditional French bakers) may lead to low air cell stability and a more open, irregular crumb. R. C. Hoseney points out that perfectly round gas cells have had no external

*R. C. Hoseney explained that these blisters "are caused by gas being lost from the outer layers of the crust faster than new gas can diffuse into the cells. Thus the cells decrease in size and many are lost completely. Upon baking, the water in the crust will accumulate in the small cells remaining and form the blister" (personal communication).

forces on them as they were set. The more irregular the cells, the more of an effect some external force had on them as they set. Such a loaf is likely to have a strong and chewy crumb.

If your hearth breads don't seem to have the open cells and strong, elastic cell walls you want, you may not be kneading long enough to develop strong, elastic gluten, or you may not be fermenting long enough or proofing long enough. Inadequate gluten development during kneading or primary fermentation leads to an open crumb, but at the expense of a smaller loaf volume and disappointing texture: the crumb seems dead. If you are sure you are fermenting adequately, your dough is not too stiff, and your loaves are rising well, but your crumb seems tight, try adding a little *lower*-protein flour to your dough. This can be especially useful in pizza dough, to make it crisp but not too tough. So-called lean-dough formulas (with no added fat or with fat less than 3 percent) will usually make a more open crumb than richer dough, and acid doughs will tend to give a more open crumb, too. Loaves retarded in proof will have a more open crumb because gas cells tend to coalesce when the vigor of gas formation (decreased at low temperatures) is overtaken by gas escape in a cool dough. A wetter, more extensible dough will also produce a more open crumb than a stiff dough.

Warmer dough temperatures during

Like crust, the nature of the crumb should be appropriate in texture to the bread being baked. A white sandwich loaf should have a fine, even crumb pattern, so jam or mayonnaise doesn't drip on your lap.

∼

proofing (the final rise before baking) can contribute to an open crumb with no adverse effect on loaf size *if the loaf is not over-proofed*. Really large holes in the loaf usually result from a failure to properly punch down the dough, poor technique in molding and forming loaves, rough handling of the risen dough, or over-proofing, leading to breakdown of the internal structure of the loaf.

If you want a tight crumb for sandwich bread, use high-protein flour, knead it well, and add a little fat, egg, and dried milk to the dough. These things will stabilize the gas cells and make the crumb even.

Cooling Bread

Bread can't be packaged or sliced easily when it comes out of the oven: it's too hot, and it's too soft. Truth be told, the best bread flavor develops when it has cooled off a bit, allowing some of the strong alcohol and other volatile flavors to evaporate. If it is cooled too rapidly the bread will shrink too fast and the crust will crack excessively. Research has shown that an air temperature of 75 degrees Fahrenheit at a humidity level of 85 percent is best to prevent excessive cracking and shrinking of typical commercial pan bread. Crusty loaves are going to crack somewhat, regardless of what you do. If bread is to be sliced cleanly (for sandwiches, for example) it should be allowed to reach an internal tem-

This roll is full of basil from the garden and fresh, organic Parmesan from Blythedale Farm in Corinth, Vermont (photo: Medora Hebert).

perature of about 90 degrees Fahrenheit, which will take about an hour and a half in room air.

Bread that is packaged too soon will develop an unpleasant, gummy crust, as moisture from the interior arrives at the crust with nowhere to go. That kind of crust will develop mold quickly if the bread is left at room temperature. A slightly damp crust is probably fine if the bread is to be frozen in a tightly sealed bag and reheated or partially rebaked before serving.

Stale Bread

Fresh bread is delicious. Stale bread isn't, but it's not obvious *why:* the feel, smell, and taste of the crust and the crumb just aren't right.

The crust is gummy and bitter. The crumb is stiff and crumbly. The aroma and taste are flat.

As it leaves the oven the outer crust of a loaf of bread has about 2 percent moisture. After cooling, it still has less than 10 percent. The crumb (the interior of the loaf) has about 45 percent water. In fresh bread the crust is crisp and dry, but storage of the bread (especially in a plastic bag) allows moisture from the interior of the loaf to migrate to the crust, making it soft and gummy. The dry, highly gelatinized starch in the crust is water-loving, and attracts moisture from the crumb and the atmosphere. The moisture content in the crust of wrapped bread will increase to nearly 30 percent after four days. As the crust hydrates it begins to have a bitter taste, brought out as the heavily caramelized crust becomes moist. Thoroughly reheating the bread will again dry out the crust and restore some of its texture and flavor—if it isn't wrapped in aluminum foil the whole time it is in the oven.

The crumb of a loaf becomes firm and sliceable as it cools to about 90 degrees Fahrenheit (32 degrees Celsius) because chains of amylose (a straight-chain starch) interlock and stay interlocked as the bread cools.* From that point on some of the gradual stiffening of the crumb as it becomes stale is due to a change in amylopectin (a branched chain starch), a change that is the reverse, in a sense, of the one that occurred as the bread was baked. This is called starch **retrogradation**, a process in which water is given up. Bread that contains a higher level of certain dextrins (amylase products) is slower to form these links, and that is one reason some commercial dough formulas include substances

*In whole grain breads interlocking of starch with cooling is delayed—up to 24 hours for whole rye (perhaps it is inhibited by pentosans) and 6 to 8 hours for naturally leavened whole wheat bread. In Denmark, where most bread is made from 100 percent rye, some bakeries do not offer it for sale until the day after it is baked, when it has "set" and can be sliced without gumming up the knife.

that increase dextrin production. Of course, elevated dextrin levels make dough unsuitable for hearth baking by weakening its starch structure. Remember the supermarket bread I mentioned in the introduction? Over-enrichment with dextrin-enhancing ingredients does not lead to great bread.

Bread does not go stale by drying out, although stale bread may seem dry because it becomes stiff with crystalline starch. Bread that is a little dry (overbaked) stales quickly, but bread that is baked very dry (for instance, *biscotti, zwieback,* or old-fashioned ship's biscuit) doesn't experience this change and thus stays fresh much longer.

Bread that is very damp, like rye Vollkornbrot, and whole grain naturally fermented breads such as Desem do not stale quickly, either, although they may mold if the crust stays damp due to storage in plastic bags. Breads made from refined flours (without bran) dry out rapidly in comparison to whole grain breads, in part because some of the non-starch polysaccharides in bran hold on to water better than starch does. The presence of these bran polysaccharides is one reason whole grain breads take longer to "set" after baking. It is also one reason that they keep longer—certainly for a week. Alan Scott has one customer, a commercial salmon fisherman, who orders Desem once every five weeks, and says he doesn't freeze it!

Retrogradation is temperature sensitive, and can be prevented by freezing the bread, which locks the gel in its amorphous struc-

Bread that is twice-stale is hopeless—except for pudding, pigs, or compost!

~

ture. Ironically, crumb staling occurs most quickly when bread is stored in a refrigerator, although it also happens (more slowly) at room temperature. As with the crust changes, the crumb texture changes can be reversed to some extent by thoroughly reheating the bread, but this usually only works once. Bread that is twice-stale is hopeless—except for pudding, pigs, or compost!

The poor flavor of stale bread crumb is due in part to loss of volatile organic flavor compounds such as alcohols, aldehydes, and ketones. Recent research, for instance, has looked at two aromatic Maillard products which are responsible for roasted smells and malty smells (and which mask unpleasant fatty smells that are prominent in stale yeasted supermarket "French" bread). Levels of these aromatics fall quickly after bread cools, with half of the original content gone in four hours. Eventually the gas cells will contain air, and the bread will taste stale. Reheating will boil any remaining aromatics into the gas cells, and some new Maillard aromatics may form; this will approximate the flavor spectrum of fresh bread. This revival, however, will last less than an hour, as the aromatic levels achieved are so low. Reheating, then, gives a small bump to the flavor of slightly staled bread, improves the hydration of its starch, and may re-establish the moisture gradient between the crust and the crumb—but the trick will only work once.

The following techniques will help you avoid stale bread without using additives:

- Use natural leavens, as the persistent swelling of gluten at low pH will deprive starch of some of its potential water, and thereby prevent it from retrograding so quickly.
- Don't over-ferment, as this contributes off-flavors that may predominate as the bread stales. Also, over-fermented bread has poor volume, which accelerates the retrogradation process.
- Eat fresh bread. If the rest of the bread is to be eaten that day or the next, leave it out—turned up on its cut surface—or put it in a paper bag to allow it to breathe, while the crust stays dry.
- Bread that won't be eaten within thirty-six hours should be cooled to 90 degrees Fahrenheit or below, then frozen in a sealed plastic bag at 0 degrees Fahrenheit or below. When you take it out of the freezer, leave it in the plastic bag while it thaws until visible signs of water on the outside and the inside of the bag have disappeared. Then take it out of the bag. Bread that is thawed at room temperature will be palatable, but can be made nearly as good as fresh bread if it is thoroughly reheated and allowed partially to cool before serving.
- Don't store bread in the refrigerator (Ever! Because it goes stale quickly!) unless you are going to use it for croutons!

CONSULTING *and* MARKETING SERVICES

South San Francisco, California

CMS PROVIDES SUPPORT to operations of all sizes wishing to make naturally fermented European breads. I went there on the recommendation of Kathleen Weber at Della Fattoria, who paid them for both advice and equipment when she was starting out and feels she got good value. Because CMS is a technical support organization, I am going to spend plenty of time at the end of this section relaying some of the technical tidbits I got there. Believe me—what I put in is only a small part of what I learned in a visit of just a few hours.

CMS is run by Michel Suas, a classically trained pastry chef from Brittany. After passing his exams in the 1970s he worked at a three-star restaurant in Tours, the only one in France at that time making its own bread in a wood-fired oven. While there, he met and was inspired by the very enthusiastic Professor Calvel (who was reintroducing naturally fermented breads in France), but it was clear that in the hierarchical world of European cuisine it would be years before Michel could have his own operation.

He therefore came to the United States, but without much knowledge of either English or our geography and climate. He worked first in Chicago, then traveled by microbus around the country and eventually to Louisiana, where his wife went to school in Art and Architectural History. He found that in this hemisphere his knowledge of baking bread was in great demand; people were desperate for advice on formulas and techniques. One of his first consultations was for a bakery in El Salvador, and on his way home he stopped in San Francisco—which has been his headquarters for the last ten years.

Six people work at CMS, including two consultants. They work with a full range of clients, from people who have no experience to those who have been successful for years but now want a larger operation or a better one. Michel requires that clients have a commitment to make "real bread." For example, he will work with a supermarket only if it is willing to put in the time to train a staff that is dedicated to and capable of quality work. Some large operations are resistant to these strictures, but others have come around: Michel says that bread is now a "destination" item that will bring people into stores, so having good bread may be worth such a substantial commitment. Not having good bread will drive customers elsewhere to buy wine, cheese, and meat. Like Alan Scott, Michel says that bread is no longer just a gimmick. Supermarket customers were initially tricked by great-looking, tasteless loaves of factory bread made from frozen dough, but "before we are a customer we are a human being. We can be tricked a few times, but after that it's over."

CMS offers its services nationwide. Startup operations may be big (the startup of Acme's third division) or small (Della Fattoria), but they are relatively straightforward to organize. Transforming a successful small bakery (the La Brea bakery) into a well-organized larger operation is often more of a challenge, because everything may have to change without losing the heart of what the operation is all about.

When consultants go into an existing operation they look first at the kinds of bread a client is baking and at the procedures currently in use. Then they ask what the client wants to achieve. They look at the installed equipment, and at the size, location, and nature of the facility. Eight hundred square feet? Michel says you need two thousand square feet to make twelve hundred to fifteen hundred loaves of good bread per day, including a retail store, and you need a realistic budget. If you don't have enough money to make any one particular change, it may be better to do the best you can for now, and only expand when you are strong enough to do so. This can be a step-by-step process. If people love what they do, Michel doesn't want to make them struggle, and turn enjoyable lives into a grueling business. He feels his clients need to be able to sleep at night, without worrying about debt. Maybe the first step is just to buy a better mixer, making sure to get equipment that won't be obsolete with the next step. Plan for the long term.

Michel, like Alan Scott, feels that the first steps of breadmaking are the most critical: ingredients, ferment, mixing/kneading—problems that develop here cannot be corrected later. Often Michel's client will have a planetary vertical mixer, and these are not really designed to properly condition a dough for a hearth bread that proofs and bakes without external support. They may be fine to start out with, but if you want to do better and you have the budget for it, Michel recommends that you get a better mixer. He says the improvement in the bread can be dramatic when a dedicated dough mixer is installed in a bakery.

Along with a good mixer, an important part of an efficient bakery is the kind of consistent procedure used at the Acme Baking Company. A small operation can jump a batch ahead in the time line to the oven, if it is developing too quickly; a bigger operation can't do that. Michel recommends that almost

If people love what they do, Michel doesn't want to make them struggle, and turn enjoyable lives into a grueling business.

~

109

*We don't have a
culture that expects
to buy fresh bread
every day*

⌇

every type of naturally fermented bread be retarded in primary or secondary fermentation, or both, with these procedures giving the baker more control over fermentation, and more consistent and highly flavored (ripe) breads. They prevent panic on the bakery floor.

As for the dough, retarding gives more time for the dough to relax, which is going to give better crumb texture, flavor, and moisture retention. The crust will be better as well. These benefits are most pronounced when bread is retarded during primary fermentation, rather than during proofing (which has other benefits)—the flour becomes more hydrated and the dough relaxes from the work of the mixer, as wavy stress lines and kinked structures in the dough align in sheets.

Decisions about oven types for Michel's clients are tied in with the volume of bread that will be produced and the sophistication of the regional market. CMS actually chooses proper locations for bakeries in part by looking at other stores and supermarkets in the area. Is anyone carrying good fresh fish, good vegetables, herbs, mineral waters, good cheese? If the market hasn't been demanding products like these, it may not be ready to support naturally fermented bread, either—population and population density alone do not determine this market. We don't have a culture that expects to buy fresh bread every day (and most European countries don't, either, anymore).

In order to expand its educational services CMS has recently started the San Francisco Bread Institute, an academy of baking with courses and seminars on all levels, located in a large new facility in an industrial area of South San Francisco.

Michel spent much longer discussing the technical aspects of baking than did the other bakers I met. I egged him on, as obviously I am inclined that way myself. I hope some of the things we discussed are interesting to you, too. Here goes:

- Michel feels starter leavens should be made from organic flour, either whole wheat or at least a high ash, high extraction type, or with added rye.
- He recommends a relatively liquid (batter thickness) leaven, as I do. He finds that a relatively liquid ferment expands starch better, and makes

the dough tolerate mixing better. Whatever thickness you use, be consistent, as thickness does affect the activity of otherwise similar ferments.

- The decision about when a sponge leaven is ripe is based on flavor, or on pH; it should have doubled in bulk or more, with vigorous gas production. Plenty of small bubbles, not big ones. A liquid starter should not break apart into lumps when it is poured. If your starter isn't right (ripe) at this stage, you are going to have problems with the bread.

- In any fermentation, the less you handle the dough, the better structure you will have. Every time you cut a piece of dough, you are cutting the structure, and you have to handle it just right to repair the structure. Even then, there will be a scar. Tearing the dough is even worse, and at any stage of the process, you want to work with the biggest piece you can. That's one reason for tilting devices to unload the mixer.

- Timing of retardation should be based on the volume change that results from fermentation, or on pH development, but you have to give the dough enough time to start rising in the first place, before you retard it. If you keep a dough at room temperature for four hours and retard it for six (ten overall), things will be fine. But you can't expect adequate fermentation if you shorten that first four-hour part too much, and take the six hours out to eight. It is better just to give it four hours up front, then retard it as long as you must—let the retarding protect it from over-fermentation. And there is a limit to the benefit that retarding dough will confer—don't overdo it.

- A cool dough at the end of proof will allow you to proof to a higher volume without having the loaf collapse, at any given degree of hydration. Also, the cooler loaf will expand more in the oven, as a cool loaf can hold a greater mass of gas in the same volume.

- Retarding will produce bread that keeps better—because of acid level, hydration, etc. Bread should be a fermented product, like wine or cheese. Then it will keep. If you just blow it up and cook it, it won't keep. That's why the *baguette* in France today doesn't keep. No acid. Commercial yeast. They are now adding some fermented dough to the *baguette*, to extend its life (called *la vielle pâte*, or *pâte fermentée*).

CONSULTING *and*
MARKETING
SERVICES

Some bakers are adding a portion of liquid starter to give better elasticity to the yeasted dough, with better keeping of the bread—*fermentation mixte.*

- To get a nice lift and curl on the slash, let the surface of the bread dry out a little before it is slashed, to make the skin a little stronger. Allowing some skin to form on the bottom of a loaf as it is proofing in a retarder or in open air may improve the appearance of the bread—a better bottom crust and a better curl to the slash. It also makes the loaf tolerant to handling as it goes into the oven, and protects the bread and traps gas during fermentation—this may make a loaf that keeps better. A little skin on the upper surface of a loaf helps to make a clean slash and helps the slash to open.

- Uncontrolled ripping or shredding of bread that has been slashed occurs when it was not mixed enough (the gluten isn't extensible), when the loaf is not uniformly shaped (especially if it bursts on one side), when the heat in the oven is uneven (the loaf is too close to another loaf), when the loaf is under-proofed, or when the oven doesn't have enough moisture, and the crust dries out, then bursts.

- Flavor comes from the crust and from the crumb—both have to be tasty. If you want flavor, you have to bake the bread well—it may look a little dark.

- Baking with whole grains or whole grain flours: people who want whole grain bread grant some "mercy" to the baker, since they expect whole grain bread to be denser than bread made with white flour—but the baker should not abuse this privilege. Use proper milling and mixing procedures, but there is no reason to pursue high-protein wheat flours, as the presence of sharp bran particles prevents very high loaves by penetrating the larger gas cells and deflating them as the bread rises.

CHAPTER SIX

MASONRY OVENS OF
EUROPE *and* AMERICA

I mentioned in the introduction to this book that I saw my first masonry oven at Heather Leavitt's in Barnard, Vermont. I had heard about "ovens" for a couple of years; I had even sent to Alan Scott for his plans catalog (a year before), but I hadn't baked in one. Truth be told, Heather hadn't really baked in her oven either, since the party to which I invited myself was her oven-warming party.

It was a wonderful scene when I got there with my bowl of dough. The Leavitts had a tent set up in case of rain and there were kids tearing around everywhere, jumping up and down. The fire was roaring in Heather's clay oven, under a free-form roof framed with saplings from the woods behind the oven. Even the oven tools looked great, made out of natural crooks of trees and odd lumps of steel by Randy Leavitt.

I introduced myself, formed up my *batards*, had a beer, met some nice folks, and got ready for the bake. Though Heather now teaches weekend workshops in masonry oven baking and is cool as a cucumber about it, on *that* day it was almost as new to her as it was to the rest of us—none of us knew exactly what was going on. We overheated the oven and then we didn't wait long enough for it to equalize its hot spots and cool down.

No matter. We put my *batards* in, because we did know skinny loaves could take a little extra heat. A little extra heat? They were golden brown in eight minutes, though it should have been at least twenty.

Maybe they *were* a little underdone in the crumb, but who cared? When we pulled them out they were beautiful, cracking and popping as they started to cool, bursting with steam as we ripped them open and ate them without butter, with butter, with Vermont cheese, with imported Brie. Every man, woman, and child ate those loaves, and they were gone in a couple of minutes—it was like wolves on sheep.

Building your own clay oven is really a hands-on experience (photo: Alan Scott).

Then we stopped, looked around, smiled, and baked the larger loaves. When I went home (much later) I knew I was going to build an oven. I didn't know then that I would meet Alan, or that I would build my oven on a trailer, but I knew that I would build an oven.

Oven History

My oven is descended from Heather's oven, which is descended from the old ovens of Quebec, descended in turn from French rural ovens of the 17th century. Ovens in rural Europe have traditionally been horizontal retained-heat ovens based on the Roman model. The basic design has never changed in two thousand years. The oven consists of an arch of masonry covering the

masonry oven floor, or hearth. Often there is a second arch underneath that supports the hearth and creates a space used to store ashes, bundles of brush, or logs. Roman-style ovens are direct-fired: the wood is burned in the baking chamber itself, and the exhaust pours out of the door of the oven and up a flue located just above and outside the oven door (if a flue is provided; often ancient ovens have none and the smoke just pours out and disperses). The oven is then swept clean and dough is put in to bake in the retained heat of the fire. This type of oven is also called a **black** oven, because the soot is never completely burned out of the baking chamber by the heat of the fire. The **beehive** oven built into the fireplace mass of American Colonial and Federal period houses is basically a small version of the Roman oven that shares a flue with a fireplace. The front of the oven is either flush with the back of the fireplace (which receives its smoke) or the oven is beside the fireplace but connected to its flue by a short connecting flue controlled by a damper.

Although the basic plan of black ovens did not change much over the years, the social and cultural context of baking has varied from time to time and place to place. Some ovens were small and used by a family; some were large and used by a professional baker. In much of Europe, however, ovens were controlled by nobility or the church, and this was in part a reflection of the role the church played in introducing grain growing and bread baking to continental Europe. A book by the Swiss author Pierre Delacretaz, *Les Vieux Fours a Pain* (Old Bread Ovens) reviews the history and sociology of the traditional communal oven from the 12th century onward in the French/Swiss border country. These ovens, called banal ovens because of the rules regulating their use *(les bans)*, were of the type used throughout rural France.

The following passages are paraphrased from his text, with translation assistance from Laurence Baudelet and the permission of Monsieur Delacretaz.

Although anyone could use the communal oven for a fee, the oven belonged to the lord, and he controlled its use. He had the right to fine anyone who avoided the use of his ovens, his mills, his presses, his bulls, or his sawmills; these fines were called *bans*. Originally these ownership rights *(banalites)* belonged to

the Carolingian kings, but they were gradually usurped by certain nobles who had the right to act as magistrates, and who could impose fines. . . . By the 15th century the lordly rights had evolved further, and were usually preserved as a license or lease *(fermage)* which the lord sold to a master of the communal oven, who then could sublet its use to individuals, or could bake for a charge (the person who actually ran the oven was the *fournier*). . . . Comparisons of 15th-century sources with those of later centuries show that rules relating to ovens (construction, repair, use, rents, taxes) changed little over half a millennium. . . . The major change occurred when the lordly rights were taken on by municipal authorities (at or near the time of the Revolution). . . . That did not make it less expensive for its users; the working rules became harsher for everyone.

Delacretaz points out that the heat remaining in the oven was considered to be owned by the *fournier* for a certain span after he finished baking, and no fruit or wood could be dried without his involvement. Many crops could not be dried in the oven at all, by published rules. Municipal records even referred to particular damaged trees that could be burned by the oven man, as wood at that time was precious. The right to clean the ashes out of the oven was sold, as the ash could be used for fertilizer. Even the sweeping up around the oven was regulated, since crumbs could be used to feed chickens.

In light of these restrictions on what common folk could do with an oven in medieval France, it is interesting to learn what the families of Quebec did with their clay, brick, or stone farm ovens—ovens that were continuously constructed over a span of nearly three hundred years, and in general use until fifty or sixty years ago. In a book about the Quebec ovens, Boily and Blanchette (see bibliography) mention that families cooked many things besides bread: pork and beans, meat pies for the winter holidays, and cookies, buns, and desserts throughout the year. Occasionally the ovens were used to sterilize the feather stuffings of pillows and mattresses: the feathers were washed, then dried in the warm oven for five or six days in sacks to kill odors and parasites. The bed linens and eating utensils of the sick were treated the same way. Flax was dried in the oven before it was processed into linen, and newly woven woolens were put wet into the oven for fulling (shrinking). Herbs, fruit, and even lumber for furniture making were all dried in the oven when necessary.

Similarly, in much of England, where the lord's ownership of the mill and oven was not so persistent, families in many districts baked their own bread. Even in cities public bakeries were uncommon. In Manchester, for example (which in 1804 had a population of ninety thousand) there was apparently not a single commercial bakery. Thus for several centuries the English, like the Quebecois, had ovens in or about the house, and used them for a variety of purposes.

After the Revolution most French rural ovens became public property (owned by the municipality, the *commune*). According to research by Nancy Iott (see bibliography),

these communal ovens continued in regular use in small villages until after World War II. In larger towns bakers used their commercial ovens in a trade originally controlled by guilds. The old village ovens were usually built into a small building that resembled a chapel, placed at the center of the village near the well, the church, and the wash house. Oriented to take advantage of prevailing winds, the oven had a foyer or outer room that was a popular gathering and gossiping spot for the town—and a meeting place in the evening for courting couples.

Most early French communal ovens did not have flues (chimneys), and the foyers of the oven houses were of necessity open so the smoke could pour out and drift away. This roofed room had counters around its walls for baskets and bread. According to Iott, most of the names for parts of the oven and its house were taken from church architecture: the building was the "chapel" (*la chapelle*), the outer hearth the "altar" (*l'autel*), and the stone water jug the "font" (*l'auge*). The open end of early oven buildings was vaulted to support a stone gable formed by stones called *pignons,* giving the oven houses a Gothic look (this stepped stone gable may have originally protected the edge of a thatched roof from embers). The buildings themselves were built of stone or of rammed earth (*pisé*), with a roof of slate where it was available. The foundation of the oven was usually of stone formed in an arch. The oven face was stone, and the floor of the foyer was either rammed earth or paved with small stones.

Each family baked once a week or once every other week; in the mountains, all the bread for the winter was sometimes baked in

Alan Scott built the oven, George Gonzales cut and laid volcanic stone from the Sierras, then a land-scaper rolled in some boulders. This oven is the American equivalent of the great stone ovens of Europe.

the fall. Bread was often eaten stale—hacked apart and softened with milk or soup. The oven itself might be in more frequent use, depending on the size of the village. There was typically a wooden plaque on the outside face of the oven building on which tags were hung to indicate the order in which village families were to bake their bread. The dough was proofed at home, then carried to the oven on a long, wide board. The loaves going into the oven were slashed with distinct patterns so each family got back its own—really its own, since the grain from which it was made was grown on their farm. The leaven was carefully kept from baking day to baking day, in a stone jar in a cool spot. In the winter the leaven was revitalized by putting it in a warm bed. Then pots of coals were placed below the mixing trough *(petrin)* to keep the dough warm enough to ferment. Leaven might be shared between families, depending on the baking schedule.

The eventual decline in regular use of these rural ovens after World War II reflected a general movement of the French population to larger towns, coupled with the availability of better transportation so that commercially-baked bread began to be sold even in hamlets that did not have a baker. It was easier (no extra firewood to cut, no kneading, no time at the oven), and the bread was not expensive, as the basic price was subsidized and set by the government. Now some French villages with ovens have a festival each year when the oven is heated and used. In a few towns there are diehards or enthusiasts who bake more often. One of Iott's informants told her, "It isn't tradition that assures the survival of our bread; it is the bread that assures the survival of our traditions."

Vertical and Horizontal Flat-Bread Ovens

In much of the world it is difficult to grow the kind of wheat that can be made into highly risen loaves that would be cooked in a closed oven. The flat breads of many countries are therefore made of durum wheat (in which the gluten is less elastic), oats, rye, or other flour cooked on a hot rock, a griddle, or in an open-topped vertical oven like the Indian tandoor, a large bell- or barrel-shaped clay pot that is usually plastered with mud or a mixture of sand and cement. A fire is kept burning in these vertical ovens (there is a small draft opening at the bottom) while a quick slap of the hand plasters a disc of sticky dough onto the inner surface of the upper oven where it will bake in a minute or so, producing a flavorful bread that is mostly crust. If the oven is well shaped, little of the radiant heat of the fire escapes through the upper opening, although the combustion gasses are rapidly lost and the

walls and floor are not insulated. Therefore, efficiency is low.

Some Mediterranean flatbreads (such as pizza) are baked in horizontal ovens on the Roman plan, but with the fire maintained in one side or at the back of the oven chamber, not raked out. These ovens bake by a combination of retained heat and continuous heat, but they are somewhat more efficient than the tandoor for baking large quantities of bread, if well designed so an excessive draft is avoided. They do not require the same mass of masonry (the walls can be thinner) as retained-heat ovens.

19th- and 20th-Century European and American Commercial Ovens

The plans in this book are for only one of several possible types of masonry oven. It is worthwhile to consider several of the common types of historical and modern ovens, for comparison.

WOOD-FIRED EUROPEAN COMMERCIAL OVENS

The ovens of the commercial bakers in French towns were of two types. The first were large internal-combustion (synonyms: directly fired, Roman, black) ovens, like rural communal ovens but somewhat larger. The second type is typified by the *gueulard* oven, a hybrid in which a firebox below the front third of the oven is vented into the oven itself through a removable cast iron elbow, the *gueulard*. The floor of the oven is inclined a few degrees, making the oven easier to load and unload with a peel, increasing the draft during firing, and effectively holding in steam during baking. The oven is exhausted

A variety of ovens: 1. Hot rock; 2. Pottery dome on hot rock; 3. "Roman" oven; 4. Tandoor;
5. 19th century commercial coal oven; 6. Modern rotary oven (sectional view); 7. Deck oven;
8. Gueulard oven (sectional view: oven door is to the left).

This French oven is thought to be 700 years old. Nancy Iott has noted that communal ovens and wash tubs were often built side by side (photo: Nancy Iott).

production. They were in regular use in larger establishments for many years, and are used today by some French artisan bakers. An old book features a woodcut of this oven, with the caption *Four L'Idéal*—the ideal oven. A French oven of similar plan was made to fire with gas, using a burner that terminated at the base of the *gueulard*. English ovens were made on a similar plan, but burned coal.

Oven moisture for such hybrid ovens comes from a boiler blowing steam into the oven through a pipe, a system that drips water into hot cast iron containers, or from a water spray. Most European hybrid commercial ovens had a hearth about ten feet long and eight feet wide. Although we call the typical hybrid oven *French,* the French called them *Vienna* ovens when they were introduced in the second half of the 19th century. Similarly, the long loaves introduced at that time were *Vienna* loaves, though they are now French loaves to us.

Although the typical French wood-fired hybrid commercial oven does have a certain glamour (and allows the bread to be sold as coming from a wood oven) it perpetuates one of the basic failings of all internal combustion ovens, including the ones described in this book: The inner surface of the oven is heated more than the outer masonry during a firing, so the outer masonry is not able to offer up retained heat until the inner masonry has cooled somewhat. Either the oven can only be partially heated (which is what the French do, heating the oven several times a day), or there must be a pause after refiring, to allow dissipation, equalization, and some inevitable loss of heat.

The indirectly fired **white** (or externally

through a rear flue which can be shut with a damper. The oven door is metal, and is counter-balanced so it may be easily opened and held out of the way, or closed. These ovens have the advantage that they are easier to refire, and so permit more continuous fired and vented) oven, which has an external firebox, flues around the oven, and external exhaust, is better in this regard, but it is much more difficult to construct correctly and has to have access for cleaning the flues. Externally combusted (white) commercial masonry ovens made to burn gas, coal, wood, or oil have been essentially replaced (for the commercial production of hearth breads) by the closest modern equivalents: the deck oven and the rotary oven.

WOOD-FIRED AMERICAN OVENS

American commercial bakers used ovens on the Roman plan into the 1850s, when ovens began to be built with fireboxes located on one or both sides of the front of the oven for easier feeding and clean-out. In the later part of the century, many big bakeries used immense externally fired masonry ovens. These were gradually replaced by gas-fired metal ovens of several types as factory-produced pan bread came to dominate the market. A common hybrid oven in England in the last century was fired internally with wood once a day, but kept hot during the day by a small coal fire in a chamber under the back of the oven, with a flue that passed around the oven. Some hybrid ovens are still in use in bakeries and pizzerias in New Haven, New York, and Rochester. Other old ovens are internally fired with coke or coal that burns in part of the oven all day. In some of them the fire is separated from the body of the oven chamber by a wall, but the exhaust still passes through the chamber on its way to the flue while the food is cooking, which is said to impart a distinctive flavor to the pizza (and presumably some poisonous combustion products at the same time).

RUSSIAN AND SCANDINAVIAN OVENS

Both the Russian (at that time Soviet) and Finnish governments have sponsored research into wood oven design. In the case of Finland, this has led to a somewhat standardized small commercial oven plan with two chambers, both with low domes (eight and one-half inches in the center of the dome). Wood is burned in one oven chamber, smoke is routed through the other oven chamber on its way to the flue (the path of the smoke is similar to that of Finnish masonry heaters), and both chambers are used for baking, after a rest or heat-soaking period of two hours. This makes for a very efficient oven, but one that must be built by a master builder. A 36 x 70-inch oven will bake twenty-eight loaves of pan bread in each chamber, using one pound of wood for each pound of dough.

DECK OVENS

The outside of a modern steam-tube deck oven looks like a big commercial pizza oven except that often the doors have glass panels. Inside, each level (there are usually several) has a hearth slab of refractory concrete. Heat is delivered by sealed metal tubes containing a small amount of water. When these tubes are superheated by a fire (usually gas) anywhere along their length, terrific steam pressures develop. This heat and pressure pass instantly and evenly along the length of the tube, and from the tube to the masonry deck (hearth) of the oven. The slab doesn't have to be very thick, as the heat lost to baking bread is continuously replaced. Steam injection or water spray onto a segment of superheated cast iron humidifies the oven.

ROTARY OVENS

Rotary ovens are shipped prefabricated from Spain and erected on-site. An immense round tray of refractory masonry is suspended on a central post in such a way that the baker can turn a wheel next to the oven door and spin the hearth and all the bread on it around in a circle, like a Lazy Susan. When bread is to be loaded or unloaded the section of the hearth to be used is moved into position at the oven door, which is hinged at its base and counterbalanced so that it swings down and inward. It moves out of the way when the peel is pushed against it. Although many rotary ovens are fired with wood and have a masonry base and firebox, almost all of them are indirectly fired ovens—the flame is outside the oven chamber itself, which is built of metal. Because these ovens are frequently faced with brick, they are often called brick ovens, but they are more accurately rotary deck ovens. The manufacturer does offer a directly fired version.

CONVECTION OVENS

The concept of a convection oven is simple: air is heated in a separate chamber and is then circulated to the oven by fans. Big convection ovens are called rack ovens, because one (or more than one) entire rack of bread pans can be rolled in or out while the heat and the fan are off. Humidification is by steam injection.

Although there are several other oven types in common use, none of them are much competition for the ones described here for baking small or moderate quantities of what the industry calls **hearth breads**—breads not baked in pans.

Your Masonry Oven

If you follow the plans in this book, you will be building a direct-fired masonry oven. You may call it a Roman oven, call it a black oven—it doesn't matter. The next chapter will tell you what to consider before you start building.

AMERICAN FLATBREAD

Warren, Vermont

I HAVE GOOD FRIENDS in the Mad River Valley of Vermont, and for some time before I met George Schenk I had been hearing snippets of stories about him. Mostly about how great his pizza was, but also about his funky oven, his wonderful barn, his wild posters, his flourishing business. Eventually I visited George, and since then I have also been telling little snippets of stories about him and his wonderful operation, American Flatbread. Several weeks after my visit I got a copy of the Mission Statement of American Flatbread:

1. To produce good, flavorful, nutritious food. Food that gives us joy and health;
2. To create pleasant and fulfilling work for those of us who bake Flatbread;
3. To produce, package, and distribute our product in as environmentally conscientious a way as our resources and imagination allow us. To be proactive in this: to discover new ways of doing these things better;
4. To support with our voices and buying power: local, regional, and sustainable agriculture; the forces of peace and understanding; the cultural, economic, and environmental needs of native peoples worldwide; the ecological needs of the wild fauna and flora;
5. To be an educational resource to our community;
6. To be a good neighbor;
7. To laugh and be of goodwill. To be grateful and forgiving;
8. To profit from this work.

George originally trained as a biologist "down country," but on coming to Vermont he took a variety of jobs, including dishwashing. Eventually a chef asked him if he would like to "learn how to use a knife," and he began on-the-job training in the kitchen. By the mid-1980s he was cooking a regional American cuisine at a different restaurant and making backyard experiments with ovens of drylaid stones, experiments based on primitive stoves and ovens he had built as a Boy Scout and an oven he saw on a trip to the Alps. From the first, George was surprised at how well these simple ovens baked. His efforts with stone, clay, and dough began to produce food that people loved, he started a baking business, and it grew and grew.

George now sells frozen gourmet par-baked pizzas (American Flatbread, "All-Natural Pizza Baked in a Primitive Wood-Fired Earthen Oven") up and down the East Coast and as far west as Chicago. His bakery is located in a barn on the grounds of a country inn in the bottom of the Valley, and on Friday night (all year) and Saturday night (summers and winters) the bakery turns into a restaurant, with hundreds of diners eating at tables in the barn and (in summer) on the lawn. The inside of the barn is covered with hand-painted posters, puppet parts, and thank-you letters from visiting kindergarten classes. On a summer night servers move in and out with pizza, beer, and homemade pie, while people waiting to be served lounge all over the place, some sitting on the lawn, some in the garden, some at a wonderful outdoor fire pit. One evening I saw a hay wagon being unloaded into an adjacent barn as the yellow afternoon sun finally set and the night (and the dew) descended.

George does a *big* business but has not lost his vision of preparing simple, healthy food. Everything comes out of the same rustic oven, and he uses certified organic white wheat flour with restored germ for his doughs, which are topped with fresh herbs, vegetables, and BST-free cheeses. (BST is Bovine Somatotrophin, a synthetic growth hormone that many people consider unhealthful and/or a threat to small-scale dairy farming.) The pizza boxes are recycled boxboard, printed with handset antique type.

George's oven is fascinating. He based the proportions on the classic Quebec oven, but turned 90 degrees, with the door on one of the long sides. This creates two alcoves (to the right and left) for cooking flatbreads while the fire is burning. The oven was built by piling wet clay blocks fortified with straw and wood ashes over an armature of saplings. An arch of stones forms the oven doorway but the oven remains an unruly pile of clay, like a flattened beaver house with a stone arch in it. The necessary 4:7 ratio of doorway:dome height is preserved, but the floor of the oven is divided into three: a central fire channel and two raised soapstone cooking slabs on the ends. There is no chimney—a copper draft hood is hung a few feet above the oven door, and a large metal smoke pipe leads to a high-temperature exhaust fan up in the dim recesses of the barn's gable.

This arrangement makes perfect sense for the mass production of pizzas.

The lowered fire hearth means that little ash can get up on the baking slabs even though a bright fire is maintained at all times. Little smoke is visible and the reflected radiant heat of the fire browns the tops of the pizzas quickly. Although the slab temperature is somewhat uneven because the fire is only touching one side of the slab, several pizzas (three sixteen-inch restaurant pizzas, or five of the twelve-inch ones to be frozen) are on each slab at all times, and they are moved, rotated, and replaced constantly, evening out the heat. One of the neat features of this arrangement is that while the baker works at the oven (feeding the fire, turning the pizzas, removing them when they are done) one of the pizza "assemblers" may run up to thrust a loaded peel in the oven—the peel put in from the right goes to the left slab, while the one from the left goes to the right. It is highly entertaining to watch, but it is so functional that it does not seem showy.

This kind of oven could be built out of any masonry material that could take the heat, and might be a good alternative for a restaurant that will specialize in flatbreads and roasting. Although at the end of the day George and his staff often bake loaf bread in the oven for their own use, an oven with an easily sealed doorway, a door on the longitudinal axis, and a less conductive hearth material would work better for loaf breads. The crew also has a take-apart oven that they move to festivals and fairs—it gets rebuilt for each event.

After I left American Flatbread, I learned by chance of their ongoing program of social and community action. I called George to ask him about it. It is called Medicine Wheel Breads and has three parts.

- Individual-sized pizzas are made (mild sauce and cheese) to appeal to the tastes of hospitalized children who have lost their appetite for institutional food. These pizzas are delivered to pediatric units at the University of Vermont Medical Center in Burlington, to the Yale–New Haven Medical Center, and to the Shriners Burn Institute in Boston.
- The "seconds" from the regular pizza production are frozen and delivered to residents of the Mad River Valley who are ill or injured and unable to cook for themselves or their family members.
- Lastly, all the leftover dough from the restaurant operation is brushed with garlic-infused olive oil and baked as "garlic bread" for delivery to the Vermont Food Bank.

The oven was built by piling wet clay blocks fortified with straw and wood ashes over an armature of saplings. An arch of stones forms the oven doorway but the oven remains an unruly pile of clay, like a flattened beaver house with a stone arch in it.

∼

AMERICAN FLATBREAD

Talking about Medicine Wheel led us into a discussion of George's life and vision, and the meaning of his business. He has been amazed by the reception of his work and considers Flatbread to have been "a gift in my life in many ways" because it has allowed him and his employees to be "self-defined"—the company can be anything they want it to be, and each turn in the road has been supported by the market they serve. He can decide to spend time with his children, or to make food for hospitalized kids, or the company can go out and bake pizzas at a festival. On the other hand, the market's acceptance of his products has brought on a little of the agony of success: he knows that "food is not a widget" that can be produced as well or better in a factory that is twice as big, or a hundred times as big. Homemade or handmade food carries with it a quality, a remembrance of the hands that made it and the "heart" that animated those hands. George feels that when the heart's intention changes (toward a predominantly financial goal, for instance) the food reacts to that phenomenon, and things change. Grandma may make wonderful cookies, and eating them in her kitchen is an act of devotion. Eating cookies made by machine to her recipe, bought from the store in a plastic package? No.

George sees that the marketplace has a problem absorbing the cost of handmade food at the same time that there is a society-wide hunger for natural and healthful food. He feels his food carries with it much of the nurture that goes into it, and he wants to share it with more people, if that is possible. He thinks about providing a good standard of living for his employees, and wonders if more production could secure that. Perhaps if he duplicated his operation in a team-based facility like Lionel Poilane's new "old-fashioned" bread factory in France?

Self-definition at American Flatbread is a continuing process. Just thinking about this man and his business always sets me thinking about my own self-definition. I mean, how am I doing, what am I doing, what could I be doing? How well am I following my path? And of course: Should I drizzle more olive oil on my flatbreads, or less?

THE CHEESE BOARD

Berkeley, California

T HE CHEESE BOARD does not use a masonry oven. This bakery, pizza place, and cheese store in Berkeley, California, is in this book because I found their organizational lessons more important than the baking techniques they use. The Cheese Board has been a successful "consensus egalitarian worker's collective" since 1971. There are forty-six employees who all make the same hourly wage (regardless of years of service), bring in no capital when they come, and take none when they leave.

The Cheese Board vision is to make good tasting, attractive, hand-formed bread that people want to eat, and to provide an honest living and enjoyable workplace for the members of the collective. Work schedules are flexible, work duties rotate, and there are added benefits of group action: the members collectively own a cabin in the mountains! Could this kind of organization be the answer to some of the thorny questions faced by self-employed bakers, such as: Who will be working when I am sleeping, if I don't want to have employees? Will my business fail if I take a week off? What if I don't have capital? Won't I be lonely if I'm in the bakery all the time? Who will run the cash register? Do I want to be in business for myself?

The bakery operation at The Cheese Board grew out of the cheese business in the mid-1980s, a time when there were surprisingly few options for people seeking rustic, handmade bread, even in the relatively sophisticated East Bay. This diversification was fortunate, since the dramatic increase in the bread business has coincided with a gradual decrease in the cheese business. Because the store was already set up to sell cheese by weight, bread is also sold by weight, which saves time as the loaves are formed: 1996 prices ranged from $1.50 per pound for simple breads to $2.50 per pound for Asiago cheese bread and $3.50 per pound for sticky buns. Other products (rolls, scones) are priced by each piece. Some products are available every day, others are only made one day a week, and regular customers get a schedule and price list to keep at home.

Most of the breads at The Cheese Board are naturally leavened, made from recipes and baking techniques that evolved in-house as a collective process over time. Here are some of their techniques to make baking easier and safer:

THE CHEESE
BOARD

- The leavens are kept in five-gallon buckets on a low stainless steel counter/sink. That way they are easy to lift by the handle, and if one becomes too active and bubbles over, the mess is easy to clean.
- There is an electric chain hoist on the ceiling at the front of the big vertical mixer, and a steel yoke and chain setup that can lift the mixing bowls—once they are up, another chain and hook may be fitted into a hole drilled into the bottom rim of the metal bowl. That way, lowering the hoist will tip the bowl, making it easy to empty.
- To better control the schedule, many doughs are fermented in a cooler or proofed overnight in the temperature- and humidity-controlled proof room, with the temperature set to 60 degrees Fahrenheit (15 degrees Celsius). The proofing room is reset to a typical proofing temperature as other batches are made during the day.

Five years ago the collective began an unusual pizza operation that has been very successful: pizza is baked like mad (for the lunch hours only) in a leased storefront next to the main store. Only one recipe is available each day, and most of it is sold in slices at reasonable prices to a long line of hungry people who wind their way into the store. The operation can produce a slice every ten seconds (a pizza a minute), and this determines the maximum rate at which the line can move. By-the-slice customers sit inside and out on French folding chairs at metal tables, eat pizza while listening to the piano player, then head off down the street. Whole, fully baked pizzas are available but other customers buy partially cooked pizzas to take home. The pizza operation is so well adapted to the needs of its customers (many of whom are getting a quick lunch between errands before going back to work) that it is almost a public service. At the same time, limiting the hours that the operation is running allows very efficient use of the the collective's strongest asset, the morale of its workers.

The lesson I received at The Cheese Board was similar to the one I got at the Upland Bakery and at American Flatbread: A bakery can be run for the benefit both of the producers and consumers of bread. The Cheese Board, though, shows that it can be done on a much larger scale. Now their collective has established a program to help similar ventures get started in other cities.

CHAPTER SEVEN

PREPARING *to* BUILD

A MASONRY OVEN

Because most people these days have little experience with masonry construction and have neither seen nor built a masonry oven, I think it wise to provide an introduction to the choices involved. This chapter will review the features of directly-fired masonry ovens, and the safety considerations inherent in their construction and use.

Fire Safety

Ovens built to plans similar to the ones in this book have been approved by building inspectors in many states under the portions of the building codes that deal with fireplaces, but building codes do change and interpretation and enforcement of these codes varies greatly from jurisdiction to jurisdiction. Therefore you *must* discuss your intentions with the building code enforcement team in your area *before* you build. If you live in an unregulated area, show your plans to the chief of the fire

department, and document your conversation. Failure to show reasonable diligence in fire safety could void your fire insurance. Of course, in no case can I (nor the publisher or any other party) be considered responsible for your actions, your oven, or any problems (such as a structural fire) that may result from building an oven—you have to assume the responsibility yourself, and act according to that burden. I will get you started by describing some common code requirements later in this chapter.

Design Lessons from Historical Ovens

You know that traditional bake ovens are called internal combustion, **retained-heat ovens** (or direct-fired) because wood is burned, the ashes are removed, and the bread is put into the fire chamber to bake. Like traditional rowboats and hand tools, internal combustion ovens possess a functional elegance honed by hundreds of years of trial and error. Every element of the oven is necessary and every necessary element is in place.

Although ovens can be built (and used) that do not follow the guidelines given in this chapter, they may have drawbacks. For example, ovens built with a rectangular or oval floor plan (like the one in this book) are more practical to load with loaves than round ovens, even though low-roofed round ovens are just as fuel efficient. Ovens with accessory flues and no way to recycle the heat carried out in the exhaust are usually less fuel efficient than ovens that vent out the door.

Many old books refer to the desirability of building an oven with an oval floor plan and a low door, without explaining why. Lise Boily and Jean-François Blanchette (in their 1979 book *The Bread Ovens of Quebec)* were the first to make a summary of the design criteria for successful ovens. By making detailed measurements of scores of existing ovens built of clay in eastern Canada, they distilled for the first time the principles that make these things work. It is fortunate that Quebec ovens are built to a vernacular design brought from France three hundred years ago and little changed over time, since most similar ovens were replaced long ago in urban Europe, where larger hybrid ovens operated by apprenticeship-trained bakers became the norm.

Oven Essentials— *Internally Fired Ovens*

Internally fired ovens can be used in both direct-heat and retained-heat methods of cooking. By **direct heat** I mean that a fire continues to burn in the oven chamber while the bread is baked, as in the Indian tandoor or in Italian roasting and pizza ovens. **Retained heat** means that the fire is removed before the food is cooked. This is the way loaves of bread are baked.

Because retained-heat ovens can only deliver heat that was stored in the masonry as the oven was fired, these ovens must be heavy and thick. Their mass must be sufficient to store enough heat to bake the bread. This requirement for oven mass is one of the factors that affects retained-heat oven usefulness and efficiency, but other factors

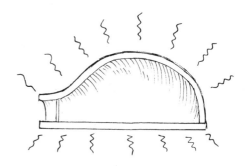

An oven in which the walls and hearth are too thin won't retain enough heat for baking loaf breads.

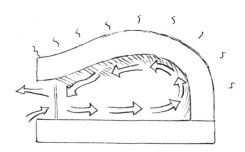

An efficient directly-fired oven will have a door that is about 63 percent the height of the inside of its dome.

are also important, such as insulation and the dynamics of oven air flow. Even more important is the operation or management of the oven (chapter 10), because firing a cold oven to baking heat requires heat that will never be recovered by baking bread. (This has been referred to as the **preheat** by oven-efficiency researchers.) If at the time a fire is started an oven is still warm from a previous use, but not hot enough for baking, only a small firing is necessary to get it ready for use. This marginal or incremental heat could be called the **baking heat**.

The efficiency of a masonry oven can be

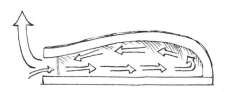

An oven that is too flat will lose too much of its heat out the door, and the door will be too low for loading.

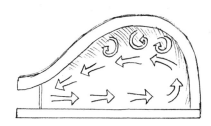

An oven that is too tall will have cold spots in the top of the dome that never get fully heated.

a hard number to pin down, as it is going to vary with patterns of use even in the same oven. It is always greater when an oven is in daily use because no preheat is necessary. A retained-heat oven designed for daily use may therefore be especially massive, so the heat storage is great and the oven temperature is stable. For intermittent use, overall efficiency will be higher in lighter ovens because the oven must be preheated each time it is used; the preheat cost is less for a less massive oven. The drawback of a light oven is that the oven temperature will be less stable if it is used in a retained-heat mode—it will cool off more quickly as it is used. The oven will need to be fired more often if a great quantity of bread is to be baked, even though a light oven may be perfectly suitable for prolonged use in a direct-heat mode (for pizza, for example).*

Each penetration into an oven's baking chamber represents a potential site for losing oven heat and steam, so an internal combustion oven should draw in air and exhaust out smoke through the same door. If the oven has a chimney, it should be in front of and above the oven door. If an ash-drop slot is provided, it should be outside the door as well. Preserving the sealed integrity of the baking chamber permits retention of heat when the fire is removed and retention of steam during the early phase of baking.

This lack of air vents and internal chimneys in an internal combustion oven places restraints on its geometry, since air must flow in the open doorway, fan the fire, heat the oven structure, and flow out without restriction. A too-low oven roof or a too-high oven door will allow the fire and its heat to spill out the oven doorway and up the flue. Heat

*Eric Shirey and John Selker measured the baking heat efficiencies of several uninsulated vernacular retained-heat ovens in undeveloped countries (ovens in use every day) and found that these average about 0.45 kg of flour baked per kg of wood burned. Efficiencies in large externally fired ovens (**white ovens**, in which the fire and smoke did not go through the baking chamber) were much greater, but white ovens are much more complex and expensive to construct.

will be wasted. On the other hand, an excessively high roof—like the roof of a typical hemispherical oven of the Southwest—will cause the smoke to stall unless air vents are provided. Firing will be difficult and the roof of the dome will be underheated. (You can sometimes see a coating of soot in the dome that shows that part of it was inadequately heated.) Ovens that are deeper (longer) than

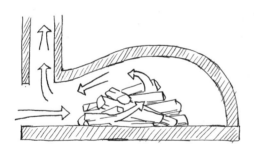

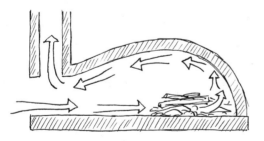

Start the fire in the front of the oven. Add wood when the fire is burning well, and let it burn all the way to the back of the oven.

they are wide tend to draw well and are probably more efficient than round or square ovens, although careful construction of the area just inside the door of a round oven can offset this problem somewhat.

Boily and Blanchette determined by direct measurements that there is a critical best ratio between the height of an oven door and the height of the oven dome. That ratio is 63:100, or 63 percent. (Folk tradition sometimes holds 4:7 to be the ratio, which is 57 percent—quite close!) This represents the average ratio for Quebec ovens that do not have supplemental air vents, which was one of the ways that Boily and Blanchette were able to determine which Quebec designs worked best. The further from these proportions an oven is, the more likely it is to have—or need—a supplemental vent.

The Quebec oven floors are egg-shaped (longer than they are wide, slightly wider in back than in front). This shape allows a large baking area at the rear, yet allows a smooth flow of air and smoke. It encourages the fire to sweep into the far reaches of the oven and turn smoothly back and then out of the oven. This is especially important since most Quebec ovens are built outside, without chimneys, and therefore without the extra draft chimneys provide. This flow of the fire leads to even heating of the masonry, and the vase-like shape makes it easy to see into the whole oven and to use long-handled ash scrapers and dough peels.

CLAY OVENS

From the outside, a good Quebec-style clay oven has a graceful shape, like half a pear lying on its cut side. The shape is strange, but pleasing. This is possible because the basic material of the oven—clay—is a plastic and forgiving medium that is easy to form into smooth curves and shapes. Unfortunately, clay has some drawbacks for oven building, even if reinforced with stone or brick:

- Good native clay can be difficult to find and is hard to dig out and prepare in the quantities needed for an oven.
- Clay is water soluble, and the outside of the oven will never get hot enough to fire the clay into terra-cotta or brick, so it will soften and slump if it gets wet.
- Clay is not a good insulator, so the oven will not hold heat well from one day to the next.
- Some clay ovens wear away from the inside (drop pieces of clay) and eventually need to be repaired.

Some of these problems can be overcome when a clay oven is made of tempered high-temperature clay and fired in a kiln, when it is built up of individual hunks of clay soil that have been dried and are then bonded with wet clay (adobe), or when the clay oven is roofed over. In Mennonite communities on the Canadian prairies the outdoor ovens were built by farm women, using native clay as mortar and cladding for an arch of used bricks. The ovens were then covered with burlap, pasted to the outer layer of clay with a mixture of flour and water. When this was dry the oven was whitewashed, giving sufficient rain protection for a dry region.

Although these techniques will extend the usable life of a clay oven, for most intents and purposes it is more practical to build ovens out of more durable and easily available building materials. The oven construction details I describe later are suitable for an oven built out of red brick, firebrick, refractory cements, stone, concrete, steel angle, and so forth, each used in such a way as to provide a balance between aesthetics, cost, and efficiency.

PROPORTIONS AND MATERIALS FOR BRICK OVENS

Practical experience has shown that a ceiling height of fifteen to eighteen inches is optimal for baking loaf breads, because a lower ceiling will necessitate an impractically low door, and a higher one will reduce the moisture content around the loaves and reduce crust formation. (This rule does not have to be followed so exactly for an oven built primarily for pizza or for mixed baking and roasting. The door and dome may be somewhat higher, but still at the 63 percent ratio.)

Experience also shows that the thickness of uninsulated masonry in the hearth or floor of the oven should be slightly greater than that of the oven walls and dome, so that a little extra heat from the hearth can flow up into the oven during the baking cycle. Heat from the hearth is very important to good baking of loaf breads.

A masonry thickness of eight inches in the hearth and about seven inches in the dome works well for an oven that is used intermittently, or is used for both bread and pizza (the fire is pushed to the back of the oven but continues to burn while the pizza bakes). An oven used only for pizza can make do with two and one-half to three inches of masonry in its walls, and five inches in the hearth. (This may not pass the building code

Richard Freeman has two brick ovens in one: an inner arch of bricks, a layer of insulation, and an enclosure of bricks.

in some areas, and may require the use of a much thicker outer oven, or enclosure.) Such a thin oven will be easy to bring to proper heat. An oven used to bake loaf bread on a *daily* basis should have at least ten and one-half inches of masonry in the dome, and a little more in the hearth.

A good brick oven is insulated below the hearth mass, all around the walls, and above the dome mass. This allows the use of the gradually decreasing heat in the oven over a period of days (for cooking casseroles, drying herbs, and similar uses). The heated mass of the oven should be isolated from the foun-

dation to reduce heat loss and to prevent cracking of the foundation when the oven is heated.

Modern internal combustion ovens will retain the advantages of their predecessors while avoiding the drawbacks mentioned above by employing these critical features:

- one door and no vents;
- external chimneys and ash drops;
- the 63 percent ratio of door and dome;
- baking chamber is deeper than it is wide;
- oven mounted on a slab that can expand

and contract without cracking the oven foundation;

- a smooth neck to permit unhindered air flow and easy ash and bread removal;
- well insulated;
- mass and wall thickness appropriate to their intended use;
- thermocouple (heat sensor) systems to assess firing and baking conditions;
- firebrick hearths that transfer heat to the bread at the correct rate when the oven is properly heated.

Externally Fired and Exhausted Ovens—White Ovens

The principles for the construction and use of white ovens are different than those for the internally fired black ovens, and a detailed discussion is beyond the scope of this book. Such ovens were once common, and some are still being made (see the visit to HomeFires Bakery). In good designs the thickness of the masonry of the oven serves to temper the heat delivered, as well as to store it—several inches of masonry (at least two inches) separates the fire and its exhaust from the cavity of the oven. The added cost and complexity of this type of oven construction (which requires a firebox, a double wall, and multiple flues and clean-outs, all of which must be built by or under the guidance of an expert mason) only make sense for a commercial oven, or if a masonry heater is being built at the same time, incorporating the oven. Masonry heaters are usually expensive, but including an oven may create little additional expense.

Planning Your Oven

A little thought ahead of time will save you a lot of head-scratching later. Let's look at the major areas you must consider.

SIZE AND STYLE

The size and style of your oven must be appropriate for its intended use. A brick oven should not be depended upon to heat a room or a house, unless it is built as part of a masonry heater. It is possible to recover some heat from any indoor oven when it is not in use, but this is a secondary effect. If the primary goal is house heating, several designs of commercially available masonry heating appliances incorporate a small oven, and there are masons in the United States with experience custom-building masonry heating appliances on-site that have ovens, or in which the firebox can be used as an oven when the fire is removed. Another possibility is to build a small oven (as described in this book) and have it share a foundation but use a separate flue in the chimney of a new fireplace or wood stove. All of these are better ways to heat a house than to try to build an oven according to the plans in this book, and then try to heat your house with it.* That said, a masonry oven is the *best* way to bake bread and cook other foods you need, and it can be a powerful architectural statement in or outside a house or restaurant/bakery.

Sizing the oven to your intended use is important. A 4 x 6 foot or 6 x 8 foot oven may bake ten large pizzas or ninety loaves of pan bread at a time, and will always require more wood than a small oven. A more modest oven makes better sense for domestic use, indoors or out. Masonry ovens work

*Members of the Masonry Heater Association are sorted by geographic area on their Internet website at: www. mha-net.org. See the Sources list.

A Finnish-style masonry heater, built by Doug Wood, with a bake oven above the fireplace (photo: Doug Wood).

OVEN SIZING BY INTENDED USE

What do you intend to bake? In general, those who wish to make predominantly pizza will want the widest possible oven and the widest possible door (and thinner masonry in the dome), while those who concentrate on loaf bread will want a deeper, longer oven with a smaller door. Some oven builder/owners have chosen to build very small ovens (20 x 30 inch) because they were sure they would not want to cook more than a few loaves at a time, only to discover that the bread was so good, they wished they had a larger oven. Besides, it's not easy to leave a fire going while cooking a series of pizzas in such a small oven.

The smallest oven Alan Scott recommends is a 24 x 30-inch size, while most household ovens are the size of the one presented in this book: 32 x 36 inches, with a door that is 16 inches wide and 10 inches high. Larger family ovens are 36 x 48 inches; interestingly, this is the size of most old farmstead ovens in this country and Europe, where all the bread for a family was baked once a week. By using modern thermocouples, you can estimate how much firing you need to bake several batches once the oven has been heated. Changes in the way you manage your oven will let you bake two or three times as much bread as the nominal capacity of your oven, when you need it (see "Oven Management," chapter 10).

Commercial ovens for small bakeries are typically 4 x 6 feet up to a practical limit of 6 x 8 feet (larger ovens are possible, but are usually fired with gas, or are either hybrid or white ovens). The maximum practical width for the mouth of such an oven is about 24

better for cooking loaf bread when they are fully loaded, or nearly so, since full loading keeps the moisture level up in early baking. A smaller oven will bake just as well as a larger one, but it will bake a smaller load. As Selker and Shirey point out, the geometry of a dome shape means that the radiant heat reaching a loaf from a small oven is the same as for a large oven, if the masonry is equally hot (see bibliography). Of course, the conducted heat from the hearth is dependent on its temperature and the specific heat of its brick, not on the size of the oven. You should avoid an excessively large oven; if necessary, a small oven may be refired (reheated) if you occasionally need to bake a larger quantity of bread.

inches. Some restaurant ovens are higher, wider, and shorter than the ones described here; they are designed for roasting as well as for bread and pizzas.

DECIDING ON THE MATERIALS FOR AN OVEN

The next question you must answer is about materials for your oven, especially in two areas: the concrete for the slabs and the bricks for the dome. The charts on pages 204 and 205 show that the temperature at the interface between the bricks and the concrete cladding gradually increases when the oven is in use. If the oven is only fired a few times a week, the concrete will never get much hotter than 450 degrees Fahrenheit (230 degrees Celsius), and standard Portland-based concrete will handle that just fine; even at 700 degrees Fahrenheit it retains 50 percent of its strength. If, however, your oven is both insulated (keeping the heat in) and in use every day (as in a restaurant or bakery oven), concrete temperatures may be excessive, especially in view of the thermal cycling that occurs. In that case, it is advisable to use alumina-based refractory concrete for the hearth slab and dome cladding (see the following chapter on materials). Constant use (for bread, not pizza) becomes easier with a thicker oven because the oven temperature is more stable. Of course, a thinner oven will be more economical with fuel if you plan to bake only one or two loads each time you heat the oven.

A masonry oven is the best way to bake bread and cook other foods you need, and it can be a powerful architectural statement in or outside a house or restaurant/bakery.

∾

This same kind of reasoning applies for using red brick on the oven walls and dome: red brick will last your lifetime if you heat your oven gradually and bake a few times a week, but it will probably last only a few years if the oven is in constant use or is exposed to rapid temperature fluctuations, especially from excessive water sprays or mopping. In the latter cases, it is better to use firebrick. In some jurisdictions that follow the Uniform Building Code, oven domes may need to be 10 inches thick (including bricks) when lined with red brick, and only 8 inches thick when lined with firebrick. That could be a deciding factor for you, if you want an 8-inch dome. Also, some code enforcers may require that the outer walls of the oven (the enclosure) be 8 inches thick if the oven chamber is lined with red brick, and only 4 inches thick if it is lined with firebrick.

SPACE PLANNING

Ask yourself what will be taking place in the area surrounding the oven. Consider that ovens draw people together and become a focus of activity, indoors or out. It is a good idea to plan not only the extra space necessary for manipulating the long oven tools, but to allow plenty of room, somewhere near, for the peanut gallery (people love to watch!). It is essential to have a flat surface onto which you can place dough, pans, boards, cornmeal, your fire gloves, and everything else you need. Of course, you need

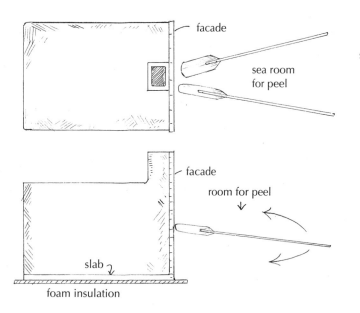

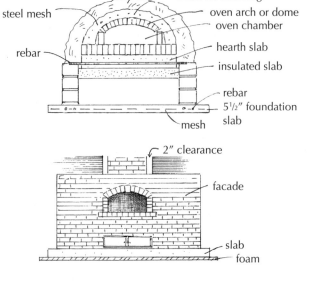

A 32" x 36" oven with a 10" x 16" door.

a table, a rack, or baskets for the bread you have baked. For outdoor ovens, it is good to have a covered area in front of the oven, with a counter at hearth height running out from the side of the oven facade. Also consider the locations of the hose connections, neighbors, and the prevailing wind. Cross drafts should be avoided, but can be managed with a draft door if necessary. If possible, position the oven downwind from the house. Try to keep the oven close to the kitchen door, or if indoors, close to or in the kitchen, and not in the basement. Plan now to store your pans, baskets, flour, etc. in shelves, racks, and bins that will be close to the oven.

INDOOR OVEN SAFETY—AGAIN!

I have cautioned you to build a safe oven, and that you need to get it approved. This is especially important for an indoor oven.

Since it is new construction it won't cost much more to do it right the first time, and it will be very expensive if you have to tear it out. Go to City Hall or the town clerk's office and find out how fireplace construction is regulated in your area. If detailed drawings are necessary, the plans in this book may be copied for submission, although they may need to be modified for your situation. Let's look at the areas the code officers may want to address.

1. Type of chimney: Officials may say that you need either a Residential Appliance-type Chimney (good for 1,000 degrees Fahrenheit) or a Low-heat Industrial-type Chimney (good for 1,400 degrees Fahrenheit). Usually the Residential-type is sufficient. Either of these requirements may be satisfied with a prefabricated metal chimney or with

a masonry chimney. In masonry, both use a $^5/_8$-inch fireclay or refractory liner joined with medium-duty refractory mortar. The wall of the Residential chimney need only be 4 inches thick (one brick), while an Industrial chimney must at least 8 inches thick. The building code uses a graph to determine minimum cross-sectional flue area, but this will be met by an 8 x 8-inch square or a 7-inch diameter round flue for all residential ovens.

2. Chimney reinforcement: In seismically active areas, masonry chimneys must be reinforced with steel and strapped to the frame of the building at each floor, even (in some cases) tied to the oven foundation. Regardless of reinforcement, in no areas are chimneys allowed to carry any of the load of the frame of a house unless specifically so designed and approved.

3. Spark arrestor: In dry regions code may require a metal mesh spark arrestor if the oven is within a certain distance of trees, brush, or flammable roofing.

4. Foundation: The stock building code language requires a foundation that is a foot thick and that extends at least 6 inches outside the oven wall. That portion of the code allows for exceptions, which you should seek—a foot is thicker than you need, if your foundation slab is adequately reinforced.

5. Clearances: There should be no combustible material within 2 inches of a chimney, or 9 inches of an oven wall. This distance can be reduced (under National Fire Protection Association rules) if heat deflectors are installed. Note that these distances are not the same as those that apply to "range appliances" such as wood-burning stoves made of metal, which have much higher surface temperatures than the outside of oven enclosures, and must be much further from combustible surfaces.

6. Hearths: This section may require that the hearth extend at least 16 inches from the inner oven door, which is longer than is practical. This is one area where fireplaces and ovens really are different, and so you should argue if questioned. The fire in an oven is much farther from the front of the hearth than the fire in a fireplace.

7. Centering: All combustible formwork and centering (wooden work used to support arches during construction) must be removed before the oven is used.

Use the charts in chapter 10 if you have to convince the authorities that the outside of the oven insulation will not be hot enough to be a danger. These are records of tests on installed ovens. Plan to vent the area between the insulation and the surround, regardless of the adequacy of your insulation. If any part of the surround is not masonry, use metal studs and framing and insulate with a granular material like vermiculite or perlite (preferably with a thin layer of diatomaceous earth right next to the walls and dome of the oven), which can sift into and seal any potential cracks. Line your enclosure with a noncombustible material before you apply wooden siding. Consider building an insulated masonry enclosure, then strapping

Consider that ovens draw people together and become a focus of activity, so allow plenty of room to work, and enough for the peanut gallery.

the outside of it with metal studs, and putting wood siding over that. Be safe.

OUTDOOR OVEN SAFETY

In most districts an outdoor oven is considered a barbecue (Section 3102.2 of the UBC), and in most districts these are fully regulated. You should ask, to be sure your insurance is not jeopardized. You may need to follow the same structural guidelines, and you may need a screen over the top of the flue in areas prone to brush fires. In addition, there may be a zoning issue—you must observe property-line setbacks. In any case you will still be responsible for any fire you cause due to poor construction or unsafe handling of the fire, the coals, or the ashes. If there is no hose faucet nearby, mount a fire extinguisher to the oven base somewhere, to back up your bucket of water. Watch the oven during the early part of the burn, when it might throw sparks.

Bakery Fires— It Can't Happen Here!

It *could* happen here. I know of two fires in small commercial bakeries, caused in each case by both structural deficiencies and improper oven management. Neither of these fires caused major structural damage, but that was mostly luck.

In the first case the structural problems included both an inadequately thick cladding (that allowed cracks to form) and the use of a fibrous insulation that did not seal the cracks, that allowed soot to build up, and was porous enough to allow combustion air to reach the hot soot. The management problem was the routine use (over a period of years) of

the oven to dry wet firewood. This allowed volatile wood gases to escape from the oven through the structural defects, then condense as soot. Fortunately, the smoldering soot in the fibrous insulation made enough smoke that the bakers were alerted and there was little additional damage. The oven has since been rebuilt and improved, and they no longer bake (the technical word is "coke") their firewood in this fashion.

The basic cause of the other fire was overfiring an oven that was too small and too thinly clad for the production asked of it. This small oven was often overheated to attempt to get extra bakes from each firing, and the result was cracked bricks and cladding. This second oven had an unventilated wooden enclosure—more no-nos. Although the enclosure was damaged in the fire, the bakery building was not damaged. Again the oven, the enclosure, and the management of the oven were changed.

To review: Drying wood excessively in a masonry oven is not recommended (see chapter 10). Wood enclosures are not recommended unless applied over fireproof materials. Build an oven wall that is at least 8 inches thick. Do not insulate a brick oven with loose fiber insulation such as rock wool or fiberglass. Use vermiculite and/or diatomaceous earth that will sift into and seal cracks that develop. Loose fill insulation like these won't pass enough air to support combustion, either.

The Health Department

You need to get in touch with your local health department if you are going to sell some of your bread. Rules and their interpretations vary too much for you to make assumptions. For instance, some states are very lenient with small-time producers, and you may find you can sell quite a few loaves a day or a week without any interference. In other areas you are not supposed to sell anything without some kind of permit. Regulations usually cover the storage of ingredients, air gaps on the sinks, drains in the floor, sewers or septic tank connections, and trash and garbage receptacles. Find out what you need before you set up your bakery, otherwise you run the risk of facing expenses later.* Keep rodents and insects out of the grain and the bakery area itself.

Some artisan bakers have had trouble with their local health authorities because of wooden work surfaces, or because linen *couche* cloths or baskets are not normally washed between uses. You must realize that the person from the health department will probably never have seen a bakery like yours before, so you must know the codes yourself and establish a working relationship with the inspector by providing information about artisan baking. (The Bread Baker's Guild of America can provide copies of articles on this subject.) Having the inspector try a little of your bread is a great way to break the ice. If the inspector is going to write you up for things you believe are safe practices, remember that brick ovens and linen *couches* are probably *not* covered in the code book, and I know of no documentation that they constitute a health risk. Don't roll over and play dead. Get an attorney, if necessary, and go through the appeal process. You will probably win.

Construction Preview

Let's review the basic elements of your masonry oven.

FOUNDATION SLAB

The most practical foundation for an oven is a slab of reinforced concrete, resting on well-drained soil or sand without other footings or frost walls. In a cold climate, the slab should rest on rigid foam insulation or a rubble footing. This will prevent freezing and heaving under the slab, and will allow you to omit the customary frost walls.

Commercial concrete is purchased transit-mixed out of a truck, but most companies won't deliver less than a cubic yard without an extra charge. This charge may be reasonable if you are not far from the batch plant, or if you need to make a foot-thick foundation under local code. The alternative is to mix it yourself unless you are in an urban area where small transit-mix trailers are available.

ASH SLOT AND CHAMBER

It is best to provide an ash chamber under the oven, with masonry walls and/or a fireproof metal container for the ashes that are scraped off the floor of the oven after firing. A metal door that closes off this chamber will keep children, pets, and rain out of the ashes. The bricks on the floor of the oven rest on a bed of clay and sand above a reinforced concrete slab, which is supported by the walls on the sides and back of the ash chamber. The oven floor slab is made smaller (shorter and narrower) than the outline of the supporting walls and the slab's grid of steel reinforcing bars is left to extend out above those walls

*See whether there is a category for small kitchens like those in schools and camps—that category could apply to you and is usually less restrictive than the general commercial category. Also check on packaging rules in your area—some jurisdictions require closed bags.

The elements of the chimney base: the arch in the oven facade, the outer hearth, the ash slot, and the doorjamb bricks.

*The original red bricks in the back of the fireplace of my house are just now wearing out. I haven't replaced them, though, since they aren't clearly worse than they were ten years ago, and my house is more than 200 years old!

and rest on them. That way, the slab is free to move slightly with changes in temperature. It also means that outdoor ovens may be fairly easy to jack up and move to a new location, to be set on a new foundation if need be.

HEARTH

The floor of the oven, the *hearth*, is built of firebricks, turned on edge; no mortar is used to hold them in place. Firebricks last much longer than red bricks when in direct contact with coals. Although soapstone slabs make an attractive and durable hearth, they are more expensive than firebricks, and they store and transfer so much heat that the bottoms of loaves of bread tend to get burned by the time the tops of the loaves are baked. Soapstone is fine for flatbread, but why limit yourself to flatbread? Some people say that firebrick is too porous for a hearth, and recommend some form of pottery. In practice, though, the heat of the next fire will burn up any traces of fat

or other liquids that have dripped onto the hearth, and firebrick is more resistant to thermal shock than pottery.

WALLS AND DOME

The inner walls and dome of a home oven may be built of hard red brick or firebrick. Red brick is cheaper, attractive, easily available, and long-lasting in this application, if it is not sprayed excessively with water.* Most people use firebrick for the hearth, walls, and dome, though, and some masons are shocked by the idea of using anything else. Firebrick is much more resistant to the type of erosion that occurs on the floor of an oven when wood embers are fanned by combustion air, but this only happens to a limited extent at the walls and dome of an oven. Firebrick is more resistant to being splashed with water when it is hot, but even firebrick will not last forever if it is abused that way.

The wall bricks are set vertically, mortared together with a thin line of mortar so that the long edges of the bricks face the oven chamber. This gives a brick thickness of about four inches, and an additional two and one-half to six inches of reinforced concrete is poured outside them (depending on the size of the oven and its use). The dome bricks are mortared into an arched vault, again with the long edges facing the oven chamber. A layer of aluminum foil laid over the bricks of the dome prevents the brick layer from sticking to the surrounding reinforced concrete. The reinforced concrete holds the walls together so the brick arch cannot collapse, while the foil allows the bricks in the dome to heave enough so that no big cracks can form. An insulation layer and an enclosure with a brick or stone facing complete the body of the oven.

THERMOCOUPLES

Thermocouples are metallic thermometer probes that can be buried in the wall and floor of the oven. Wires then lead to a gauge that will tell you the masonry temperature at a glance. The details of these devices will be covered in the chapter on oven management (chapter 10), but what you need to know here is that it is helpful to have a series of them at various levels of the thickness of the masonry. That makes it easy to see when the oven has been heated enough and easy to see when the stored heat in the masonry is too low to continue baking. The main drawback to thermocouples is cost—both the probes and the gauges are expensive.

OVEN DOOR

Most ovens with a flue above and outside the oven doorway do not have a hinged metal door or pair of doors to close off the mouth of the oven itself, because they are not necessary. Hinged lightweight metal doors are often fitted to close off the outer opening of the chimney recess of indoor ovens to ensure no smoke enters the house, to screen the occupants from the heat of the oven, and (in some counties) to meet fireplace codes. If this kind of door is closed when the oven is fired, draft air must be available through the ash slot or through draft slats or controls in the doors themselves.

Instead of hinged doors, most ovens have simple metal or metal and wood doors with a D–handle on the outer side. These are easily placed and removed as necessary, and they sit on the lip between the ash slot and the oven

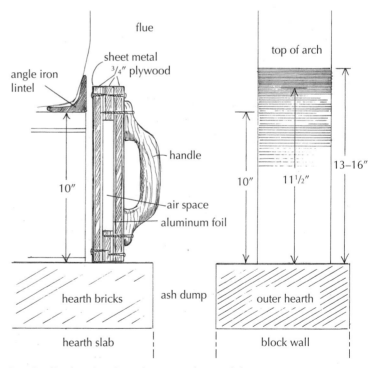

Longitudinal section through an oven door and the outer oven doorway.

door. This kind of door is used whenever the oven is used to bake loaves, and it is left out when pizza is baked with the fire pushed to the back or side of the oven.

The exception to this discussion about removable doors is for small commercial bakeries, where it is more convenient to use counterweighted doors that either fall away in front of the peel or lift up out of the way (into the chimney recess) when activated by the baker.

ENCLOSURE

A vented enclosure, preferably of masonry or metal, protects the outside of the oven and its insulation. The minimum thickness of the enclosure may be dictated by building codes. The enclosure includes the facade of the oven, its outer sides, and its back and cap. Make an access and inspection door in the top of the rear of the enclosure.

CAP

Many ovens have a masonry cap that rests on the enclosure walls and closes off the space around the oven dome. The cap is essentially the top of the oven structure. It is typically made of reinforced concrete. Many other ovens are capped with sheet metal. Some are capped with wood, but experience (and, in most locations, the building code) indicates that is not a good idea.

ROOF

Outdoor oven enclosures are either roofed over with a separate roof, or the cap of the enclosure itself can be of some non-combustible material, pitched to shed rain. I favor separate roofs, as they make the outside of the dome more accessible. Because most forms of heat-resistant insulation will stay wet if exposed to water, and because stucco will crack if parts of the outside of a stuccoed structure are heated to different temperatures, covering an entire oven with stucco requires perfect detailing. I don't really favor depending on stucco for waterproofing, because I live in a wet climate with large temperature extremes. I favor a masonry cap (a thin, reinforced slab) that is completely watertight and can be removed if you need to modify your oven in the future.

A stucco enclosure and roof combined, however, is something that lots of others have done in drier and more temperate places. If you want to try it, be sure to space the stucco mesh or plaster lath out a few inches from the oven and the chimney, then cap around the chimney with metal or stone, creating a thermal and structural break. That way, the stucco will heat more evenly. If an entirely masonry oven enclosure is what you have in mind, consider a brick, slate, concrete, or stone roof, and you will make it watertight.

CHIMNEY MATERIALS

The chimney recess is built of brick that is tied to the brick or stone of the facade. Above the recess the chimney (for an indoor oven) must be lined with formed clay flue tiles or approved metal flue pipe. Indoor ovens need a damper so that warm air from the room is not drawn up the chimney when the oven is not being fired or used for baking. Outdoor ovens should have a chimney cap in rainy climates, and a spark screen in dry ones.

Oven enclosures.

145

Design choices

You will be more familiar with masonry materials after you have read the chapter on materials (chapter 8). If you are going to build your own oven, you need to buy a basic book on masonry construction or get one from the library. It would be wasteful to duplicate all of that information here. After educating yourself you must still make several decisions:

1. Do you want a slab and block walls as your foundation (as is presented in this book), or some other arrangement, such as a heavy-duty welded metal stand?

2. Are you in a cold climate, where the foundation should be insulated or placed over a rubble footing to prevent frost heaving?

3. Do you want an ash slot in the hearth? They are convenient for bread ovens but optional for pizza ovens, where the fire is pushed into the back or side, not raked out.

4. What is your comfortable working height? For most people it is a little below elbow level. Remember that this is the height of the finished hearth, not the height of the ash-dump walls or the height of the top of the hearth slab. The traditional height of a European hearth is 90 centimeters—about 35 $^1/_2$ inches; however, many bakers like a higher hearth. A lower one will *not* do, unless children will be actively involved with the oven, as at a school.

5. Will you use firebrick or red brick for the walls and dome? If you use firebrick for the walls and dome you need 10 percent fewer bricks than the standard plans call for, because firebrick are larger than red brick.

6. Will you use Portland cement or alumina-based concrete for the hearth slab and cladding of the oven, and how thick will the cladding be? Use alumina and a thicker cladding if you are going to be baking every day, or if you want to bake more than three loads per firing.

7. Do you want thermocouples, and how many? I recommend at least one in the wall or dome, and one in the hearth, but having a series of three of them in line somewhere in the dome is even better.

8. What will the facade of the oven look like?

9. What type of arch do you want at the opening of the chimney recess, and what type of brick, stone, or tile is to be seen on the facade?

10. Do you want a stone slab or bricks for your outer hearth?

11. Will you insulate the bottom of the hearth slab to save heat? This will be worthwhile if you plan to use the oven more than once a week, and it adds little expense or labor.

12. How will you insulate the dome and walls of the oven?

13. If outdoors, what kind of roof and enclosure do you want? If indoors, what kind of outer oven finish do you want? Brick, stucco, stone?

14. Will your flue run straight up, or does it need to snake around somewhere to get out of the building?

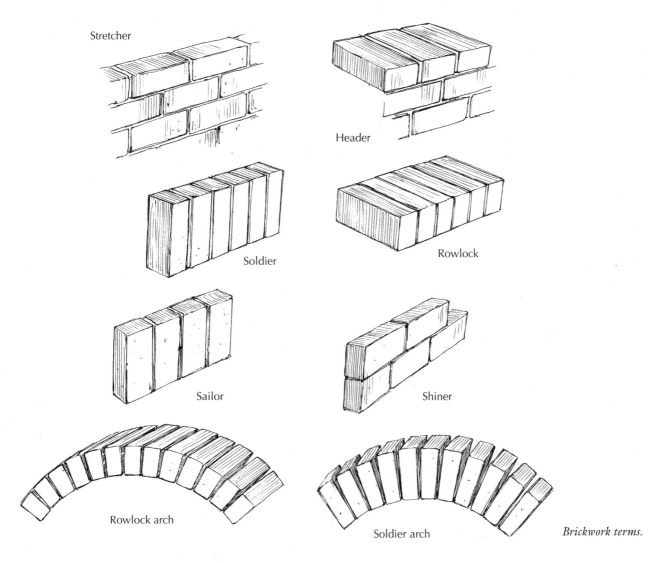

Stretcher

Header

Soldier

Rowlock

Sailor

Shiner

Rowlock arch

Soldier arch

Brickwork terms.

As you can see, there are many questions that must be answered—and this list is by no means complete. Building a masonry oven requires a certain amount of forethought, but remember, the more consideration you devote in the planning stages the more smoothly the construction processes will proceed and the more satisfied you will be with the final outcome.

Buying an Oven

As this book is written I know of only one company making modular masonry ovens designed primarily for baking loaf breads—Dietmeyer, Ward, and Stroud of Vashon Island, Washington, makes both retained-heat and white modular ovens in small, household sizes—but beginning in the early 1980s, several companies began to import or manufacture multipurpose ovens designed primarily for baking flatbreads and for roasting, but usable for loaf breads. Some have domes of refractory concrete, some of high-fired refractory clay. Some have hearths of dense, nonporous high-fired clay, and some use less dense ceramics formulated specifically for hearths. Please see the Sources list for contact information for these suppliers.

If you are considering purchasing a manufactured, modular masonry oven, and plan to bake loaves, keep these important characteristics in mind:

1. The masonry of a retained-heat oven should be at least four inches thick to guarantee that enough heat can be stored for two bakes without refiring.
2. The hearth material should have a density and conductivity not greater than medium density firebrick (130 pounds per cubic foot, and 8.5 btu x in/hr x ft squared x degree Fahrenheit or, in metric units 2.06 g/cm squared and 1.23 W/m x degree C.)
3. Get one that has been approved by a national testing agency. Otherwise you may have problems with the local code officers, since the wall of the oven is going to be less than 8 inches thick.

Some suppliers furnish ovens in parts that require assembly, but that are easily carried to the site. Some supply prefabricated ovens that don't require assembly but may need a forklift or a lot of ingenuity to unload and install. Some ovens can be ordered with metal bases that are lighter than concrete block; these may be installed on an existing floor. Some suppliers don't have much to offer in household sizes. Some supply oven tools as part of the kit. Make your selections carefully to be sure you get what will work for you.

MUGNAINI IMPORTS

Watsonville, California

Pottery oven liners were built in Devon, England, for hundreds of years, exported, and widely used in colonial houses in this country. In other parts of Europe there is a similar tradition of prefabricated, kit, and modular ovens—such ovens are now being imported to the U.S. by several firms.

Andrea Smith's company, Mugnaini Imports, began by importing wine and oil, then architectural ceramics. In the late 1980s, she began to bring in small ceramic ovens handmade in Italy by the Valoriani family, and now she handles their full line of ovens for houses and restaurants, including machine-made heavy-duty models for sustained use.

Andrea is partially of Tuscan descent—her mother is the Mugnaini in the family. The Tuscan hills south of Florence are the source not only of Chianti, but also of *cotto*, a high-alumina clay soil that can be formed and fired into a relatively nonporous and highly conductive ceramic. For fifty years the Valoriani family firm has been making home and commercial wood-burning ovens of this material. According to Andrea many Tuscan houses have a small oven in the courtyard that is in constant use for roasting, cooking flatbreads, and baking loaves. The ovens she sells are designed for that kind of use, in which a small fire is left in the oven all day after the oven has been brought to heat with a larger fire. A draft door is left in place when the heat is to be controlled, and also used to seal the oven if the fire is removed altogether and loaf bread is loaded. The refractory pottery floors of these ovens cannot stand sudden temperature swings, so the hearths are swept with a brass brush after the fire is pushed back and to one side. They are never damp-mopped.

These modular ovens are not ready to use when they arrive, though the kits do include the pieces that will form the hearth, the dome, the base of the flue, the outer oven doorway, and the first layer of insulation, in addition to the oven door and a kit of basic oven tools. Prices are $1,200 or $1,800 for the two sizes of home oven, with a shipping weight of 750 pounds. Although the company can supply other parts of an oven enclosure, a typical installation will require on-site work by a mason or handy owner, since the oven base and oven enclosure are similar to those of site-built ovens. The smallest oven (the "Piccolo") is often enclosed in a rounded dome formed of rebar, metal lath, and stucco, while the larger home ovens (the "Medio") usually get a roof and walls.

The domes of the Valoriani ovens are insulated with blankets of kaolin-based ceramic fiber insulation, then 6 inches of loose vermiculite. No attempt is made to insulate the hearth, which sits on a site-built concrete and sand sandwich that is fourteen inches thick overall. The oven dome is much thinner than that of a site-built bread oven, and so stores less heat. The modular ovens are thus better and more efficient for cooking flatbreads, for roasting with a fire in place, or for cooking one load of bread loaves, but they will not cook multiple loads of loaves without refiring.

I visited Andrea at her California-Mediterranean hillside house, with its hillside stone and terra-cotta terrace and sweeping views of the central California coast. Talk about Italy—I came away with a powerful impression of the potential for elegance that an outdoor oven offers in such a setting. It becomes a lifestyle statement that Americans can interpret, Andrea says, through their long experience with barbecues and fireplaces. I also realized that there are plenty of people who don't *want* to build their own oven, and there is no reason they should. They can have someone else do it, and using a modular oven kit will probably lower the overall cost of professional installation. On the other hand, it was clear to me from my visit to Mugnaini and my review of the catalogues of the other companies in this business that a site-built oven will be better for loaf bread than anything that is currently commercially available, because the masonry of site-built ovens is thicker.

TECHNICAL POINTS

- Although Andrea supplies thermometers that may be used in the ovens, she advises her customers to learn to judge the heat in the oven by direct observation—for example, pizza edges and toppings should bubble in thirty seconds and a plate-sized pizza should cook completely in three minutes. This means that the oven temperature is between 650 and 750 degrees Fahrenheit (345 to 400 degrees Celsius). The desired 450 to 500 degrees Fahrenheit (230 to 290 degrees Celsius) oven for roasting is maintained by observing the cooking food, feeling the heat with a hand in the oven, then adjusting the draft door, fire, and the exposure of the food to the fire. She recommends a cooler oven for loaf bread,

This Mugnaini modular oven is part of a nearly completed house in California (photo: Mugnaini Imports).

achieved by closing the oven for several hours (usually overnight) after it has been used for other cooking.

- Andrea likes the nonporous hearth tiles, in preference to more porous firebrick, because she does a lot of roasting, and liquid spatters and food odors don't get into the tiles. Also, the large size of the tiles combines with their high conductivity to evenly distribute heat in the hearth—hot spots are not a problem. Of course, the downside is the relative delicacy (to thermal and mechanical shock) and rapid heat transfer rate of the tiles, which theoretically could be a problem when she bakes loaves instead of flatbreads. Since she usually waits until the next day to bake bread and the ovens have no hearth insulation, it may be that she avoids burning the bottom of her loaves because the hearth becomes slightly cooler than the dome.

- Andrea was arranging a regional distribution system for the ovens when we met, and may in the future be able to make referrals to local distributors and/or installers. Up to now, she has shipped everything from warehouses in Watsonville and Los Angeles, though she has a new office in New York.

- Although it is environmentally appropriate and economically sound to use locally available materials and labor when possible (which is certainly possible when ovens are built of native clay, or of bricks made from native clay, or of a refractory mixture of alumina cement and heat-resistant native rock), not every part of the U.S. has good clay, a local brick kiln, or a source of heat-resistant rock. The scratch materials you buy may have been trucked two thousand miles, while a prefabricated European oven will have been shipped to this country by water, a relatively efficient method, and trucked a few hundred miles.

SAN JUAN BAKERY

San Juan Bautista, California

and

HOMEFIRES BAKERY

Leavenworth, Washington

The sourdough starter and sourdough bread recipe are unchanged in fifty years

⁓

NOT ALL BRICK OVENS were made to be fired with wood—coal-fired ovens are still common in New York City, and large oil or gas ovens were built in many areas into the 1950s and some gas-fired masonry ovens are being built today. Let's look at two such ovens, one directly-fired (a burner pointed into the mouth of the oven) and one externally-fired (with a burner in a separate fire box with its own fuses).

There is an early gas oven in the small mission town of San Juan Bautista, California, where in 1938 Reno Cornaggio got tired of the recurrent flooding in his oven room and bought the building across the street. He hired Paul Metz, a well-known oven builder from Oakland, to build a large gas fired brick oven—its inside dimensions are about 12 x 12 feet. It has been in continuous use since it was built, by Cornaggio (who often sang opera in the street), by Bill and Gladys Paradis (who baked everybody's turkey, all of them at once, at Thanksgiving), and for the past sixteen years, by John House, now in his mid-sixties. The sourdough starter and sourdough bread recipe are unchanged in fifty years, the recipe for Portuguese orange nut bread was acquired by Bill Paradis before he bought the bakery, and the horizontal paddle mixer, the slicer, and the oven are unchanged.

The oven's heat storage is immense, as the hearth bricks rest on 13 inches of sand and the dome bricks are covered with the same amount. The oven is fired for two and one-quarter hours at the end of the afternoon each day so the heat can equalize by morning. On Sunday (his biggest baking day), John bakes two hundred and forty yeasted French loaves, two hundred sourdough loaves, and any number of loaves of herb and onion, garlic Romano, pesto tomato, cheese and jalapeño, potato, and Portuguese orange nut breads, in addition to pastries and cookies. Hundreds and hundreds of loaves on one firing of the oven—the massive heat storage of this oven does the trick.

There is a very different gas-fired oven a few miles outside the Bavarian/Tyrolean-theme town of Leavenworth, Washington: a "white" or externally-fired and vented masonry oven, built in 1985 by Dietmeyer, Ward, and Stroud, of Vashon Island, Washington, under the guidance of Ernst Heuft, a fifth-generation German stove mason who lives in British Columbia. The style and the workings of this oven are typical of small

SAN JUAN BAKERY
and
HOMEFIRES
BAKERY

commercial masonry ovens in Germany, Austria, and Switzerland, and many of the oven parts were imported from Europe. Although built for wood-firing, it was converted to propane seven years ago; it can be converted back to wood-firing in a matter of minutes, should that ever be necessary.

The efficiency of external-firing commercial ovens may justify their complexity, since the purpose of any firing schedule for a masonry oven is to heat the outer part of the mass to a temperature above that required by the baking bread. That way, heat will flow into the oven as bread is baked, without over-heating the bread early in the baking cycle. With a directly-fired oven, this is achieved by carefully timing the firing, clean-out, resting, and baking operations. There is little recourse if the oven is not hot enough when you want to use it, or if you want to bake extra loads. With externally fired ovens, however, the heat is always coming into the oven from outside (where it is generated), and continuous or intermittent firing can provide heat at the rate it is used, while retaining the hearth conduction, radiant heat, and high moisture advantages intrinsic to masonry ovens.

What is the downside? Cost and complexity. The HomeFires oven cost about $15,000 in 1985, and that was about $5,000 lower than it otherwise would have been because the constructors wanted to gain experience with the techniques used to make it. With inflation and currency changes (for the same imported castings), the same oven would cost about $50,000 in 1997 dollars, which is a lot to pay for an oven that has half or a third the hearth space of an equally expensive deck oven.

What is the oven like? It is a large rectangular masonry structure with a brick front and stuccoed sides. In its face there is an iron oven door that slides upward on iron tracks, its weight counterbalanced by iron weights on the end of two chains that run from the upper corners of the door over two toothed idler sprockets, then down to two iron weights. There is no outer hearth, but there is an inner transition hearth of smooth stone that slopes sharply up to a gradually sloping oven floor of refractory blocks. At the far corners of the oven there are small cooling vents, controlled by big chrome-plated damper handles on the front face of the oven, while on the right inner oven wall there is a small opening in the brick oven lining to let in steam. Steam is generated by allowing water to run into a copper funnel mounted on the stucco wall. From there it runs to a thick-walled metal box on the side of the

John House at the San Juan Bakery. The pipes behind him serve the gas burner and the steam injector. The rigid gas pipe is jointed, and can swing into the mouth as the oven is fired. See how high this hearth is? The door is counter-weighted (photo: Dina Dubois).

firebox, where it instantly boils, releasing steam into the oven. Because this is an open system on both ends there is no risk of steam explosion, and if scale builds up it is easily removed.

The firebox is under the rear of the oven, with an iron door that opens on the right side of the oven base. Dampers direct the flame into vertical (for starting the fire, or to reduce heating of the hearth) or horizontal channels. The first pair of horizontal channels run the full length of the oven, under and on each side of the center line of the hearth; they then double back, still under the hearth but under its outer aspect. They end in vertical tubes that take the smoke above the oven and empty it into horizontal channels over the outer aspect of the oven roof; these take it forward, so that it can be sent back again in two (more centrally located) channels that finally join at a vertical tube that dumps into a last horizontal channel. At its forward end this is controlled by the main draft damper. After the smoke passes this damper it reaches the chimney; a flap-type barometric draft there automatically adjusts the force of the draft as the oven is fired. In all, the smoke makes five passes across the oven brickwork, transferring heat to the masonry. Two internal dampers control the firebox, two control the cooling vents, and there is one main smoke damper and one barometric damper. There is a cleanout door at each 180-degree bend of the smoke channels.

Structurally, the masonry arch is retained by metal ties that run through sand layers above and below the oven. Since the sides of the oven are insulated, the retaining plates at the ends of these ties are not visible. However, there are additional, smaller plates that stabilize the outer wall and attach it to the inner brickwork—these stand proud of the stucco. The roof blocks of the internal smoke tubes under the lower sand layer are cast as trapezoids that keystone with adjacent blocks that are supported by the brick walls of the smoke channels.

There are two penetrating niches in the oven face beside the loading door, one for an oven light, the other for a metal-stemmed dial thermometer that reads the oven air temperature. There are no thermocouple probes in the brickwork, but there is a probe in the oven air next to the thermometer; its wire lead connected to a high temperature limit control for the propane burner. Since the oven is in daily use, it never falls below 300 degrees Fahrenheit overnight. In the morning the burner is fired (main damper open) until the oven temperature is 385 degrees Fahrenheit; the oven will then coast to 425 degrees Fahrenheit. More heat will come in as loads are baked, but the oven temperature is usually quite stable. If necessary the burner may be fired, or the firebox dampers may be opened, or the cooling dampers may be opened.

The reasons the D-Litzenbergers changed to propane? There were several: one was the uneconomical expenditure of time, space, and effort required to deal with 25 cords of softwood (that is what is available in Leavenworth) a year. Another was the persistent fine soot and fly-ash that burning that amount of softwood produced, which filtered onto everything near the bakery. Lastly, there is the greater degree of control that gas firing provides.

CHAPTER EIGHT

MASONRY MATERIALS,

TOOLS, *and* METHODS

You may wonder why I would spend a chapter discussing materials, since I am also going to give you a set of plans and a list of materials to buy. I am doing it because some people just won't follow directions! And if you are one of them, and want to modify, customize, or interpret as you go, a question about materials may come up in your planning or construction process that cannot be answered by the people at the building supply, masonry supply, or even the refractory supply store. I hope you will be able to answer it here.

Masonry Materials

Brick, stone, concrete, and sand are masonry materials. Although masonry materials are strong, most of them are brittle. They are stronger in compression than in tension (that is, pushed together as opposed to pulled apart), and will fail if exposed to vibration or shearing forces. Though resistant to heat, they will fail if rapidly cooled. Metal reinforcement must be used cautiously in heated masonry, as it expands and contracts differently.

CEMENT, CONCRETE, AND MORTAR

The essential material for most masonry construction is cement. This bonds the other materials together. When sand and small stones are bound together, the product created is called concrete. Common mortar is sand in a cement (without small stones) with lime added to increase adhesion and flexibility. It is placed between bricks, blocks, or stones to bind and bed them.

Powdered clay may be added to make the mortar easier to work, but it decreases the mechanical strength of the mixture, without increasing its heat resistance unless the mortar is primarily clay, with little cement present. At that point the mortar is weak, but heat-resistant. For concrete, heat resistance is dependent on the type of cement and the type of aggregate (filler) used. When the cement is resistant to high temperatures, it is called **refractory cement**; mixed with an appropriate aggregate, it becomes refractory concrete or mortar. When cement cures by taking up water, sets under water, and is resistant to water when set, it is called a **hydraulic** cement. Most other types of cement are **air drying**, although some refractory mortars are heat-setting.

Straight cements don't have a great deal of strength when bridging large gaps; they require a filler material, or aggregate, to correct this potential weakness. The aggregate bridges the gaps and provides many of the qualities of the finished product. These could include compressive strength, a low coefficient of thermal expansion, uniform grain size, light weight, or high thermal insulation performance. Choosing an aggregate requires balancing physical properties desired against the cost and local availability of the aggregate. Common aggregates are mined in their final form (sand, gravel) or are produced by a simple mechanical process (crushed stone).

Specialized aggregates are manufactured from raw materials by subjecting them to heat (as is the case with perlite, expanded shale, and vermiculite).

PORTLAND CEMENT

The most common type of cement is Portland cement, so-called because of the resemblance it bears to a type of limestone quarried near Portland, England. It is produced by burning clay or shale and high-calcium minerals to produce cinders that are then ground very fine to make a wettable powder. The hardening of Portland cement and the concrete and mortars made from it occurs as the result of hydration: the cement takes on water.

For general masonry work, the advantages of Portland cement include its high strength, relatively low cost, widespread availability, and versatility. It can be used in concrete and a variety of mortars when modified by other ingredients. Its limitations in oven building are its slow acquisition of strength as it sets, the loss of strength development

Concrete gets its strength from its aggregate. Sharp aggregate that is varied in size makes stronger concrete.

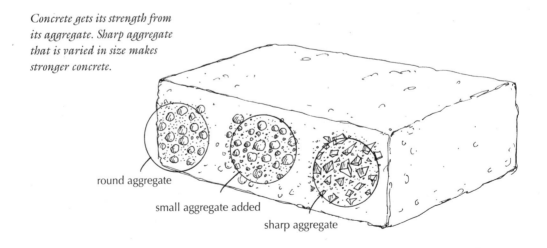

round aggregate

small aggregate added

sharp aggregate

if the cement is mixed with too much water or is prematurely dried, and its relatively low tolerance for heat. Cured, Portland has full strength up to about 450 degrees Fahrenheit (235 degrees Celsius), half strength at 750 degrees Fahrenheit (400 degrees Celsius), and no strength at 1,150 degrees Fahrenheit (625 degrees Celsius). *Strength does not return when it cools.* Even at temperatures in the moderate range (700 degrees Fahrenheit, 370 degrees Celsius), repeated cycles of heat are not well tolerated. Portland cement contains silica compounds and breathing cement dust is best avoided. Also, Portland and all other hydraulic cements will suck moisture from your skin, even when the cement is in a watery phase. This may lead to chapped or even broken skin.

MASONRY CEMENT

Masonry cement is a Portland cement modified by adding lime. This allows mortars made from it to grip more tightly to brick, stone, or block, and it makes the working (trowelling) qualities of the mortar better. There is no increase in heat resistance.

SACK MIX

This product comes premixed and bagged, and is sold at hardware stores, lumberyards, and by masonry suppliers. It is available as either mortar or concrete mix. All you add is water (directions on the bag say how much) and elbow grease to mix up small quantities. Sack mixes are more expensive than home-blended cement products, but you may save enough in aggravation (moving sand, dealing with half-used bags of cement) to make them worthwhile on an oven job.

Sack-mix mortar is useful for laying block in the ash pit walls, and sack-mix concrete may be used for the foundation slab. It may also be used as the cladding of a household oven. When determining how many bags to purchase, read the label carefully: it takes a lot of bags to pour a slab. Also, be sure you don't overload your pickup truck and your back—arrange a delivery if you can.

The major concern about sack-mix concrete is the aggregate. Often these are rounded gravel and quartz sand. This leaves the concrete with fairly low tensile strength as well as relatively poor heat tolerance. Sack mixes are fine for a slab on grade, adequate for the cladding or the hearth slab of a home oven, but are best avoided for cladding or hearth slabs of ovens larger than 32 x 36 inches, or ovens used every day—regardless of size. Refractory concretes are better in these applications.

TRANSIT MIX

Transit-mixed concrete is the kind that is delivered in big trucks, coming from a central plant. It is great stuff, but the minimum orders are too big for most oven work, even for slabs. Sometimes you can pay an extra fee to have a small order delivered, though.

CALCIUM ALUMINATE CEMENT

Calcium aluminate is a cement that is similar in use to Portland, but which avoids some of its problems. It is made of bauxite (ore that contains alumina) and limestone. This cement reaches good compression strength in one day (it is always weaker in tension than Portland). It is sold both for this early strength quality and for its heat resistance. It is the heart of refractory concretes, and buying it in the form of calcium aluminate cement and making your own refractory concrete is cheaper than buying proprietary brands of refractory concrete.

The most extensive line of this cement is from LaFarge Calcium Aluminates, Inc., with an office in Virginia (1-800-524-8463) that can refer to local distributors or ship directly. Their least expensive cement is *Fondu,* at 38 percent alumina. This product is resistant to heat of at least 950 degrees Fahrenheit (510 degrees Celsius) when made into concrete with quartz aggregate, 1,500 (825) with traprock, 1,900 (1,150) with vermiculite, 2,000 (1,200) with expanded clays, and 2,400 (1,300) with crushed firebrick. Progressively more heat-resistant and expensive cements are available, with higher alumina contents, but for oven construction, all calcium aluminate cements should have less than 45 percent alumina, so that they remain resistant to thermal cycling.

Of the aggregates mentioned, the most common one used in heat-resistant oven slabs and claddings is traprock, a widely available crushed basalt. Using LaFarge *Secar 41* (41 percent alumina cement) the mix would be:

- cement—94 pounds
- traprock, $^3/_4$ x $^3/_8$ inch—230 pounds
- fine manufactured sand (traprock)—188 pounds
- water—not to exceed $4^1/_2$ gallons

If getting all those materials is not possible, consider a premixed alumina concrete like LaFarge's *Fondag,* if it is cheaper in your location than a proprietary castable refractory

of the same strength and heat resistance. Calcium aluminate cement costs three to five times as much as Portland cement and is much harder to find, but in appropriate applications it will not add as much in cost as it will add in longevity and convenience. A word of caution: even a little of this product in uncured or dust form may drastically accelerate the setting of Portland cement products, creating so-called flash setting. Don't mix them.*

FIRECLAY

Fireclay is a heat-resistant clay that is available in a dry powder form to use as an additive to mortars. It imparts little of the refractory qualities of firebrick to mortars made with non-refractory cements. Its chief benefit is the plasticity it gives to mortars, allowing them to be smoothly buttered into place. It reduces the tensile strength of conventional mortar significantly, but this is not much of a concern because mortars are not relied on for strength except in compression. Thick (mortar consistency) suspensions of fireclay with a little fine crushed firebrick or pottery grog (crushed ceramic) and a small amount of Portland cement (to thicken them) can be used to set brick used for dome and arch constructions that are exposed to high heat and compressive forces. Joint lines in that case should be narrow (approximately $^1/_8$ inch).

Naturally occurring fireclay is the basic ingredient in common firebricks; its resistance to heat and its dimensional stability come from its relative lack of minerals that would serve as flux for its further fusion. Its heat resistance increases with its alumina content.

REFRACTORY CEMENTS

There are many types of commercial refractory cements, mortars, and concrete, known by a confusing range of trade names but assigned to groups by their properties and uses. Dry-shipped castable refractories are the largest group, sold to be mixed with water, then poured, pumped, trowelled, or shot from a gun. Refractories may be either hydraulic or air-drying. With each type of installation a range of properties is available, such as density and insulation characteristics, increased resistance to thermal shock, abrasion, shrinkage, thermal expansion, etc. All of them have strict mixing requirements (not too much water, avoid overmixing) that must be followed to preserve their thermal cycling endurance.

In general, castable refractories do not shrink or expand markedly with air curing or shrink much after fire curing, although they do expand slightly while hot. Refractory mortars made with refractory cements and aggregates tend to reduce loosening of the bricks in oven walls and domes because of their good dimensional stability. Lightweight castables contain lightweight aggregate and have thermal conductivities that are one-fifth to one-half of conventional castables.

Buying refractory materials can be frustrating because salespeople usually don't know

Buying refractory materials can be frustrating because salespeople usually don't know much about the uses and technical specifications of the products, and the product names are often not helpful. Ask for the name of an engineering representative who can help you.

∼

much about the uses and technical specifications of the products, and the product names are often not helpful. Ask for the name of an engineering representative who can help you (in person or by phone) and get the manufacturer's catalogs and data sheets on the products you plan to use. Any castable which is exposed to thermal cycling should have an alumina content of 35 to 45 percent, and a porosity of 20 percent or more, to reduce cracking. Avoid using steel reinforcement in refractories exposed to high heat (oven hearths or inner domes). Put the steel in an outer cladding or slab that has smaller temperature cycles.

HEAT-RESISTANT MORTARS

These include factory-made clay-based mortars consisting of fireclay and fine sand, homemade clay mortars made of rehydrated dry clay mixed 3 to 5 parts fine sand to one part clay, and the same clay mortars with 3 to 8 percent Portland cement added to help the mortar stay "fat"—to resist slumping. Heat-resistant mortars also include two general types of refractory mortars, both with pulverized firebrick as aggregate. One type is based on calcium aluminate cement (convenient since it sets at room temperature and can bridge larger gaps) and the other is based on waterglass, or sodium silicate, which sets at temperatures of about 1,000 degrees F.

All heat-resistant mortars are applied in narrow joints—never over $1/4$ inch for calcium aluminate mortars and never over $1/8$ inch for fireclay or waterglass mortars.

FIREBRICK

Firebrick is the solid equivalent of castable refractories. It is available in full density or lightweight (insulating) makeup in several types and grades. For ovens, it is fine to use standard low-duty "fireclay firebrick," which costs $1.00 to $1.50 a brick. This is manufactured by adding fireclay to ground firebrick (grout), sand, alumina, and silicate rock and is good to about 2,700 degrees Fahrenheit (1,500 degrees Celsius), which is far above the temperatures you will ever achieve in your oven. Higher-percentage alumina firebricks are more resistant to heat and abrasion (good for pizza hearths), but they have a disadvantage in bread ovens: the higher-alumina brick is more conductive, and may transfer an excessive amount of heat to the bottom of the loaf. Also, high-duty firebricks are actually *less resistant to cycles of heating and cooling* such as those experienced by oven brickwork, and are *more* likely to crack, spall, and fail than standard firebrick: low-duty firebrick contains tiny voids into which the solid material of the brick can expand when it is heated. One modern design for a French hybrid-style bread oven specifies a firebrick hearth of 25 to 28 percent alumina. This is approximately the percentage in standard firebrick, with a conductivity about 75 percent that of medium-duty firebrick and 60 percent that of super-duty firebrick. In Finland, France, and other European countries, special materials are maufactured for oven hearths that are even less resistant to heat

*Standard firebrick corresponds to ASTM C 27 or C1261.

than standard firebrick, but more resistant to thermal shock. If they wear out mechanically, they are simply replaced. If you are experiencing premature mechanical wear in the hearth of a bread oven because of gas firing or excessive mopping, medium-duty brick is probably the most heat-resistant brick you should consider.*

RED BRICK

Brick or red brick is made by pulverizing clay or shale (which geologically is basically old and compressed clay), then compressing it into a block, drying it, and firing it until it is fused (vitrified) by the action of mineral fluxes present in the clay. The vitrification temperature is reached in six to eight hours. Faster heating might cause the green brick to explode. The temperature reached in firing in part determines the hardness and porosity of the brick. The density of the brick derives from its constituent materials and the force with which they are pressed together. Uniform, high-quality red brick is easily available for use in ovens. Some types of irregular bricks or used bricks may be more attractive for oven fronts or exterior oven walls where aesthetically appropriate. Brick is available in a variety of shapes, including a bull-nose brick that makes an attractive lip on the front end of the hearth of a masonry oven. The rounded end is also resistant to chipping.

Not all red bricks offer the same mechanical qualities, and not all have been fired to the same temperature. Some masons believe that high-fired bricks are better for exposure to heat because they are thoroughly vitrified and will not further change shape or size. Others are adamant that high-fired bricks are too brittle for use inside an oven, and recommend low-fired bricks for such locations on the grounds that they will be more resistant to thermal shock, though less strong.

Most of these opinions grew out of common and practical phenomena, related to the way bricks were originally fired and to the historical lack of specialized firebrick in colonial America. When bricks were fired in big open-air stacks or primitive kilns, some would be fired more than others. The higher-fired bricks were more resistant to water damage and weathering, and were used on the *outside* of a chimney for that purpose. The rest of the bricks were softer, and were used in the fireplace itself, where resistance to water was not important. If exposed to excessive heat, those bricks could revitrify to a higher temperature.

Gradually the rule that soft bricks were used in fireplaces developed, but according to Greg Borchelt, an engineering consultant for the Brick Institute of America, there is little or no functional advantage to using soft bricks there; any well-made brick will do. In ovens, relatively light (and therefore soft) red bricks were historically used for the hearth (and replaced frequently) to prevent burning the bottom of the bread—not because they were particularly resistant to heat.

American-made bricks are fired to 1,950 to 2,900 degrees Fahrenheit (1,050 to 1,600 degrees Celsius), but some lumberyards also carry common red brick from Mexico that are low-fired, contain a lot of quartz sand, and are quite porous. Because these bricks may not have been fired beyond the temperature at which quartz undergoes a change in structure, sand could pop out of these bricks at high temperature. Avoid these inferior bricks by buying domestic ones.

Finally, the maximum heat resistance for red bricks and common firebricks is about the same. Red bricks have a greater rate of expansion, however, and are more likely to spall or flake when unequally heated. This can occur when a hot fire is built and the surface of the brick is heated too quickly, or when a jet of water is sprayed on the bricks. If an oven is gently managed, there is little advantage for firebrick, except as I have mentioned.*

BLOCK

Concrete block is manufactured by using Portland cement to bind an aggregate of sand and fine gravel, which is forced into molds that produce the various shapes of block required. Some block is made in a shape that allows it to run along in a wall, but not to terminate a wall or turn a corner. There are, however, blocks for ending walls and turning corners. Most blocks have holes that run vertically through them, called cores. Blocks are available in a variety of sizes for walls of different thickness, or to act as spacers in a wall as necessary.

Blocks may be made out of lightweight aggregate to make them easier to lay and to provide some insulation value. Extra insulation can be obtained by filling the holes in the blocks with lightweight mineral products. A block wall is usually reinforced with steel bars embedded in mortar or concrete and placed vertically, horizontally, or both. Although blocks are usually mortared together, mortar does not provide much adhesion to the block, and unreinforced walls don't tolerate lateral forces well.

*Facing bricks used for oven enclosures outdoors should meet ASTM C 62, grade SW, or ASTM C 216.

BASALT

Basalt is a dense and hard volcanic rock, crushed and sold as traprock and manufactured traprock sand. It is good for heat resistant, high thermal mass concrete when mixed with calcium aluminate cements.

GRANITE

This is a strong, igneous rock containing 20 to 50 percent quartz, held with other crystalline minerals in a granular arrangement. It is moderately dense and moderately heat-stable.

OLIVINE

Olivine is a rock found with basalt, serpentines, and soapstone in areas of past volcanic activity. It is often used as an aggregate in refractories and high-temperature concrete because it has very little thermal expansion and good resistance to heat. It is very dense—sometimes over 3.5 times the density of water. Oven temperatures do not usually require such specialized aggregates, but olivine sand is used by some manufacturers of precast refractory oven components and it could be used to increase the mass of any masonry layer. Because it is used in foundry operations, it is widely available.

QUARTZ

The most common mineral on Earth, quartz is silicon dioxide, with a density of 2.65 times that of water. When heated to 1,600 degrees Fahrenheit (870 degrees Celsius) it undergoes a change in crystal structure, with a 15 percent change in volume. This temperature may well be reached at the inner surface of an oven, so quartz aggregates should be avoided for high-temperature use unless, as in high-fired brick, any quartz present has been previously heated. Quartz is a component of granites and is a water-carried deposit in many other rocks.

SERPENTINE

Less dense and softer than olivine, this is one of the minerals commonly used in Europe in past years for building or lining ovens and for making urns, vases, and ewers. Although it is closely related to asbestos, there is no particular health risk in non-fibrous serpentine.

SOAPSTONE

Soapstone is very dense and resistant to heat. It is often used for the hearths of pizza ovens, but it should be covered with firebrick in bread oven hearths, as it passes too much heat to the bottom of the bread. It can be carved into beautiful doorways and outer hearths.

STONE

Stone, as crushed rock is commonly called, is usually made by mechanically crushing hard rocks. The resulting stones are screened to size, and have sharp edges that interlock when used as aggregate. This makes concretes made from stone stronger than sack-mix concretes made from rounded gravel. Heat resistance depends on the type of rock used.

GRAVEL

Gravel is a natural product of generally rounded small stones that are sized according to the size of wire screen they will pass through. Gravel is a common aggregate for concrete, but tensile and shear strength is not as great for concrete made with gravel as it is for concrete made with crushed rock, because the stones do not interlock. Gravel usually represents a mixture of rock types, and the thermal resistance and expansion qualities of the rock cannot be predicted. For these reasons it is probably better to use a known type of stone or crushed rock in concrete that will be used in high-heat parts of ovens (such as a refractory concrete exposed to flame). Some gravels are quite homogenous and resistant to heat (like the famous gravel in Devon that was used as aggregate to temper the clay ovens made by the potters there).

EXPANDED CLAY AND SHALE

Expanded clay, slate, and shale are lightweight, insulating, heat-resistant aggregates made by rapidly heating clay and shale that contain carbon and sulfur (especially iron pyrite, or fool's gold). Gas is generated at such a speed that it expands the mineral as the material becomes glassy. This material is used in such huge quantities by makers of lightweight concrete block that they will usually give you as much as you can cart away in a small truck, or sell it to you cheaply. At 90 pounds per cubic foot, concrete made with this material can provide good levels of compressive strength (2,000 pounds per square inch, or psi) with a thermal conductivity that is less than half that of conventional concrete. It can be combined with other lightweight additives to further increase insulation values.

PERLITE

Perlite is a lightweight insulating aggregate made by heating volcanic glass quickly to 1,600 degrees Fahrenheit, where it pops as water vaporizes, forming tiny bubbles. It can weigh from two to twenty-five pounds per cubic foot (pcf) and is not affected by temperatures to 1,600 degrees Fahrenheit. Perlite concrete as light as twenty-four pounds pcf are extremely good insulators and retain compressive strengths of 200 psi, about that of extruded styrene insulation. A mix of 1:6 cement and perlite will give a 24 to 30-pound pcf concrete. Adding expanded shale to the mix will make a heavier and stronger insulating concrete, but be sure to avoid heavier aggregates and extensive power mixing, which can crush the perlite granules.

Perlite is not expensive. Because the little rounded balls of perlite run into cavities like water, most of it is used to insulate the cores of block walls. That makes it easy to get, but means that perlite sold in bags at masonry outlets is often coated with silicone, which reduces its adhesion in concrete. This isn't a problem when perlite concrete is used nonstructurally as insulation, but locate a source of the nonsiliconized material to use it in a load-bearing element.*

VERMICULITE

Vermiculite is a lightweight aggregate made by expanding mica. It forms into little worms and flakes that are similar to but much smaller than styrene packaging peanuts. The little worms are very light and soft and resistant to heat; they fill cavities almost as well as perlite. Vermiculite is less easily available, as some of it is contaminated with small percentages of asbestos. Use a mask when you pour *any* particulate masonry product.**

*Perlite should conform to ASTM C 549. It is also available in a rigid form, ASTM C 612.

**Vermiculite should conform to ASTM C 516.

Masonry Tools and Methods

It is not feasible or appropriate to describe all the techniques of masonry construction and formwork in this book. Good, basic books are available at the library or can be purchased at a masonry supply yard, lumberyard, or bookstore. Consult one of those texts as a supplement to this book. What you do need to know, however, is what tools you will need.

CEMENT MIXER

Although a mechanical mixer may be used to mix the mortar and concrete for an oven, the small quantities required may also be mixed by hand in a trough or wheelbarrow. The entire amount of concrete and mortar that goes into an oven is rather small, and its use is spread out over several days. Therefore, it is not too much to mix by hand.

SHOVEL

Cements and aggregates are usually measured by the shovelful, using a square or round shovel that can also be used to slice into a bag of cement or to clear away the topsoil for a foundation slab. You have to have a shovel, and it is best to have both types.

WHEELBARROW

This means a concrete type of wheelbarrow, with a metal or plastic pan that is balanced over the wheel when the handles are lifted. A wheelbarrow is good for mixing concrete and mortar by hand and for carrying concrete, sand, and other materials to where they are needed.

The tradition of wearing mortar-boards (with a tassel on top to signify a trail of mortar falling off the board) goes back to the graduation ceremonies of the middle ages, when masons were made masters of their trade.

TROWEL

It is convenient to have three trowels on an oven job: a triangular traditional bricklayer's trowel, a flat concrete finishing trowel, and a notched tilesetter's trowel, which is used to score the surface of the sand and clay layer on which the hearth bricks are set.

Along with your trowels a few pieces of plywood measuring 18 to 24 inches on each side will come in handy as mortarboards from which you can trowel up mortar as necessary. Apparently the tradition of *wearing* mortarboards (with a tassel on top to signify a trail of mortar falling off the board) goes back to the graduation ceremonies of the middle ages, when masons were made masters of their trade.

JOINTING TOOL

You don't need one of these for interior brickwork. Get a mason's or tilesetter's sponge instead. Tooling joints is a good idea for exterior brickwork, as the compressing and sliding action helps seal the mortar against water, and forces the mortar into a tighter bond with the brick. Jointing tools are available in several profiles, so be sure to choose one that makes a pattern you like.

SPONGE

Tilesetters finish off grout lines by sweeping them gently with a damp sponge after the grout has partially hardened. You can do the same thing with the mortar in interior brick-work joints. Just don't make the sponge too wet, which would make a mess of the joint and brick and also wash some of the cement and strength out of the mortar.

LEVEL

This job requires several types of levels. Test individual bricks for level (the eye can lie) with a plastic or metal torpedo level. The bigger the bubble, the better. Typically these levels are the length of a brick, so they can be placed on a brick while it is tapped level with the trowel handle or a wooden mallet. The foundation forms may be leveled with a water level, a builder's optical level, or even with a four-foot level taped onto the edge of a straight piece of 2 x 4 lumber; the slab is small enough that a small deviation from absolute level won't matter that much. A two-foot and a four-foot level will come in handy for leveling and plumbing the block walls as they are laid.

MASON'S CORD

Many people find it convenient to lay out square, level, and plumb lines to guide construction with brick and block. This is done with sturdy, colored string, stretched between stakes or between bricks set at each end of a course of bricks to be laid.

CHALK LINE

A chalk line is convenient for laying out the pattern of the wall bricks on the hearth bricks, before the walls are laid. This is not critical; a thick pencil and a straight edge may serve as well.

WOODEN MALLET

Use a wooden mallet to tap brick and block into place.

THREE-POUND HAMMER

Use a three-pound hammer with a brick set to cut bricks to size, and to make half-bricks for corners. A three-pound hammer works better and is safer than an ordinary carpenter's hammer for this job.

BRICK SET

A brick set is a big blunt chisel that is used to score or stress bricks until they break along the line. A brick should be placed on a piece of wood or a somewhat yielding surface (soil, sand) when it is hit. Flying chips are *common* and protective lenses are a must.

HACK SAW

You need a hack saw to cut reinforcing bar.

Basic Carpentry Tools

Carpentry tools are necessary on this masonry job to build forms for concrete, to make braces, and to build forms or centering for brickwork. A circular saw, some saw-horses, hammers, tool belts, squares, measuring tapes, wood chisels, and so forth are all needed.

Now that I've previewed the basic elements of a masonry oven and the tools and materials required to build one, it's time to start construction.

MATERIALS LIST FOR 32' x 36" OVEN

Exclusive of foundation slab, insulation, enclosure, and roof

Concrete

Hearth slab: Six 90-lb bags of sack mix or
equivalent concrete—see text

Oven cladding: Ten 90-lb bags of sack mix or
equivalent

Concrete block

For base 38" high at hearth: Fifty-three blocks
16" x 8" and two blocks 8" x 8"

Mortar

Portland mortar to lay this amount of block
and fifty bricks (four sacks mortar mix
approximately)

Portland fireclay mortar to lay one hundred
twenty-five bricks OR

Refractory mortar to lay one hundred twenty-
five bricks with $1/4$" joint lines

(Fireclay mortar willl require one sack Portland
cement, one sack fireclay, and three 100-lb
sacks of fine mortar sand)

Reinforcing mesh

Oven cladding: 6' x 7' approx. of 6" x 6"
10-gauge

Reinforcing bar

Hearth slab: 60' of $5/8$" bar (20' lengths
preferred)

Block walls: (optional) 120' of $1/2$" bar

Lumber

Hearth slab form: One sheet of $3/4$" CDX
plywood; four 8' lengths of 1" x 4"
softwood

Bricks

Hearth: Ninety-six standard-duty firebricks

Oven: One hundred twenty-five best-quality red
bricks (10% less if using firebricks, 10% more
if using modular-size bricks)

Outer arch and flue throat: Fifty best-quality red
bricks

Chimney: flue tile and red bricks to suit

Outer hearth: bullnose brick or stone slab to fit

Below outer hearth: Sixteen red brick splits or
pavers

Lintels

For block base: Two 2" x 2" x $3/16$" angle iron
64" long

Oven doorway: One 2" x 3" x $1/4$" angle iron
22" long

Foil

Below oven cladding: Two rolls heavy-duty
house-hold foil

CAFÉ BEAUJOLAIS

Mendocino, California

Three hours on winding roads up the scenic route from San Francisco, Chris Kump and Margaret Fox work day and night to turn out memorable meals at Café Beaujolais in the North Coast town of Mendocino. Chris grew up in a chef's family and didn't start to bake until he was in college, although he remembers visiting Lionel Poilane's basement oven in Paris as a boy, and always held the visual and gustatory memory of hearth-baked European bread up against the bread that was available to him on the North Coast.

At first Chris and Margaret tried to bake in the restaurant's ovens, but try as they might, it wasn't great bread. Chris learned about Alan Scott and began negotiations for an oven, but was inhibited by the cost not only of the oven, but of a building to put it in and the wages of the people who would bake in it. Then, in a farmer's market in a little village in southern France, Chris saw a plume of smoke coming out of a shabby trailer with a line of people outside it. In the trailer was a brick oven, and in the oven was a batch of the kind of real bread that Chris *had to have* at his place. He came home and said, "If he can cook bread like that in a trailer, I'm going to build the oven!" Chris got back in touch with Alan and they decided to build the biggest oven Alan had done up to that time (4 x 6-foot interior) and to do it as a student workshop to offset some of the cost and increase the excitement. They named the new bakery the Brickery.

The Café already had a walk-in cooler in an adjacent shed so the Brickery construction was a renovation and addition on that shed, creating both the bakery and a prep room for the Café. The face of the oven is on the short west wall of the bakery room, with the mass of the oven outside. The south wall of the bakery has windows looking over the organic garden of the Café, down toward the Little River cove. The room is oblong and open, to allow free use of the peel, ash rake, and hearth mop. There is a skylight to reduce glare and the room is full of natural light, with a concrete floor, a homemade proofing cabinet, one sink, and two Formica-covered counters. The proofing baskets are stored in a set of shelves over the counter and the sink, the *baguette* pans on another shelf near the proofing box.

The Brickery runs on a twenty-four-hour cycle, six days a week; most of the bread is naturally leavened. Until 1996, the *levain* was made in the

CAFÉ BEAUJOLAIS

Chris Kump and Margaret Fox, Mendicino, California.

morning—doughs containing 30 to 35 percent of this *levain* were made up at night by the restaurant staff, well after the bakers had gone home, and this dough had most of its primary fermentation in the walk-in cooler. Dough mixing by the cooks led to some variability in the doughs and was a strain on the restaurant staff, distracting them from their primary duties. Because there are three or more naturally leavened doughs prepared each day and because they use an *autolyse* to achieve a well-hydrated dough, this evening work took up to two hours. In 1996, they changed to a dough process similar to that described by Nancy Silverton, and they changed the timing of their retarding step from primary fermentation to proofing.

Now doughs are mixed in the early morning by the bakers, after the first bake of loaves is in the oven. Only the leavens are mixed in the evening, and this chore is relatively brief. By 11 A.M., the doughs have had their primary fermentation, rounding, and shaping; after one hour at room temperature, all of the proofing baskets are put in the cooler, to be taken out and baked the next morning. Aside from the naturally fermented breads, the most popular bread at the restaurant is a yeasted Austrian Sunflower Bread that contains ten kinds of seeds or grains; these require soaking to soften and are mixed together and wetted in the evening so the dough may be made up, fermented, and baked the next day.

For a number of years, the Café Beaujolais oven was fired with fireplace logs first thing in the morning, after the wood had dried overnight in the cooling oven. This delayed baking for several hours, the heat on the hearth was uneven when baking began, and the wood sometimes overdried. An overnight firing program was developed in 1996, in which the oven is loaded (still with fireplace-sized wood) at the end of the baking day, but not lit. That wood is dry (but not excessively) by the time the evening staff comes in to mix the leavens. They light the oven; when they leave it is burning brightly, allowing them to place a draft door over the oven doorway, with room at the top for smoke to exit, but with control of incoming air (with adjustable air intakes on the door). This gives a burn of about six hours, allowing more bakes the next day without as much use of a supplemental gas burner between bakes. The oven has a portable gas jet that can be fired in the oven for fifteen to twenty minutes to raise the temperature by 25 degrees Fahrenheit (14 degrees Celsius) if there is a pause in the baking and there are several loads still to go. The overnight burn also allows baking to start as soon as the oven is cleaned out and rested for half an hour, baking the retarded loaves shaped the day before.

Although the hearth heat is now even, there is a tendency for the hearth to be a little overheated relative to the dome. Since the first bread baked each day is a load of *baguettes*, this extra hearth heat has not been a big problem: they are baked in perforated stainless steel pans that hold them up off the hearth a little. By the end of the morning there is plenty of bread, not just for the restaurant, but for wholesale clients (stores) and for retail customers who buy bread from the restaurant secretary.

What are the things that really work about this operation? First of all, Chris and Margaret could not have had a first class restaurant without first-class bread, and now they have it. Secondly, the restaurant has to have a secretary, and it is not too much of an interruption for the secretary to sell some bread in the middle of the day—but it would be too much of an interruption for the baker to sell it all. Also, the restaurant is staffed at night, and the baker

Loaves on a peel may be sprayed with water, then dusted with seeds before they are baked.

can be home when the leaven is mixed for the next day. All of the staff get to have some control over their work hours, even though bread is available by mid-morning.

What are the things that don't work so well? Well, the Brickery is only about a break-even proposition. The market in Mendocino is small and the labor is hired, so a typical one hundred and fifty loaf day may not break even. This is made up on the weekends and in the summer, but only barely. It would also have been nice to create a seasonal morning and lunch place centered around the oven, a service room for coffee and bistro food, but the construction cost was just too high. A trial some years ago of oven-baked pizza for lunch just wasn't profitable without the ambiance and seating to go with it.

Overall, though, everyone at Café Beaujolais is pleased with the Brickery. They love the bread they sell and eat, they don't lose money, they are fascinated by the process, and everyone gets some sleep at some time of the day or night.

172

CHAPTER NINE

OVEN CONSTRUCTION

This chapter is either the meat of the book—if you have been dying to build an oven—or the gravy, if you just have a passing interest in ovens, or if you are going to have someone else build one for you. In any case, these instructions are for a 32 x 36-inch oven, and they are a close description of the way Alan Scott builds an oven of that size. I only describe construction of one size of oven because it is the size most people want, and it is not feasible to give complete plans for ovens of other sizes and keep everything clear. You will have to buy plans from Ovencrafters if you want to make a larger or smaller oven. In general, though, the principles of construction remain the same.

For the sake of consistency I assume you are using hard red common brick for the walls and roof of the oven, which typically measure $2^1/_2$ x $3^3/_4$ x 8 inches, and common firebricks for the hearth, which measure $2^1/_2$ x $4^1/_2$ x 9 inches or $2^1/_4$ x $4^1/_2$ x 9 inches.

I assume that you have decided to use a slab for your foundation, and that you have already bought the materials on the list for a 32 x 36-inch oven.

Starting Out

You must mock-up the outline of the inner and outer oven walls before you start construction. A mock-up is a full-sized model or outline used to help locate and visualize construction. By taking the time to create a mock-up, you will be able to see if the oven's dimensions will meet your needs and expectations before you begin to build; you will also be able to develop a feel and sense for the project before you begin using mortar.

First you will mock-up the oven, then the hearth, then the hearth slab, then the block walls of the base. You will then be able to build the foundation, which will be in proportion to the other measurements. The foundation slab is going to extend 6 inches out in each direction beyond any finish layer/material that you use to cover the oven (e.g., a brick facing).

THE MOCK-UP

You will need a smooth surface that is *not* directly over the site where you will build the oven. Lay down a couple of sheets of plywood, or use the floor of your garage, patio, etc. Draw or use a chalk line to snap out the outline of the block walls, 72 x 64 inches outside, 56 x 48 inches inside: this equals 4½ blocks long by 4 blocks wide. Now draw or snap a line 1 inch inside the block wall layout: this is the outside perimeter of the hearth slab. At the front of the oven, draw another line 3 inches inside the block wall: this is the back of the ash slot. Again at the front of the oven, draw a line 6 inches inside the block wall: this is the outer face of the doorway of the oven—the jambs of the oven doorway. Draw a line that runs 2½ inches inside the hearth slab outline, along the sides and back, to mark the inside of the concrete cladding. The outside of the cladding will be flush with the outside of the slab.

Next, lay out the bricks of the oven wall, standing on end, starting with the bricks that form the sides of the doorway—the door jamb bricks. These two bricks are usually placed 3 inches back from the ash drop to create the ledge that the oven door sits on. They are separated by the width of the doorway, 16 inches. Space the wall bricks ¼-inch apart from each other, angling back from these two jamb bricks at 45 degrees, until the wall proper turns and runs just inside and along the line 2½ inches in from the edge of the hearth slab. At the right-angle junction of the side wall and the rear wall, one brick is placed at a 45-degree angle to make it easy to scrape the oven clean of ashes. Turning a flat carpenter's pencil on its edge is an easy way to get the ¼-inch spacing for the wall bricks.

Now stand back and consider your model. Does the floor plan of this oven meet your baking needs? Does the door opening accommodate your favorite pans and have enough width for pizzas? The plans call for a doorway that is 10 inches high. If you choose to raise the door, you will have to raise the dome height proportionately (the door height is 63 percent of the dome height). Now imagine the outside of the oven, by adding some space for insulation (at least 4 inches all around) to the line marking the outside of the cladding, and then adding the thickness of your enclosure. How does *that* look?

Consider whether the final thickness of the oven wall you have drawn (bricks, with concrete cladding, insulation, enclosure) will still fit within the restrictions of the site you have chosen. Modify the dimensions accordingly, but follow the rules that have been

By taking the time to create a mock-up, you will be able to see if the oven's dimensions will meet your needs and expectations before you begin to build; you will also be able to develop a feel and sense for the project before you begin using mortar.

reviewed previously in chapter 7, on oven principles.

Mock up the hearth by laying one row of firebricks on edge, end for end, along the side of the oven wall mock-up, and another row, also on edge, side by side across it, in front or in back of the wall brick mock-up. Tighten the spacing, because there will be no mortar between these hearth bricks. This hearth mock-up will determine the exact dimensions of the hearth, and the total number of hearth bricks you will need. This is done to the nearest whole brick, in the sense that these bricks do not need to cover the hearth slab to the very edge, but must at least fully underlay and support the bricks of the oven walls and some of the cladding. The overall width of the ash slot will be approximately 2 inches wider than the doorway, to the nearest whole brick. That way, all of the ashes will fall when they are raked out past the door jamb bricks. Refer to the plans as needed.

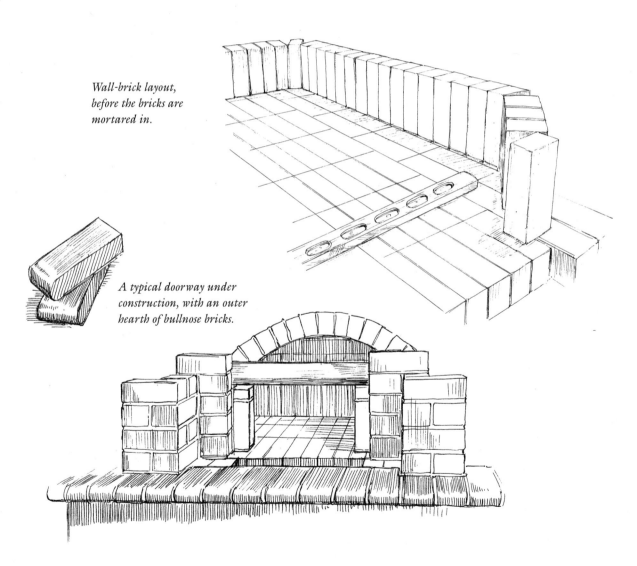

Wall-brick layout, before the bricks are mortared in.

A typical doorway under construction, with an outer hearth of bullnose bricks.

**Oven
Plans**

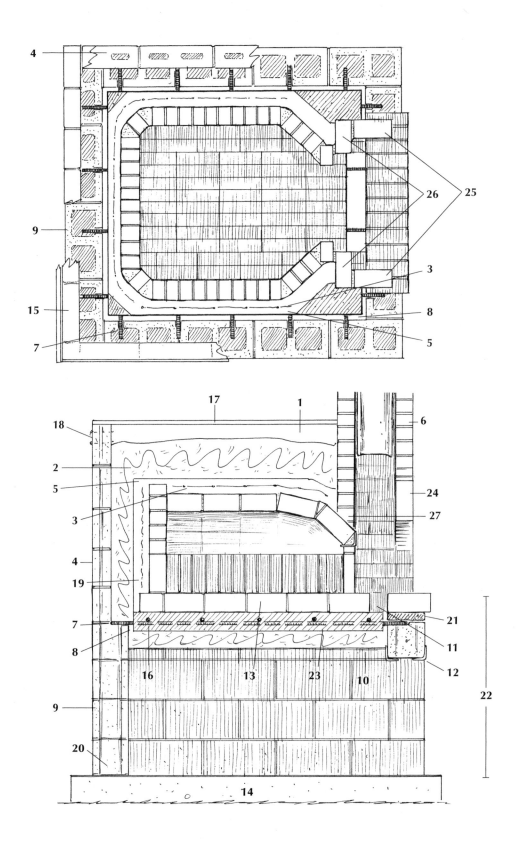

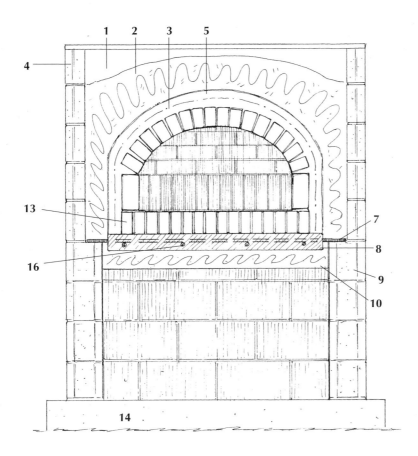

LEGEND

1. Air space
2. Loose vermiculite insulation
3. 6 x 6 x 10 x 10 mesh
4. 4" block or brick
5. Concrete cladding
6. 8" x 8" flue or 8" metal pipe
7. $^5/_8$" rebar seated in block
8. $^3/_4$" thermal break
9. 8" block
10. Vermiculite/cement mix (6:1)
11. Ash slot
12. Angle iron
13. Fire brick hearth
14. Foundation slab

15. Metal stud wall and "wonder board" etc.
16. Brick ties
17. Non-combustable weather proof cover
18. Vent
19. 1" chicken wire
20. Concrete fill
21. Pavers
22. Your comfortable working height
23. Hearth slab
24. Face arch
25. Brick A
26. Brick B
27. Brick C

The firebrick hearth will run beside the ash slot to the edge of the slab, on each side of the doorway. In other words, the side hearth firebricks will run 3 inches past the firebricks of the center, since the center courses end at the ash slot and the bricks that run beside it create its sides. You may draw or mock up the front hearth (in front of the ash slot) if you want to decide what kind of brick or stone to use there. Firebrick are not necessary for the front hearth, and many builders use bullnose red bricks, which come $11\frac{1}{2}$ inches or 9 inches in length. The back edge of the front brick is plumb with the inside of the front block wall, which is 8 inches thick. You may want to custom cut a piece of flat stone for the outer hearth. Mock up and study the relationship of bricks A and B (see plan) to the front of the oven, the front hearth, the chimney, and the facade. This will help you conceptualize the hearth and decide.

Foundation

A $5\frac{1}{2}$-inch slab can be formed with 2 x 6 lumber. When made of a good concrete adequately reinforced and insulated, this is all the foundation the oven needs. You will have to get the slab approved by the Code Officer, who may want a thicker one. Because the slab is small, thickening the perimeter of the slab is not necessary if the perimeter is steel-reinforced. (See illustration showing insulated and uninsulated slabs in chapter 7).

In cold climates, begin by digging out a trench that is level, $7\frac{1}{2}$ inches down from finished grade, and about 60 inches wider and 60 inches longer overall than the outside dimensions of the block walls you have laid out.

The foundation slab must extend 6 inches out from the outside of the oven walls, and in cold climates there should be a 2-inch-thick flat layer of foam insulation under the entire slab and skirting it by approximately 24 more inches, to prevent frost formation at the edge of or under the slab. For the 32 x 36-inch oven, the total excavation will be 124 x 132 inches, and $7\frac{1}{2}$ inches deep. Level the earth in the trench and pack it back down firmly by tamping. A hand tamper can be made by screwing a piece of 2 x 6 about 8 inches long flat across the end of a piece of 2 x 2 or 2 x 3 about 48 inches long. (An alternative to the foam and the large trench is a thick rubble footing of well-drained crushed stone, covered with plastic.)

When the tamped earth sounds solid, place a layer of 2-inch extruded polystyrene insulation flat in the trench, extending 30 inches out from each edge of the eventual block wall outline. Then make a rectangular box (the form for the slab) out of 2 x 6 lumber on edge and 12 inches wider and longer (inside dimension) than the outside of the block walls. Brace across all four corners to keep the form square and to reinforce the sides. These braces will be removed once the form has been partially filled with concrete. For a nice detail, place a rim of diagonally cut 2 x 2 lumber around the inside of the top of the form, to chamfer the lip of the slab (or use an edging trowel later before the concrete sets).

Center the form over the foam laid in the center of the excavation. You may now sift and shovel dirt back over the foam that is *outside* the box, tamp that down, and walk on it. Keep the box sides straight and square while tamping.

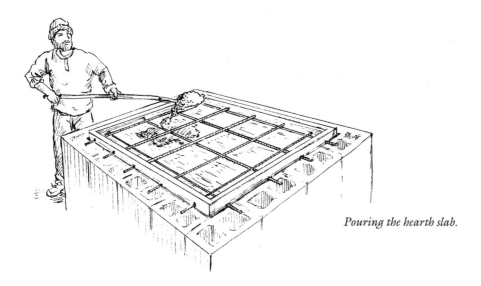

Pouring the hearth slab.

The slab for warm climates is the same, but the polystyrene foam may be omitted, the area excavated can be smaller (because the foam skirt is missing), and the excavation should be lined with 6-mil or thicker black polyethylene sheet in the trench, before the slab form is placed. This will keep water from wicking up the oven structure, which is a function the insulation serves for insulated slabs.

Place two runs of ½-inch steel rebar around the slab perimeter, located about 3 inches and 8 inches in from the form. The rebar should be supported on small pieces of broken concrete block or brick that do not touch the form at any point. Keep the rebar off the ground about one-half the thickness of the slab you have planned, and lap it well around the corners. If bending it seems too difficult, buy pre-bent rebar corners, or have the supplier bend it.

Roll out 6 x 6-inch steel reinforcing mat and tie it securely with plastic or steel wire ties to the outer perimeter rebar, supporting

it as necessary in the middle of the span on broken brick. Overlap it generously, sheet to sheet, so there are no empty areas. Re-level the form if necessary.

Next, mix and pour the concrete for the slab, letting the tamped earth outside the form hold the form in place. Use any conventional Portland-based sack mix, or mix your own, or order it from a transit mix company. Use a piece of lumber as a screed, sawing it back and forth while pushing the wet concrete along the form to level the slab completely. It helps to lean the screed back a little, away from the direction of its major movement. That way, the surface of the wet concrete is levelled, smoothed, and compressed, all at the same time. If you want the slab to be smooth, keep watching it, and float and trowel it when it is workable.

If you are concerned about earthquakes that might eventually shift the oven, use a chalk line to snap the outline of the concrete block walls on the fresh concrete. You can see where the first row of cells, or cores, are

Screeding the hearth slab.

Ash Pit/Wood Storage Walls

This is a routine block-laying job. A review of your masonry manual will help you prepare for the task. Determine the height of these walls, based on the additional thickness of the following:

1. one-half the hearth slab, or about 1¾ inch
2. the thickness of your firebrick, on edge, combined with
3. your ideal working height and
4. available block dimensions.

Remember that block comes in many sizes: you can adjust the wall height in 2- or 4-inch increments using different block. Most people use four courses of 8-inch block. The outside of the block walls will usually be about 6 inches in from the perimeter of the slab, more if you plan a masonry veneer that starts at the slab.

Try to stay square, plumb, and level as you build the walls. Remember as you lay the block courses that two pieces of angle iron are going to bridge the front of the ash pit, to hold the block lintel below the front of the oven.

Note that little pockets need to be chipped in the inner sides of the front and back blocks of the top course to hold the lengthwise rebar for the hearth slab. Note also that the concentrated load of the rebar that extends onto all the block walls would have a tendency to crumple them. This is prevented by filling all of the cores in the last course with mortar or concrete. Ideally the blocks in this last course will be not only filled, but also bonded together with

going to be while the slab is soft enough to set some short hooks of rebar vertically several inches deep in the slab, so they project above the slab in spots where the cells/cores in your block will be. Install two for each of the side walls and two for the back wall.

The best practice is to leave this slab covered with a piece of plastic for a week to cure before you start laying block. Often this isn't practical, because of time pressure. In that case, just make sure the slab stays damp for a week, even as you lay the block walls and go on to build the oven. You may pull the form box off when the slab is good and hard, and then use some of your excavated dirt to backfill smoothly up to the edge of the slab, forming a slight rise of an inch or two (for drainage) over the surrounding area. You may start laying block when the slab is hard enough to support it.

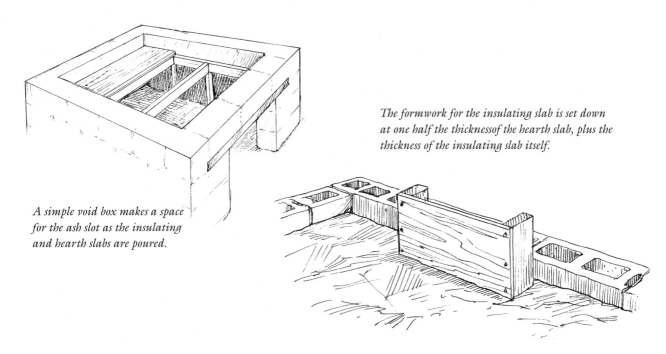

A simple void box makes a space for the ash slot as the insulating and hearth slabs are poured.

The formwork for the insulating slab is set down at one half the thickness of the hearth slab, plus the thickness of the insulating slab itself.

two runs of ¹/₂-inch rebar, all four corners included. This creates a "bond beam" that will make the whole foundation of the oven stronger and also makes it easier to pick the oven up with a forklift and move it, should that ever be necessary. Most masonry suppliers sell special block for this application, with knock-out cell partitions so you can place the rebar. You only need enough of them for one course.

To avoid filling the cores all the way down to the slab, jam the lower cores with tightly crumpled paper (concrete sacks are fine), or place some stiff metal screen or metal plaster lath over the open cores of the next-to-last course of blocks, sealing them off.

It is a good practice to fill the corner cores down to the slab, and to sink some rebar dowels down in the concrete poured in those holes. If the outer finish and roof of the oven is to be framed with metal studs, you may fas-

ten the metal sills for this part of the structure to bolts placed into the wet concrete that fills the cores in the last set of blocks. (Or wait until later and use "Tapcon" screws for that job—hardened fasteners that are screwed into cured concrete after it is drilled with a special bit.)

Hearth Slab and Hearth Insulation

The hearth slab is normally made as an open-faced sandwich with a layer of insulating concrete (vermiculite and Portland cement, 6:1) poured on a plywood form, then covered with a slab of concrete poured directly on it. If you use alumina cement, use igneous crushed rock for aggregate. The hearth slab is going to be approximately 3¹/₂ inches thick for a home oven (it would be more for a larger oven, or for an oven used every day), and the insulating concrete underneath will be at least 2 inches thick. An ash slot is formed by pouring the concrete in layers around a hollow "void box."

Although these layers should be poured one after the other on the same day to help them bond, 4-inch common nails should be placed at a 45-degree angle (one foot on center) to extend up out of the vermiculite concrete to help the separate layers stay firmly attached. Although the vermiculite concrete will run all the way from one block wall to the next, with no air gap, it is soft enough and weak enough that it will not crack the walls when the oven is heated.

Cut the $^3/_4$-inch plywood so it is about 1 inch in width and length less than the inner dimensions of the block walls, to make it easy to place and remove. As you locate the height of the plywood form, consider that the bottoms of the side-to-side reinforcing bars in the hearth slab are at the center of the thickness of the slab; this is also at the level of the top of the block wall on which it rests. The concrete is $3^1/_2$ inches thick. The bottom of the concrete will thus be $1^3/_4$ inches below the top of the block, and the bottom of the vermiculite below the slab will be 2 inches or more (depending on how thick you want it) below that. Measure down $1^3/_4$ inches (plus the thickness of your vermiculite layer) from the top of the block wall. Snap lines around the cavity and set the top of the plywood at that level, reinforced strongly (so it won't distort with the weight of the concrete) from below with 2 x 4 lumber. Put in a void box that will maintain a 3-inch-wide space in the vermiculite layer where the ash slot will be.

Pour the 6:1 vermiculite and cement layer up to a line that you have drawn or snapped to mark the bottom of the upper layer of the concrete slab, and put in the bonding nails. Now arrange the $^5/_8$-inch rebar in a grid so that no two parallel bars are more than one foot apart, and none are closer than 3 inches to an edge of the slab. The slab is reinforced with $^5/_8$-inch rebar because it is stiff enough to cantilever out over the block and hold up the slab. Each bar must extend 4 inches onto the block wall. The lengthwise bars need $^5/_8$-inch recesses chipped or cut into the block, best done before the cores are filled (see note above). Wire-tie this grid together. Avoid over-reinforcing the slab, as this may paradoxically lead to cracking in an area exposed to thermal stress.

Only when the grid is laid out will you locate and drill the rebar holes in the 1 x 4 perimeter form for the hearth slab. See the plans. A standard 1 x 4 is $^3/_4$-inch thick, but it is going to be spaced in from the block wall by $^1/_4$-inch wedges or strips of wood during the pour. When these are pulled out, the 1 x 4 lumber will pull free. To make the 1 x 4s removable, cut their lower edges with a hand saw or saber saw, twice for each hole you have drilled, to make a slot for the rebar. The

Form and steel reinforcement, in place for the hearth slab pour. There are small spaces in the end blocks for the longitudinal rebar.

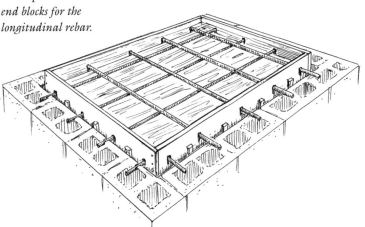

THE BREAD BUILDERS

concrete that will fill these holes may be easily knocked out after the forms are pulled.

Now set the form boards in place over the grid, with the outside of the form boards wedged in place, 1/4 inch from the block wall. The form must be level and secure, as it is the level to which your slab will be screeded. Fasten the corners together with sheetrock screws. Maintain the 3-inch space in the front of the slab that is the void for your ash slot—the rebar grid is going to run right through it. Since the 1 x 4 and wedge takes up 1 inch, the ash slot void box will be 2 inches thick, front to back, for the hearth slab.

Remember that the concrete for the upper layer of the hearth slab may be Portland concrete or alumina concrete, depending on the intensity of oven use. Use a 3:2:1 concrete mix (stone, sand, cement), and screed it off by seesawing along the top of the form. The slab must be level but it does not have to be perfectly smooth.

Lay a row of **pavers** flat across the width of the front wall to make up the height of the slab above the top of the wall. Use regular mortar. Cover the slab and leave it to cure overnight.

The Hearth

To start, measure the centerline of the slab and mark that line all the way out on the block walls, so it will still be seen when the slab is covered. Then choose the best (unblemished) firebricks you have, and set them aside for use in the center of the oven.

Mix up a thick, spreadable paste of water, 1 part fine mortar sand, and 1 part fireclay, and trowel it onto the slab 1/4-inch thick, using a 1/4-inch notched tilesetter's trowel to finish it off and make it completely even. Snap a line down the center of this layer of sand and clay, and begin to lay hearth bricks, with this line as a guide. The first brick laid (at the edge of the ash slot) must be very carefully plumbed and leveled, as all others are leveled from it; each brick must be gently slid into place against the preceding brick so they meet the clay/sand bed absolutely square on—not at any angle at all. Each is then tapped into place with a soft mallet. No mortar is used between the hearth bricks so that no mortar sand gets in the bread and the bricks are replaceable if that is ever necessary.

MOVING *the* OVEN

If you suspect that you may have to move the oven in the future, leave enough room so you can get a rented forklift in to pick it up. You will take the hearth slab and oven. Moving to a new location, in a different state? I have a masonry oven mounted on a trailer (the whole thing weighs nearly 4,000 pounds) that I can take from place to place! It is made of refractory concrete.

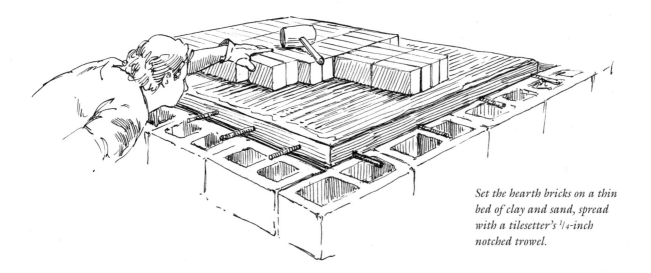

Set the hearth bricks on a thin bed of clay and sand, spread with a tilesetter's ¹/₄-inch notched trowel.

Start placing hearth bricks at the edge of the ash dump and run them all the way to the rear, then fill out the rest of the hearth. Do not place the bricks that go in *front* of the ash slot. These will be set in place with mortar.

If you want a surface thermocouple in a hearth brick, drill a ¹/₄-inch hole for the tip into the bottom of a center brick and a corresponding hole down into the slab beneath. The tip of the probe should be ³/₄ to 1 inch from the hearth's upper surface and the wire must be long enough to reach a meter mounted on the front of the oven. The thermocouple is mounted in place using furnace repair cement, squeezed from a tube in a caulking gun. Finish the floor as you laid it out, and check that it is smooth, tapping with the mallet.

Now lay the hearth in front of the ash slot. This may be firebrick, red brick, or stone, and should be mortared down to the pavers that you put in earlier. The upper surface of this outer hearth should be level with the inner hearth.

Oven Brickwork

The oven bricks are held together with narrower (thinner) joints than regular structural brickwork. Portland-based mortar modified with a little added fireclay to make it sticky holds up well in home use. (The traditional proportions are 10 parts mortar sand, 3 parts cement, and 1¹/₂ parts fireclay. This modification gives the hardened mortar an expansion rate that is similar to that of the brick, as well as making it sticky.) You can also use a proprietary refractory mortar from a refractory supplier, and in most jurisdictions this is required by code, as it has greater heat resistance. When firebricks are laid in modified Portland mortar, they should be briefly dunked in water (not soaked) before they are laid, to help keep the mortar workable and sticky. If you use refractory mortar, follow the directions on the container about wetting the bricks.

Before you mix mortar, be certain that the wall bricks are where you want them, especially the *doorjamb* bricks, which must be exactly opposite each other and backed off from the front of the ash slot by 3 inches. Mock the walls up again on top of the hearth, then mark the hearth at the inner edge of each brick with a thick line from a carpenter's pencil. Then remove the bricks, and mortar them in place, buttering each brick carefully on one side and the bottom before it is placed, starting with the two doorjambs. Set all the wall bricks in position on the hearth, with the 1/4-inch spacing preserved at the inner edge of the bricks, and 1/4 inch of mortar under the bricks, as well. Each brick may require tapping with the mallet. Finish with the middle of the back row. The last brick will have to be buttered on both sides, placing a wedge of mortar on the brick that is thicker at the top. The adjacent bricks should be lightly buttered with a wedge of mortar that is thicker at the bottom, so the mortar wedges join as the last brick is dropped in. Go around the ring and fill any gaps you see in the mortar, and cut the mortar off flush.

Next, mortar in place the bricks that make up the chimney base and the entrance to the oven. These will stack up beyond the top of the doorjamb bricks and will thus brace the angle iron lintel when it is laid across the doorway. Typically, four courses are enough. It is convenient to start with a brick laid crossways on each side (brick B), then a lengthwise one (brick A). As you go up, you will be leaving two sets of gaps: out

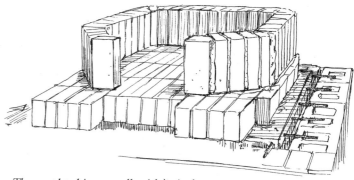

The completed inner wall, with 1/4-inch mortar joints.

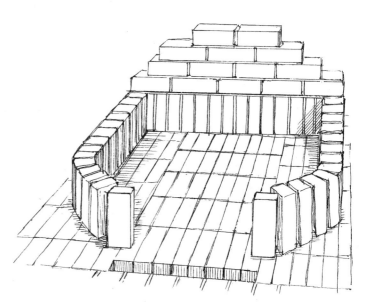

The back of the inner oven wall is built up with bricks set stretcher-style.

front and alongside the doorjamb. You will need to cut half-bricks with your brick set and hammer to fill in next to the doorjamb. Don't worry about the outer gaps; you will fill them in later as you tie into the facade. Set the inner edge of the crossways bricks (brick B) 2½ inches wider on each side than the edge of the jamb bricks. This step-back from the jamb makes it easier to manipulate oven tools into the front corners of the oven and creates a generous lip for the oven door to seal to. As you go up, sponge off excess mortar before it sets hard, and keep the faces of the bricks clean. Put a drop cloth or plastic sheet over the hearth to keep that clean as well.

The Dome

Mortar in place the bricks of the top of the rear wall—the bricks that rest on top of the vertical bricks you have already placed. These upper bricks are laid flat, with ¼-inch mortar joints, and their pattern has to be tall and wide enough to allow them to be mortared to the edge of the first arch of roof bricks as those are laid. The top of the rear wall will be four or sometimes five courses high.

Place the angle iron for the oven lintel on top of slices of brick mortared to the tops of the upright doorjamb bricks, to give the oven doorway its finished height of 10 inches (or whatever you have determined it to be, according to the plans you have made). See that the lintel and jambs line up on the same plane (viewed from above) so the door will seat and seal well.

Place the last of the outer entranceway bricks (A and B) up a full four courses, so that the angle iron lintel will be well braced as the final roof course is laid up to it.

You must make two plywood templates for laying the arch. These templates are going to be placed with their flat bottoms at the level of the top of the oven walls as the roof bricks are laid. Along the straight bottom edge of a sheet of ½-inch plywood, mark off a distance equal to the inside width of the oven walls. This will be the bottom edge of your template. Assuming that the wall bricks are 8 inches high, and that the oven doorway is 10 inches high, you will want an oven dome height of approximately 16 inches. You should measure up 8 inches from the midpoint of the length you have defined. If you are using 9-inch firebrick, the arch will curve only 7 inches.

Lightly sketch a pencil curve that goes

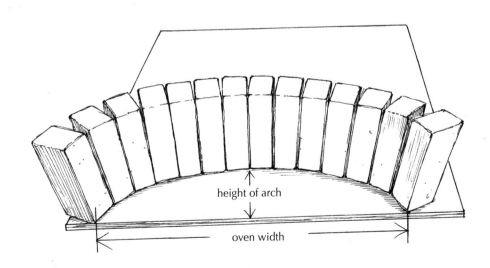

Laying out one of the templates for the oven arch, adjusting to use a unit number of bricks.

height of arch

oven width

THE BREAD BUILDERS

from each end of the baseline you have defined, and passes through the point you have fixed. Then stand up on edge the necessary number of bricks that will form that span, placing them along the rough line you have drawn, with each brick touching its neighbor on the inside of the arch, tilted to be evenly spaced on the outside. As you place the bricks, adjust the arch to fit a unit number of bricks, flattening it out a little in the center, (without making it look too shallow and weak) and bringing it down rather quickly at the ends where it will meet the wall. This will eliminate the need to saw any bricks.

Now, with a marker, trace the line of the bricks onto the plywood, following faithfully their every facet. This will allow the inner edges of the bricks to just touch and will prevent exposure of mortar to the intense flame of the fire, which tends to erode it.

Cut two identical templates like this with a saber saw. Nail them to opposite sides of a 2 x 4 that is long enough to reinforce the templates but short enough not to project above the edge of the curve. Position this new template assembly on two upright bricks at the rear of the oven, with an additional $1/4$-inch spacer at each end. The ends of the template should line up with the top of the wall bricks. Adjust it until it does.

The arch bricks exert a small outward thrust as they are laid, so it is wise to brace the wall bricks very firmly. Brace a board on edge a little way behind them and tuck some wedges in to hold the wall bricks in place as the roof is laid.

Lay the first arch in the back of the oven. Start by laying the left and right end bricks that rise off the walls. Since the outer portion of the mortar bed for these bricks is so thick, wedge some chips of brick into the joint to keep them in place. This will also stabilize the template. Continue to lay the remaining bricks, working toward the top. Be sure that each brick fits into its facet on the template, touches its neighbor, and is evenly tilted. The last brick will then fit just so with a little tapping with a wooden mallet. Don't force things or you will disturb the wall bricks.

The template may now be carefully removed (take out the $1/4$-inch spacers first, and clean off all the joints on the inside of the oven) and moved forward by the length of one brick, to support the next course. Repeat that sequence until you finish the third row, then leave the template in place. At some point in this process take a little excess mortar and fill in the ledges/pockets in the back corners of the oven, above the wall bricks.

Set the first row of arch bricks.

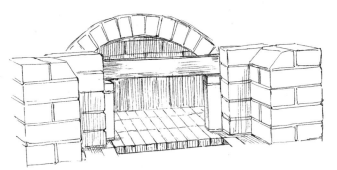

Starting the outer arch of bricks in the facade. The first brick on each side of this arch sits on a brick specially cut to accommodate it.

If you are planning to have a temperature probe in the inner dome, place it in the center of the first arch brick (the one next to the wall on either side) halfway forward in the oven, 1 inch deep to the inside of the dome. Other dome sensors might be placed at the junction of the brick and cladding and at the outside of the cladding, at the same general longitude and latitude of the oven. This array gives a profile of the heat distribution through the thickness of the masonry at any time.

Since the last two rows of bricks will funnel toward the doorway, you left the centering template temporarily in place under the third row of roof bricks. The next course to be laid is the most-forward course that is only as wide as the lintel, and which rests at an angle on the lintel (see the illustration below). The elevated back ends of these bricks may be set on two 2 x 4s (one flat, one on top of it, on edge) or on a single 2 x 6 (on edge) placed temporarily across the wall bricks where they start to taper in.

This forward row is set in a straight line across, with no arch built in, but the angle of tilt up and back is critical. It must allow for a transition to the final row of bricks to be laid, which will be shaped to bear against it and against the arched row that has already been placed. The transitions should be as smooth as possible (again, see the illustration at the bottom of the previous page).

A simple form holds up the front row of bricks as the next row is cut to fit and is mortared in place.

The final row placed is the next-to-last in position, and it is also only as wide as the lintel. It must bridge the remaining gap without being laid on a form, bridging brick by brick, with each one custom cut to best fit the shape of the cavity—a curved arch is mating with a straight lintel row, so the bricks get shorter and the angles change a little as you work sideways from the center. When this course is in position, the 2 x lumber underneath the lintel row and the arch template are removed and the final holes on the front sides of the oven are bricked in "fair as can be", and cleaned up inside with mortar. Any ledges on the inside must be mortared out, as were the ones in the back corners. Keep a drop cloth on the hearth and clean up as you go along with a damp sponge.

Lay at least the first few courses of the brick throat of the chimney before you pour the oven cladding. This will allow the chimney to serve as part of the form for the cladding. A new row of bricks needs to be laid across the lintel bricks, to join the columns of A and B bricks already in place. These new C bricks form the base of the rear of the chimney, and their lower back edges may need to be knocked off.*

Concrete Cladding

One thickness of brick will not hold enough heat for good baking, and a flattened arch of bricks without lateral support will fall down. A hundred years ago oven walls were massive and often secured with metal tie rods. That gets expensive to build and to heat up. You are going to put a layer of reinforced concrete over the oven to provide sufficient heat storage for efficient baking, and to provide the mechanical strength necessary to hold the arch. Make it $2^{1}/_{2}$ to 3 inches thick at the sides and 4 inches at the top if you will use the oven occasionally. Use 3 inches at the sides and $5^{1}/_{2}$ inches at the top if you will be baking every day, or if you want to bake more than three loads at a firing. (You need to make some provision for expansion of the arch as the oven is fired. This will be in the form of one layer of heavy-gauge household aluminum foil, laid across the brickwork before the concrete is poured. This will provide "slip" and "slack" for the brickwork, and will also reduce hot spots in the oven.)

Allow the green (fresh) brickwork to completely cure before proceeding. Ideally the bricks should be dry and somewhat warm before the concrete is poured, so they are in their expanded mode as it sets. Put a lamp or a small heater with a fan inside the oven, if the weather is cold, to help the mortar to set and the bricks to become dry and warm.

Place a plywood form $2^{1}/_{2}$ to 3 inches out from the oven by wedging it in place against the hearth slab and boxing the corners as necessary. It should be 24 inches high along the oven walls and run all the way around to the doorjamb bricks. It must be 36 inches high at the back, and the bricks at the rear of the chimney must be at least as high as the thickness of the dome cladding.

Lay three layers of the heavy duty household foil over the arches and rear wall of the oven and down the side and rear walls. Try to avoid tearing the foil in all future steps.

Form two layers of 6 x 6 x 10-gauge reinforcing mesh so they sit $1^{1}/_{2}$ to $2^{1}/_{2}$ inches off the arch and walls (depending on the thickness of the cladding you chose). Support it

*Since people treat the chimney and facade in many different ways, we have put some instructins and drawings on the Ovencrafter's Web site, www.nbn.com/ ~ovncraft.

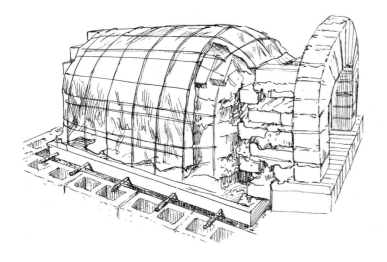

The completed oven brickwork is covered with aluminum foil and reinforcing mesh before the oven cladding is poured. The foil provides some "slip" between the two masonry layers.

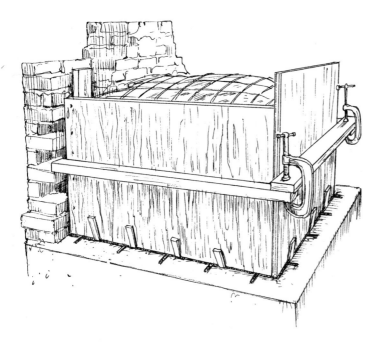

Place temporary formwork before pouring the concrete cladding.

on brick chips or temporary blocks that come out as you pour. *Do not* tie this reinforcing mesh into the slab or block wall. The oven must be free to move a little bit as it heats.

Although a full layer of mesh is not necessary across the back of the oven, one layer of hardware cloth or chicken wire in back of the oven, tied to the mesh over the walls and dome, is a good idea to make sure that the rear cladding never shifts.

Pour the concrete (Portland or Portland ready-mix, or alumina concrete for an oven in frequent use), tamping it carefully into the narrow space by the walls and hitting the form from time to time with a hammer to help the concrete settle. Keep the mesh in approximately the middle of the thickness of the cladding, and remove supporting blocks or chips as you go. Trowel the concrete in place over the dome, above the top of the form, and use a common nail protruding 2 to 3 inches from a block of wood to gauge the thickness of the cladding.

Chimney, Facade, and Finish

You will not box in and insulate the oven until it has cured for at least a week. Two weeks are better. You may use a series of *very small* fires to help dry the oven, or you may put a small electric heater with a fan in the oven, set on low all week.

In the meantime, you may complete the chimney and front facade, placing flue tiles and damper or metal flue and damper if those are called for in your personal plan. The illustrated sequences are your guides. One convenient type of top damper fits onto the upper end of a clay flue tile and also keeps rainwater out of the chimney when it is closed; it is operated with a metal cable that runs down inside the chimney throat—convenient for indoor ovens. Outdoor ovens may benefit from a metal chimney cap in wet regions, in addition to a spark arrestor.

The two most common treatments for the facade are the brick rowlock arch and the soldier arch (see illustrations), but others are possible. You will need to make a template to support the arch as you lay it. Typically the apex of the chimney arch is 13 to 16 inches above the level of the hearth. A flatter arch is better: making it too high may let smoke escape, and making it too low will restrict vision and access. The bricks that form the base of the arch interlock with the A bricks of the chimney base. The A bricks may need to be shaped to receive them.

You will insulate the oven after it has cured one or two weeks. Even if you are planning to use the oven only intermittently, you should insulate it to prevent bystanders from getting burned on its surface. I recommend an initial layer of diatomaceous earth (an inch or two), then vermiculite. If a crack develops in the oven these fine mineral sands will tend to fall in and seal the crack. They may be poured around the oven after a finish wall is built; the loose insulation may be covered with a trowelled vermiculite/cement mixture if you are going to cover the top of it with stucco, brick, or stone. (It is best to build a separate roof above the completed oven, though, for outside installations.)

There are many possible ways to enclose an oven. Most people erect metal studs on the block walls, attach noncombustible sheathing of some kind (metal or cement backer board, also known as Wonderboard or Durock) and then stucco. Others build complete

stone or brick enclosures. This is completely up to you. I recommend that all enclosures be well vented (at least two vents, screened to keep insects and mice out of the insulation) to allow moisture to escape and to release the heat that passes through the oven insulation.

Oven Door

Down through the centuries, oven doors were often made of an oak plank, carved

This framework of metal studs is for a tapering enclosure of fiber-cement board that will be covered in stucco. The metal chimney is angled back to clear existing framing.

with some rune or symbol on the outside. Oak chars, but doesn't burst into flames in this application if it is wet before being put in place. But oak is heavy, and most bakers now make an insulated door out of two $^3/_4$-inch plywood sheets, $1^1/_2$ inches taller than the oven opening and wide enough to lap onto the doorjamb bricks on each side. The inner piece of plywood is covered with a piece of sheet steel or aluminum, screwed in place. Then a layer of aluminum foil is stapled onto the other side of the panel before a spacer rim of $^3/_4$-inch stock or plywood strip is screwed on. Then another layer of aluminum foil is attached to the final plywood panel. You can use a stock replacement wooden trowel handle from a mason's supply catalogue for a handle, by screwing it in place on the outer panel, or you could make a similar one or cut a fork off a tree. Those who are going to do production baking (usually with a bigger oven) will want a door that will fold down into the oven in front of the peel, or at least a lightweight door that can be flipped back on the outer hearth. These will reduce the amount of time the oven is open, and will serve as a rest for the peel as it is moved in and out of the oven. Hinged, counterweighted doors are available from Ovencrafters.

Wow! This is going really well! You know how to build great dough and a great oven. But how do you *bake* that great dough in that oven? Read on!

DEPOT TOWN SOURDOUGH BAKERY

Ypsilanti, Michigan

To stretch out the capital, the oven was built as a hands-on oven-raising work-shop and purchased equipment was kept to a minimum

~

THE DEPOT TOWN BAKERY is the only bakery profiled here that was started with non-profit capital. In 1989, the Cooperative Whole Grain Education Association, aware that locally baked naturally fermented hearth breads were not available in their area, decided to loan money (from the successful publication of their book *Uprisings*) to Tom Kinney—a long-time baker at their headquarters bakery, Wildflour, in Ann Arbor, Michigan—to begin a whole grain, natural fermentation bakery based on the use of a wood-fired brick oven and a stone grain mill.

Tom found a space in an historic building in nearby Ypsilanti for $600 a month, and with $20,000 start-up capital from the C.W.G.E.A., plus several $100 pledges from prospective customers, he created a community sponsored non-profit bakery. To stretch out the capital, the oven was built as a hands-on oven-raising workshop and purchased equipment was kept to a minimum—primarily a 1939 Hobart mixer and a Meadows 8-inch stone mill. Tom began by making a whole wheat Desem and a sourdough whole rye bread exclusively.

He made the wheat bread from flour ground three days ahead of time. The Desem or leaven for the next day's bake was kept in the mixer overnight, set on a timer that mixed it for four minutes every hour for twelve hours. At 5 A.M. the leaven was used to make up the dough. First, Tom added water and mixed for three minutes, after which flour and salt were added and mixed for a further seven minutes, rested for five, and mixed again for seven minutes. The dough was then rested for twenty minutes and scaled to $1^3/_4$ pounds, shaped into rough rounds, rested again, and then shaped. Loaves were placed on a bed of meal on proofing peels, then placed in a heated proofer. Proofing peels are essentially boards that dough can sit on in the proofer but which also have brass fittings on their ends that allow a handle to be quickly fastened on. Then the boards become peels that can be directly loaded into the oven. To fill the oven to capacity, usually sixty $1^1/_2$-pound loaves, Tom used three sizes of proofing peels—large ones that held nine loaves to load the main body of the oven, and some smaller ones that held six, five, and three loaves to load the remaining front corners. After two hours in the proofer the bread was loaded and baked.

Tom baked three batches a day, on his own for the most part, bringing in casual help only on occasions to mix or to help shape, and did the

DEPOT TOWN SOURDOUGH BAKERY

deliveries himself in the afternoons before mixing the desem for the next day's batch. The bread was always packaged (strictly regulated in Michigan), without forced cooling, in plain paper bags, hand-stamped with the bakery's logo but with the bread unfortunately sealed inside out of sight. Avoiding the expensive cooling process and using paper bags kept the bread as fresh as possible. Less than a dozen customers made their way to the bakery itself each day. A co-op right next door retailed the bread; they were the first stop on the delivery route. Tom made a living for himself from this small production during the first years.

When competition from an increasing number of bakeries in the area drove sales below survival level, a new 33 percent lower rent was negotiated with the landlords who would otherwise have lost this appropriate enterprise in the "historic" district, and bread variety—one with raisins and walnuts and another with sesame seeds—was added to the two types Tom had been making.

The new breads kept the doors open until Tom decided to give baking a break and the bakery changed hands. The new operators, a three-person collective, found an effective way to keep folks reminded of the importance of good diet by staging bread demonstrations at their retail outlets, and this has kept the operation viable.

This bakery's history shows the viability of seed loans by non-profit organizations, and that education is an essential part of any commercial venture in whole foods—education that requires time, as well as free communication between the producer and the customer. It also shows that the time demands of a commercial bakery with a wood-fired oven, natural fermentation, and a rent bill are a lot for one person to take on.

CHAPTER TEN

OVEN MANAGEMENT

This book is about bread and ovens, and this chapter is where the dough meets the oven to become bread. First, though, the oven has to get "psyched up" for its big occasion. You have to get it fired up.

Firing the Oven

The goal of firing the oven is to end up with a clean oven that has a masonry dome temperature about 50 degrees Fahrenheit (10 degrees Celsius) hotter than the walls or the hearth. The temperature of the dome will be about 75 to 100 degrees Fahrenheit (24 to 38 degrees Celsius) hotter than the air temperature in the oven. The air temperature for most breads will be about 450 degrees Fahrenheit (235 degrees Celsius) and the temperature of the inner surface of the masonry will be 525 degrees Fahrenheit (275 degrees Celsius).

In general, logs or sticks less than 4 inches in diameter work better than larger logs for heating ovens. Their greater surface area means that more of the wood gets to burn at one time; there is also more surface area for radiation. After the fire is going, longer logs work better than short ones because they carry the fire into the back of the oven without reloading.

European bakers have often used fagots of small saplings or brush, which burn quickly and heat an oven quickly. French Canadians use full lengths of cedar (preferred because it gives such a bright fire) or other softwoods, and generally fire the oven twice, allowing two fires to burn from front to back, one after the other. An old United States Army Subsistence Corps oven manual from the 1880s mentions "bakers pine" as the best fuel.

You may burn crooked or forked pieces of wood that wouldn't fit in the fireplace or wood stove, old unpainted pallets (broken up), or sawmill slabs (cut to length). Buying

This book is about bread and ovens, and this chapter is where the dough meets the oven to become bread.

~

first-quality wood for a masonry oven doesn't make good economic, environmental, or functional sense. Since the oven takes on heat in part by radiation, a bright fire is better than a smoldering pile of thick logs,

Basic oven tools—a scraper, a poker, a brass-bristle brush, a scuffle of terry cloth toweling on the end of a handle. If you use a cotton mop, be sure to wring it well.

and hardwood is only needed when a fire is going to be maintained for some time, as in cooking pizzas.

Start by cleaning out ashes or coals from past firings, then set a small fire of crumpled paper and split softwood just inside the doorway. Add larger pieces as the wood catches, pushing the starter fire gradually about one-third of the way back into the oven. Do this before flame starts to shoot out of the oven door, to avoid overheating the facade of the oven (which could cause it to crack). You want to get a nice draft started up the chimney, but of smoke, not fire.

When the fire and chimney draft are going well, add the bulk of the wood, almost filling the chamber with full-length logs loosely crisscrossed for air flow and extending to the rear wall. If the oven is cold at the start, it takes two and one-half to four hours to heat the oven for one bake, depending on the intensity of your fire and the thickness of your masonry. If several bakes are planned, it is best to preheat the oven the day before, pushing heat into the outer masonry, or to fire the oven for six to seven hours using two burns, front to back, then close it for at least an hour to let it equilibrate.

If the wind at your place is gusty, leading to an unsteady draft, consider making a draft door, or stack some bricks in the oven mouth as a deflector. Put these in place after the oven has been loaded, adjusted so the fire has the air it needs for a clean burn. Research by the Masonry Heater Association shows that a fire needs about two and a half times as much oxygen as it will actually consume, to guarantee that it will burn cleanly.

The fire will burn at the front for an

hour or so, but when the bricks underneath are thoroughly hot the face of the fire will begin to burn as a wall, moving toward the rear and heating the oven as it moves. *Let it run its course all the way to the rear of the oven.* If you have made a draft control door it may be fitted during this part of the burn to reduce the air going into (and cooling) the oven, or the doorway may be partially blocked with stacked bricks to control the draft. Attempts to feed the fire with fresh wood will retard the process and eventually choke the oven, leaving unburned coals at the rear and an unevenly heated hearth.

If the oven needs more heat after the initial burn-out, add small pieces of wood anywhere in the oven chamber, or reload it completely. In either case, the wood will catch fire quickly. Large coals should be knocked apart at the end of the burn and spread out across the hearth for a few minutes, leaving them thin in the middle and thick toward the mouth of the oven. They will add significant heat as they burn to ash, and the center of the hearth is usually hot enough after the burn.

After the coals burn out, you should rake out the ashes, put the door in place, and let the oven rest for at least forty-five minutes (up to several hours for high-mass ovens). This will help even out hot spots. If the oven is much too hot after your burn and rake-out, you can leave it open to cool for a few minutes, then close it to let it equilibrate.*

Before you put your beautiful dough on that clean hearth, though, you need to know that the temperature of the hearth is right.

~

When the oven heat has equilibrated and you are ready to bake (meaning also that your *bread* is ready for baking!) you need to open the oven to clean the hearth a little more by sweeping and mopping before the bread goes in. I sweep my oven with a brass-bristle brush from a restaurant supply house, a brush made for sweeping pizza ovens. Then I mop with a homemade mop, a scuffle of terry cloth nailed to the end of a pole or fed through a metal ring linked to the end of a pole. Note that *mopping* does not mean *sloshing.* Perhaps a better word would be swabbing. You dip the mop in water, then wring it out before you use it. If you don't like wringing out all that dirty water by hand (it will soon be full of ash from your passes over the hearth) use a bucket with a mop wringer. The mop should be *damp*, not wet: just damp enough to clean any leftover ash from the hearth.

Before you put your beautiful dough on that clean hearth, though, you need to know that the temperature of the hearth is right. There are several ways to judge the heat of the oven, aside from thermocouple readings. The most common is to throw a handful of flour into the oven then watch the results. How long it takes to turn tan, brown, and black varies with the temperature of the hearth. For loaf bread the flour should be quite brown at 15 seconds. If it starts to burn right away, you either have to wait a while or mop the hearth again, lightly, a couple of times.

*In the 1850s, American commercial bakers fired their retained-heat ovens overnight, and always allowed two hours for the ovens to equilibrate after clean-out, with the door in place, before baking began.

Understanding Heat Management— Theoretical Considerations

Retained-heat ovens bake by transferring stored heat to dough. But how much heat should they store, and at what temperature? How much do they store? What is the best way to get the heat into the masonry, and what is the best way to get it back out? Physics can suggest some answers, but such estimates are ballpark guesses, best confirmed experimentally.

For instance, firebrick has a known ability to store heat per pound of brick, and each firebrick in the hearth has a known weight. Calculations can estimate how much heat is released from hearth firebrick if an oven cools from 550 degrees Fahrenheit to 400 degrees during a bake. Similar calculations can be done for the dome and the walls of the oven.

In reality, however, it's hard to predict how much of that stored heat will be lost in the form of hot air that escapes during cleaning of the hearth or loading, and how much will be made up with conduction of heat into the firebrick from the hearth slab. How much heat is lost as steam? Does heat loss through the outer wall of the oven contribute significantly to cooling? How soon can the heat stored in the cladding contribute to baking? How much of the heat used in baking is stored in the inner few inches of the masonry, as opposed to outer layers? Does the cladding ever get hot enough that it should be made of heat-tolerant materials? If you want to bake more loads per firing, is it better to buy more insulation, have thicker oven walls, or to wait longer between loads?

Understanding Oven Management— Practical Considerations

What are the differences between ovens managed for daily bakes and those used only once a week? How large a fire do you really need if you bake every day?

For any part of the masonry to effectively give heat to the bread, that part of the mass

---

BAKING PIZZA

To bake pizza instead of bread, push all the coals to the back of the oven when the burn is through, lightly mop or wire brush the hearth, toss a little kindling on the coals (reflected heat from a bright flame helps cook the top of the pizzas), and load the pizza. When the pizza is done, you may need to refire for a while, clean the oven again, and allow some heat equalizing time if you plan to bake loaf bread. If you bake loaves first, and then want to cook pizza, you should build a small fire when the loaves are out, and push it to the back when it is going well. (That is what I do when I have company coming—it is too nerve-wracking to try to bake fifteen loaves of bread in the aftermath of a pizza party. I have the guests come when the bread is already baked and the oven is ready for pizza.)

My oven has refractory concrete walls three inches thick. There is a full layer of firebrick in the hearth. Notice the ovenspring the hot hearth gives these loaves. The oven doorway on this oven is a little large; I would make it smaller now (photo: Dina Dubois).

must be hotter than the baking temperature (say 500 degrees Fahrenheit, 260 degrees Celsius) when baking begins. If the inner masonry is not above that temperature when the bread is put in, the bread will cook at a less-than-ideal temperature. Similarly, if the outer masonry is at less than baking temperature, it will continue to steal heat from the inner masonry, reducing the amount available to the bread. This may not matter when you're only baking one load of loaves, but it will prevent effective baking of multiple loads.

Baking multiple loads depends on the baker's ability to raise the entire thickness of the oven masonry to a temperature greater than the baking temperature. The heat stored in the outer masonry can then be recovered during baking: it is conducted to the inner masonry and transferred to the bread.

The amount of heat that can enter the masonry mass during a firing depends on the difference between the fire's heat output and the temperature of the oven mass itself (the greater the difference, the more rapid the flow), multiplied by the surface area of the mass exposed to the fire, multiplied by the time the mass is exposed to the heat. Heat transfer can be increased by increasing the intensity of the fire, the surface area of the mass, or the duration of firing. There is a practical ceiling on the maximum or safe intensity of a wood fire, and, of course, very rapid rises in surface temperature tend to cause bricks to spall.

The surface area is fixed: therefore, the easiest way to increase heat flow into the mass is to prolong the firing time. This is especially so since the heat flow from the inner surface of the oven to the outer masonry mass is also dependent on time. If the only alternative means of increasing heat storage is attempted (a hotter fire), the inner masonry will become too hot for baking, while the outer mass will not heat up enough for effective heat storage.

The airflow that supplies oxygen to a fire also cools the fire and the oven. The proportions of the oven and door are designed to make a fire easy to light and to maintain, by providing plenty of airflow and turbulence. The combustion efficiency of a fire burning in free and turbulent air is very high, but the efficiency of the whole process depends on the heat transfer efficiency—the heat that gets absorbed by the oven.

Transfer efficiency is reduced when an excess of cool air is fanning the fire. Therefore, it may be necessary to control airflow once the fire is well established, to maintain it for a longer time without wasting heat up the flue. There must be enough air for efficient combustion, but not more.

The purpose of firing the oven is to heat the masonry mass. An oven that is to be used every day (for one load or many) will work best if it is raised to baking temperature and maintained there, assuming it is well insulated. Once stored, the heat should not be wasted.

The common practice of drying wood in today's hot oven for tomorrow's fire does not make sense in this light: the moisture that is boiled off is removed at the cost of a great deal of stored heat, and that loss will make it difficult to fully saturate the thickness of the oven with heat when the oven is fired the next day. Eliminating this practice will reduce thermal cycling in the oven mass appreciably and contribute to the durability of the masonry. It is also more efficient to air-dry the wood, assuming that the wood

gets at least dry enough for a bright, steady fire. Each day's fire will then need to be only big enough and hot enough to get the mass up to the plateau temperature. An exception is an intermittently used oven: then, drying wood is a way of recapturing some of the heat in the oven. Drying must still be done safely and the wood not coked excessively, to avoid generating an explosive gas.

An evenly heated oven will bake better; it will not have hot spots, nor will it have excessive heating of the inner masonry, compared to the outer masonry. As an alternative to a longer firing, an oven may be fired briskly, well in advance of baking, then closed up for some hours. This will allow oven heat to even out, from hearth to dome and from front to back, and to diffuse into the deep mass where it will be available to the inner mass during baking. This kind of a schedule will allow you to use an intense fire for a short time (if that is more convenient for you, or just more satisfying) rather than a prolonged fire. You will rely on the seal of the oven door and the adequacy of the insulation to hold the heat when the hot fire is out. Some ovens that are used every day are fired only in the evening, and others get a small fire in the evening and a larger one the next morning. Bakeries that rely on semiskilled help have often found that the results of oven firing are more consistent with a longer, less intense firing.

An oven that is used intermittently *should* be heated in such a way that excessive heat is not stored in the deep mass. At the end of baking the remaining stored heat should be used for some purpose after baking is done, as it will otherwise be wasted. Cooking beans or casseroles, drying vegetables or fruit, or drying wood with the oven door at least partially open (to prevent coking the wood) are typical uses. The cladding for ovens that are used only intermittently should not be as thick as the cladding for ovens used on a daily basis.

Measuring Oven Temperature

There are two basic schools of thought about measuring oven temperature: those who do, and those who don't. Those who *don't* generally don't because they have turned away from the mechanical products of the industrial age, and want to rely on the heat felt on a bare arm thrust in the oven, the color of a handful of flour tossed out on the oven floor, or the burning off of oven soot. That's fine.

Those who *do* are in for a bit of a financial shock: reliably measuring the temperature in or on the walls of the oven is best done with expensive equipment: hard-wired thermocouples or infrared optical pyrometers.

Thermocouples are installed in the oven walls, with wire leads connected through a

A pyrometer reads the temperature of the oven's brickwork.

switch to an electronic device that reads in degrees. The probes themselves can be purchased prefabricated and sheathed in stainless braid or can be welded, brazed, or silver soldered up out of special wires made from dissimilar metals. There are several types of thermocouples; type "K" is the one to use in an oven. Gauges made to read the thermocouple outputs are sold by suppliers of scientific and industrial instruments and are AC-powered, run by a 9-volt battery, or powered by the thermocouple output itself. A panel-mounted setup with a switch to choose between several probes might cost $200 total. Since the manufacturers of this type of equipment are typically not interested in dealing with individuals, you may find it best to buy what you need through Ovencrafters or the scientific stockroom of your local college or university.

Optical pyrometers will tell you instantly the temperature of any surface, without touching it. You can read the wall at the back of the oven, the oven dome, etc. Until recently, infrared pyrometers were too expensive for bakery use, but recently the Snap-On tool company began to offer one (made by Raytek) for about $200 that is very easy to use. Just point and shoot, and a digital readout holds the reading for you. The only drawback is that the maximum temperature it will record is 880 degrees Fahrenheit (470 degrees Celsius). You can't read the temperature of the fire itself, but you can scan the inside of an oven to see if the heat is even and you can see how much heat (surface temperature) you lose with each batch of bread. You can combine the surface value you read with deeper readings from thermocouples to see how much of the oven wall is at or above baking temperature, and that will tell you how many batches you can bake before reheating.

Conducting Your Own Research

It is possible to track heat flows in thermocouple-equipped ovens. Probes can be placed at several locations in the oven, and at several depths from just below the inner surface to the outside of the cladding. A more basic installation has a sensor in the cladding (to read deep heat storage) and an infrared pyrometer or a subsurface thermocouple to look at the inside of the oven. The outer and inner readings will allow you to determine how deeply your oven is heated.

Alan Scott did this for the first time in 1987, with construction of an oven with six thermocouples buried in it. He was primarily interested in the distribution of heat between the various parts of the oven—the dome, the hearth, the wall, the front, the back. He also wondered what happened to the oven air temperature, and he placed a probe into the oven to record that. He was only baking one day a week, and did not study a more regular or prolonged firing

OVEN TEMPERATURE PROFILES

In the spring of 1996, Ed and Kathleen Weber of the Della Fattoria bakery placed additional probes through the thickness of their small commercial oven, which is used seven days a week. Before this experiment they (like many others) had been in the habit of drying some of their wood in the oven each day, then firing for a fairly short, hot period shortly before baking. They were having trouble keeping the oven heat up for four bakes a day without refiring, even though they had introduced the use of an infrared pyrometer to get an accurate check on the interior surface temperature of the oven. The results of their research are graphed on the following pages.

The Webers began their research recordings with their new deep probes two weeks *after* they had changed to a slow-firing schedule. They had already noted better bread color and more predictable inner surface temperatures before recording was begun.

Initial studies of the temperature profiles across the oven wall showed that at the end of firing and rake-out they had temperatures at the *outer* cladding of over 700 degrees Fahrenheit (370 degrees Celsius), with inner surface temperatures of over 675 (355). Further cleaning of the oven reduced the inner surface temperature to the baking range (just over 500 degrees Fahrenheit (or 260 degrees Celsius) but left them with a great deal of heat stored in the deep masonry. After five full bakes they still had over 500 degrees Fahrenheit (260 degrees Celsius) in their cladding, and in fact had that same temperature one inch deep in the brick. The surface temperature schedule. Graphs of the data he obtained indicate that the surface of the hearth becomes hot very quickly, that the surface of the junction of the wall and the dome (halfway back in the oven) is slower to get hot but eventually becomes hotter than the hearth, and that the interface of the firebricks and the cladding is slow to become heated.

When an oven is fired for only three hours, the outer levels of the masonry are gradually getting hotter even when the bread is baking because the entire mass is not yet saturated with heat. With one firing, the outer masonry reaches a maximum temperature of about 400 degrees Fahrenheit (205 degrees Celsius), well within the capacity of Portland cement. When an oven is briefly fired for a second day, the outer masonry starts at a temperature of about 225 degrees Fahrenheit (107 degrees Celsius) and reaches a temperature somewhat above that seen the first day, but still not hot enough to provide any heat to the inner masonry during baking.

Ed and Kathleen Weber of the Della Fattoria bakery also investigated their oven temperature profile. The Webers were having difficulty keeping up their oven heat for four

had fallen to about 400 degrees Fahrenheit (205 degrees Celsius), but this recovered to nearly 500 (260) after the oven had been briefly allowed to rest, closed.

Over the next few months the Webers experimented with more intense and extended firings; because the infrared pyrometer will only read to 880 degrees Fahrenheit (470 degrees Celsius), they used a thermocouple probe that was flush with the inner surface of the oven. They pushed surface temperatures to 1,050 to 1,100 degrees Fahrenheit (560 to 590 degrees Celsius), firing air-dried cordwood with restricted draft from approximately 9:30 P.M. to 2:45 A.M. They then spread the coals out to continue firing for two more hours with even more restricted draft. (They restrict draft by placing a careful pattern of stacked bricks in front of the oven doorway.) At 5 A.M., the coals are brought forward to heat the very front of the hearth, and at 6 A.M. the oven is raked out and left open until the surface heat drops to 670 degrees Fahrenheit (355 degrees Celsius), at which time (8:00 A.M.) they can bake a load of mini-baguettes (seven inches long) in baguette pans held up off of the oven floor by wire racks. When these are done, the surface temperature is low enough for regular baguettes, then foccacia, then loaf breads. The Webers have found that if their masonry temperature is at least 700 degrees Fahrenheit (370 degrees Celsius) three inches deep in the masonry of the dome, they can bake from 8:00 A.M. to 4:00 P.M. without refiring, and there will be enough heat in the masonry to repeat the same firing and baking cycle the next day.

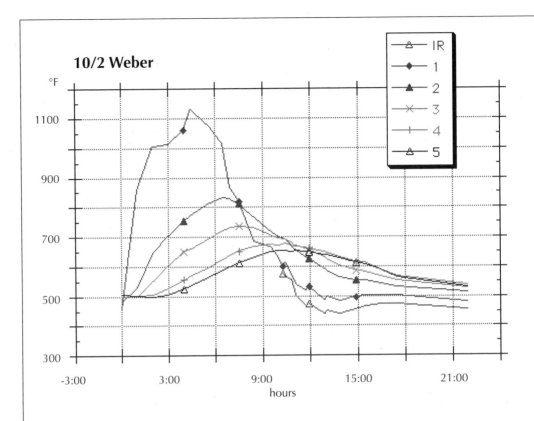

10/2 Weber

A 24-hour cycle in a commercial wood-fired retained-heat oven. The curve "IR" was obtained with an infrared pyrometer. Curve 1 is with a thermocouple probe flush with the inner surface of the brick. For curve 2 the probe is in the middle of the brick, curve 3 is at the junction of the brick and cladding, curve 4 is in the middle of the cladding, and curve 5 is at the outer edge of the cladding, inside the insulation (curve 5 begins at around 10:00 hours, as the heat reaches the probe).

A fire was started at 0:00 hours and was partially damped with a draft door when well established. Coals were spread out at 4:30, raked forward at 6:30, and removed at 7:00. The oven was closed from 7:30 until it was cleaned at 9:00. Focaccia and "mini-baguettes" were loaded at 10:00, out at 10:15, baguettes in at 10:25, out at 10:50. Three full loads of loaf breads were baked, the last out at 13:50, at which time the inner surface of the oven was 483°F. It rose to 500°F by 15:30, and fell to 480°F by 24:00.

Note that the inner surface of the brick went from 450°F to over 1100°F in 4½ hours, but that it takes the cladding 10 hours to reach its maximum temperature, just as the oven is loaded. That heat is therefore available to work its way back through the mass, stabilizing the temperature of the inner surface when it would otherwise fall steeply. When the baking and firing schedule permits, this oven is fired a few hours earlier, reducing the need to leave it open for a period before baking begins. Given the final temperature of about 500°F, additional loads could also have been successfully baked without refiring.

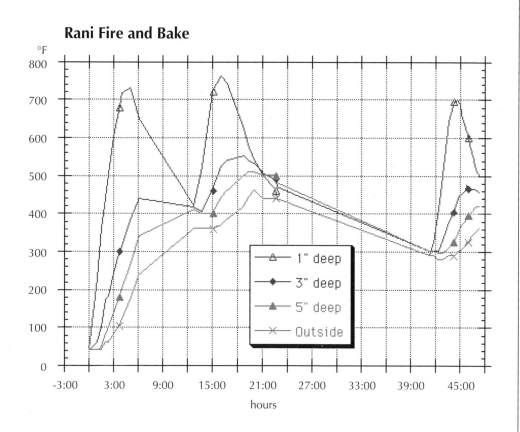

Rani Fire and Bake

Legend:
- 1" deep
- 3" deep
- 5" deep
- Outside

A 48-hour cycle in a 32 x 36-inch oven (without hearth insulation), fired from "cold" and used to bake bread on two successive days. The first curve is from a thermocouple ³/₄" deep in the dome; the next curves are from the middle of the brick layer, the middle of the cladding, and the outside of the cladding, inside the insulation.

A preheat fire was started at 0:00 hours; at 4:00 the door was placed. Another fire was started at about 12:30 and burned until 15:30. Three loads of bread (12-14 loaves a load) were baked from 18:30 to 22:00. It was refired at 41:00 and 3 loads of loaves were baked by 47:30. (The oven was a little too hot but the first loaves were fully proofed and could not wait.)

Note that from 19:00 to 22:00 hours the falling temperature of the inner masonry is being stabilzed as heat is recovered from the deeper masonry. Also note that even two firings 12 hours apart are not enough to bring the entire mass of this oven to a temperature above that required of the baking bread; the mass is never fully heated. The smaller size of the oven (greater surface to mass and/or volume ratio) and lack of hearth insulation probably account for its more rapid loss of heat, compared with the Weber oven, even accounting for the difference in the time constant of the graphs.

bakes a day, so they did some research with temperature probes. They found that switching from a short, hot firing to a longer, more gradual firing enabled them to store enough heat in the oven to make a second daily firing unnecessary.

Part of the management of an oven fired each day is to plan batches/loads so they are spaced out slightly more as the day gets late, to give the inner masonry time to recover (reheat) to baking temperature before the next batch is loaded. This can be done over and over again as long as the outer mass is still hot enough to give up heat. The Webers now know how long the oven rest periods should be, based on the inner surface temperature and the temperature of the deep mass. When data from this study was supplied to other bakers in the summer of 1996, several changed their firing and baking schedules and had results that confirmed the Weber's experience, even without added thermocouples. For example, the Pleasanton Desem Bakery was able to add two bakes a day, without refiring, when they stopped drying wood in the oven and began to space out their last bakes of the day. The firing and baking schedule was also changed at Café Beaujolais.

OVEN EFFICIENCY

Shirey and Selker explored the efficiency of several types of ovens used in developing countries using the concept of a "baking timeline" to look at fuel use. A retained-heat oven has to be more or less completely heated before baking can begin, and this fuel—the fuel used for *preheat* and the first series of bakes—can be differentiated from fuel used later to *reheat* the oven. In a theoretical example they pose, the preheat and first-bake efficiency of the oven might be 15 kilograms (kg) of flour baked per 11 kg of wood (or 1.4 kg/kg), while for reheat (for subsequent bakes) the efficiency might be 30 kg/2 kg (or 15 kg/kg) in the same oven. Retained-heat ovens are thus always going to be more fuel efficient in daily use.

The theoretical maximum baking efficiency Shirey and Selker cite is 26 kg of flour/kg of wood (or equivalent amount of other fuel), but of course this cannot ever be reached in any type of oven. One comparison of two bakeries in Somalia showed an unimproved and uninsulated retained-heat oven had an overall efficiency of 0.33 kg/kg, while an externally fired steam tube oven next door came out at 6.25 kg/kg, nearly 20 times more efficient. The most efficient retained-heat oven they found in the developing world, in Somalia, had an efficiency of 1.1 kg/kg.

Gas Burners

Brick ovens do their cooking with retained heat, regardless of the source of the heat. Most internal combustion ovens are fired with wood, but some were built for and are used with gas (see the visits to the San Juan and HomeFires bakeries, pp. 153–156), and others are reheated, as necessary, with gas if the stored heat is not sufficient for the quantity of bread to be baked in a day. Heat stored from a wood fire in a well-built oven will generally suffice for seven bakes if well managed, although the last bakes may need to be partial loads, loads of breads that bake best in a cooler oven, or bakes that are delayed for ten to thirty minutes to allow the internal heat of the oven to be replenished from the deep masonry mass before they are loaded.

Gas burners can be a heat supplement, even in an oven that is primarily heated with wood. The safest and most convenient type is the atmospheric pressure burner, which requires no compressed air or blower for complete ignition, and which may be safely turned down to reduce heat output when necessary. One of the leading manufacturers of this type of burner is the Charles A. Hones Co., on Long Island (516-842-8886). Their burners are supplied with gas at safe pressures (less than $\frac{1}{4}$ psi) and the gas flow sucks most of the necessary combustion air into a Venturi (a tube similar to the throat of a carburetor), where they mix. About 75 percent of the required combustion air comes in with the mixture; the remainder comes from the atmosphere of the oven. At least that much supplemental air must be supplied by leaving the oven door off, or placing a cut-down draft door that is used when the burner is in place and firing.

The major disadvantage of these burners is that the flame is rather concentrated and may produce local overheating (even brick damage) if the burner is left in one position too long. If the oven is fired for 15 minutes, it is advisable to move the burner several times to even the heat out, and to leave the oven closed for a few minutes after firing (15 minutes is a good place to start) to further equalize. A flame diffuser may *not* be used, because the draft of these low pressure burners would be affected, but arrays of more than one burner will produce more even heating.

To use gas as a supplement:

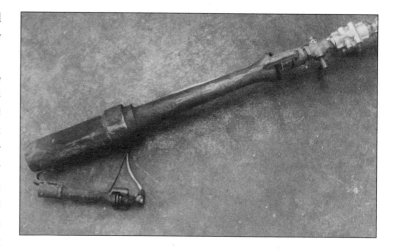

- Have the gas company terminate a metal gas line several feet from the mouth of the oven, and fit a flexible gas hose and a pilot light system that will shut the burner down if the flame goes out.
- Mount bipod or tripod legs to the burner to hold it off the floor of the oven when it is in use, or mount it on a little trolley that can be wheeled into place in front of the oven.
- Make a draft door to fit around the burner, to prevent excessive loss of heated air during firing. This door must be cut short enough to leave one square inch of exhaust area for each 6,500 BTUs of heat in the burner's rating. A typical restaurant or bakery oven (5 x 7 foot or 6 x 8 foot) will use a 100,000 BTU burner (Hones VNB 200) and will have about sixteen square inches of free space at the top of the door. Since one-quarter of the combustion air does not come through the Venturi, there must be an opening in the bottom or face of the door of about five square inches.

This is the gas burner that is used on busy baking days at Café Beaujolais.

This can be in the form of a slot that allows the door to fit over the Venturi.

- Don't let your oven cool down too much before you refire. It is better to refire a couple of times in the course of the day than to do a longer firing which will make the oven heat too uneven. Start with a fifteen-minute burn time and see what effect it has on your oven temperatures and your bakes; then go from there.

- Light the burner with a sparker (never a match), place the burner in the oven, and set a timer that will remind you to move it every few minutes. It is very handy to have high-temperature oven mitts for this job!

A final note about gas: It is certainly possible to build an oven that is heated with externally combusted gas. Such ovens use a Venturi burner to combust gas in a refractory combustion chamber below the hearth; combustion products then pass through tubes formed in the refractory slab and cladding. These tubes join above the oven in a manifold which is vented to the chimney stack, above the oven door. Obviously this is not a job for a weekend handyman. There is a real logic to externally fired gas ovens, since the heat is being generated where it will be available to the oven chamber by conduction, without overheating the inner masonry. Such an oven may be refired during the day, even as baking is underway, and the oven may still be heated with wood without alterations, if the local fire department will allow a dual-fuel installation.

By the way, masonry Roman-style ovens have also been successfully heated electrically.

If you live in an area where the off-peak rates are quite low, you may be able to heat your closed oven inexpensively in the night, using a timer or a thermostat. The utility will demand a monthly charge for a second meter to record the off-peak energy you buy, but the electricity may be cheap enough to justify it. In some areas of the country off-peak power comes from base power plants and hydros. It may be cleaner for the air than burning wood.

To fire an oven this way, you put an electrical element mounted on ceramic mounts (electric stove oven unit or a resistance coil from a ceramics supplier) into the oven, hooked to a flexible 220-volt cord. Take it out when the oven is hot. Get a qualified electrician or appliance repairman to help you with the hookup.

Managing Oven Steam

There are several factors to consider about the water/steam question. It is likely that *almost none* of the water from mopping the hearth stays in the oven. It is lost up the chimney as the bread is loaded. Therefore, the hearth should only be mopped with a damp mop, not a soaking wet mop, to remove loose ash, not to create steam.

Much oven humidity comes from baking with a full oven. Plan your bakes that way. That's the way successful large-scale bakeries such as Acme Baking manage their big rotating-stone ovens, and their crust is as well developed and colorful as anyone could want. The amount of water the Harbor Bakery in Gig Harbor, Washington, sprays for each batch in a big 6 x 8-foot oven is only three ounces. The rest comes from the bread.

A regular hose nozzle probably passes so much water, in such big droplets, that no significant portion of it vaporizes before it hits the brick, and it shocks the hot brick. Make a mist wand out of metal pipe with a three-nozzle metal greenhouse head at the end of it, and mount a valve at the base. (The Foggit company in San Francisco makes nozzles that are calibrated to deliver mist at specified rates. The 0.5-gallon-per-minute nozzle is the best for oven use.) Plaster the inside of the door with a wet towel, then give a fine spray with the wand from back to front and close the door quickly—that's all the steam you need if you bake with a full oven. In fact, if you like a crisp crust it will be important to remove the towel halfway through baking to allow some steam to escape. You can even bake for a minute with the door open at the end of the bake to crisp the crust further.

Steam injection systems requiring a boiler are too expensive, complicated, and troublesome (scaling and clogging) for the small bakery. Some brands of commercial deck ovens utilize cast iron plates onto which water is dropped or sprayed after the oven is loaded. This system is trouble-free and avoids any shock to the bricks, but requires a pipe into the oven and it requires heating up the iron. It has, however, been incorporated into masonry wood-fired ovens by those who like to use a lot of steam. Some European externally fired, internal-flame path ovens (*gueulard* ovens) have cast iron steam generator pans set into the brick on the sides of the oven, filled from outside when the oven has been closed.

Well, that is the last of the technically dense parts of the book. You can now make dough, build an oven, and bake bread. In the visits, you have met bakers, millers, consultants—all kinds of people who are excited about great bread.

While I was writing this book, though, I went to a place, The Bay Village Bakery, that embodies the kind of oven and bakery that most excites me. The young couple who run it, Chad Robertson and Elizabeth Prueitt, make wonderful bread *and* have a clarity about what they are doing that many people never get. I hope the next short chapter about day-to-day life at The Bay Village Bakery will pull together some of the lessons about baking and life that this book project brought me.

DELLA FATTORIA

Petaluma, California

Getting to know Kathleen and Ed Weber has been one of the most pleasant parts of working on this book. They operate Della Fattoria, a wood-oven bakery in Sonoma County, California, and they are wonderful people, relaxed and intense at the same time. Ready to work all night if need be, but to stop at noon for a wonderful meal of bread, fresh greens and tomatoes, great pasta, and a terrific bottle of wine. Their bakery is on a twelve-acre ranch that has been in Ed's family for years—Della Fattoria means "from the farm." Ed manages and maintains the rental units on the property in addition to doing the oven work. Kathleen does the mixing, dividing, shaping, and deliveries. Recently they have had the help of their son, Aaron, in all phases of the operation. Both Kathleen and Ed have elderly parents living on the ranch and working at home lets them provide support when it's needed.

All of the Weber's bread is sold to wholesale accounts, but at prices that exceed retail. There is practically no waste, which is good because they use only natural leavens and organic ingredients, which are more expensive. Also, they space their bread in the oven to avoid uneven loaf shape or color, and so make fewer loaves per bake. Their customers are high-end restaurants and shops in Sonoma and Napa counties which are willing to pay top dollar for a premium product that is baked to order and delivered in perfect condition. In 1996, for example, they were selling one-pound straight-flour round loaves for $2.00 and one-pound specialty breads (Garlic and Goat Cheese, Brandy/Currant) for $3.25; at the same time, retail prices at The Cheese Board, a gourmet foods store in Berkeley, were $1.50 a pound for straight-flour breads, $2.50 for Asiago, and $2.00 for Cheese Onion Dill.

Demand is constantly increasing at Della Fattoria. In the spring of 1996, they were baking sixty-five loaves on slow days, twice that many on Fridays and weekends. By the fall of 1996, those numbers had doubled, and by the spring of 1998, they were planning to have Ovencrafters build two additional ovens, to bring production to five hundred loaves a day. This would completely utilize their mixing, delivery, and human capacity, although they may add a cooler to permit retarding for more control over their schedule. The twenty-four-hour cycle of baking was grueling before they got regular help from Aaron. Kathleen is now going back to bed after two hours of work in the middle of the night, since Aaron comes in at 5 A.M. to continue the work. Although she is up later to help with shaping, she feels more rested and relaxed.

The breads are based on a natural starter that Kathleen began from organic grape skins. This is refreshed each day, left out for a few hours, and then fermented in a five-gallon bucket in a cooler until it is used the next morning. She measures all ingredients to the gram on a digital balance. Mixing is by *autolyse*—a few minutes to incorporate, twenty minutes or so of rest, then slow mixing in a medium-sized spiral mixer (massive motor, belt drive, no gears or grease) until the dough is turned into a big flat covered plastic fermentation bin. Fermentation is at room temperature, and doughs are turned over but not actively deflated at the three-quarter point in fermentation. All doughs are well-hydrated, with water content from 71 to 74 percent of the flour weight in most recipes. Doughs are quite soft when she shapes them on a 4 x 6-foot sheet of marble (her daughter found it torn out of an old building in San Francisco). She proofs her loaves in linen *couches* and in baskets placed in modified proof racks.

The 4 x 6-foot oven is on the deck of a screened and covered porch, directly outside the big double doors to the bakery. Ed uses five thermocouples and an infrared pyrometer with a liquid crystal readout to check on the distribution of heat in the oven. His oven does not have an ash slot ("too dusty") and he carefully removes ashes with a grain scoop and a big hoe. He doesn't believe in mopping the hearth; he props up the oven door on a brick in front of the oven, then blows residual ash out with a five-horsepower shop vacuum with an extended tube. This clears most of the ash, which vanishes up the chimney. Then he does the same thing with compressed air and cleans the dome with a fog of water from a greenhouse sprayer. He wants to be sure that no grain of coarse salt from yesterday's onion bread gets stuck to a walnut loaf baked today, and Kathleen doesn't want any of the bread to taste of ash.

Loaves are proofed in the bakery and the Webers use a thin beechwood transfer slat to roll the *batards* sideways onto a rectangular peel that holds four loaves. Kathleen slashes them while Ed holds the peel; he then swings the loaves through the double door and into the oven. He keeps them well separated, a maximum of 28 standard *batards* to a full 4 x 6-foot oven. The oven roof is water-fogged during and after loading, and a towel wrapped over

Ready to work all night if need be, but to stop at noon for a wonderful meal of bread, fresh greens and tomatoes, great pasta, and a terrific bottle of wine.

~

the inside of the door is soaked at the last second before the door is placed. Rather than leave the door out of the way during loading, Ed lets the door flop out like a pillow to support the peel, and he puts it back instantly after each peel of loaves is placed. He bakes seven to eight loads a day, without supplemental heat or refiring, and sets an electronic timer to remind him to check the loaves when they may need to be rearranged or pulled.

I have loved getting to know the Webers, but I am also concerned for them. Their setup teeters between being what I would call a small, conscious, and controllable family operation and a full-bore commercial effort that could engulf them. Their bread is so good that I see no end to the demand for it, but making a lot more of it may not allow them to maintain what I see as a wonderful balance in their lives. I guess if they seem to be getting too caught up in the business I will just have to show up at the right time of day and insist on a great lunch, and get Ed to get out one of his old guitars. That ought to slow things down!

RANI AND KEITH

Garberville, California

RANI MET ALAN through an old friend of Alan's who is a near neighbor of hers—although she lives miles back in the country, on top of a ridge, on a dirt road that winds slowly up from the highway. There is a loose community of souls up on the ridge, but there wasn't any really good bread until Rani built her home oven in the summer of 1996. She and her husband Keith had lived on the ridge for three years and she had been baking regularly every week or so for most of that time because the kind of bread they had eaten in the Bay area wasn't available in the nearby towns, even if someone went there to get it.

At first Rani was just kind of curious about the ovens—it wasn't something she had always had her heart set on, and she was busy enough, working as a nurse in a nearby clinic part-time, painting in her studio, working in the garden. But in the spring of 1996 she went to visit Alan, helped at a bake at his house, got his oven plans, and went back to bake again. She began to build her 32 x 36-inch oven in late May and early June, and finished it in late August. It helped a lot that Keith is a builder/boatbuilder, but it was still a lot of work, and it was more expensive than she thought it would be. Part of the effort was getting all the materials up onto the ridge, one load at a time. It was hard to find all the time needed to build the oven, given the demands of daily life.

Once it was done, Rani had to learn to fire the oven, to get the dough ready when the oven was, how to handle the peel, the hose, the door. At first she had a hard time judging the temperature of the oven—because she and Keith don't have grid electricity and she wanted to avoid the inconvenience of battery power for the pyrometer, she got a special-order unit (from Omega, a large supplier of temperature instruments) that is designed to run off of the microcurrent produced by the probe itself. It didn't work and had to be exchanged for a new unit, so while she was waiting for the replacement, she began to bake using empirical temperature tests: how long can you hold your arm in the oven, how many seconds does it take a handful of flour to turn brown and then black when tossed on the hearth?

Because this book was being written when the oven was being built, Alan gave Rani extra temperature probes to install through the thickness of the wall of her oven, so a chart could be made of the flow of heat through

RANI AND KEITH

the masonry. Once the new temperature meter and a rotary selector switch were installed, Rani found that making careful records of the temperatures allowed her to learn very quickly how to fire the oven for one, two, or three bakes of ten to fourteen loaves each, enough to feed everyone on the ridge. She and Keith had not finished insulating the oven when she began to bake (or when the graph in this book was made) and she was able to see from the records that she was losing an excessive amount of heat overnight, if she baked two or three days in a row. She also found that it took almost seven hours to saturate the mass of the oven with enough heat to make three bakes. Even if she had baked the day before, it took about four hours of firing to store that much heat—and then she actually had enough heat for an extra bake, or for some other form of cooking if she wished.

Technical points at Rani's:

- The heat kinetics of heating and baking in this 32 x 36-inch oven are really no different from those seen in the larger oven at Della Fattoria— that is what would be predicted from the geometry of the ovens, as covered in chapter 5.
- The oven is being fired with oak, but the wood is being split with a power splitter to the recommended size (about three inches), and firing is easy to manage.
- The bricks above the arch in the facade cracked when the oven was first fired, and the crack opens every time the oven is fired and closes again when the heat is gone. This is not something that has happened to many other ovens, although they all have only one thickness of brick in this area, which is exposed to intense local heat when the oven is fired, as exhaust from the oven emerges from the door and has to make a turn up the chimney. Only a small pile of wood should be lit at first, until the chimney draft is established. The fire should be pushed back part way into the oven before more wood is added.
- Rani has a kneading counter covered with a stainless steel sheet, bent down in front to lip over the edge of the counter—now *that* is easy to clean with a scraper!
- Rani built a counter that comes out from the right hand side of the front of the oven, like similar ones at Alan's and the Rabins'—this is very

handy for pans and cooked loaves, and the outer end of it is a handy place to rest the handle of the peel while she is slashing loaves.

- Rani has a greenhouse sprayer, but the gravity-feed water system doesn't make enough pressure to run it as it was designed—she may need to use a hand-pumped garden sprayer.
- The air up on the mountain is much drier than in the area near the sea where Alan usually bakes—when he went up to a bake there he had to take extra pains to keep his loaves moist as they proofed, since he proofs on boards, not in baskets. Baking remains an empirical craft!

CHAPTER ELEVEN

A DAY *in the* LIFE *at the*

BAY VILLAGE BAKERY

This book is full of "visits" because it is about two somewhat distinct topics: bread and ovens. I thought the visits would make it easier to see how they go together. Now let's bring bread and ovens together in one place in a chapter that is similar to a visit, but a little longer. This will give you a better feeling for the way the dough, the oven, the bread, and the life of the village baker are related.

I met Chad Robertson and Liz Prueitt at Alan Scott's, where they had gone to see if there was any way to turn their meager financial resources into a brick oven and a bakery. They had just returned to the United States from a year working at several small bakeries in southwestern France. Chad and Liz are young, intelligent, enthusiastic, considerate, knowledgeable, irreverent, and hardworking. If it weren't for the irreverent, they would just be too much to take. It's the irreverence that lets them keep their priorities straight, and gives them something

I can't put my finger on—something that falls between equanimity and composure. Meeting them is like meeting monks who have learned exactly who they are through years of meditation—except that Chad and Liz aren't monkish, and didn't take a vow of silence. Far from it: they love jazz, laughter, good food, and each other. But their focus, their ability to be constantly moving toward a considered goal, has brought them to a sustainable life that embodies much of what this book is about. They not only make great bread—they are developing a "right livelihood."

In the two years since I met them, Chad and Liz have gone from sleeping on a mattress on the floor of the den at Alan's house to running a successful small bakery. They are living in a charming house in an interesting town near a fascinating city, baking bread that has received rave reviews from some of the most knowledgeable people in Northern California. Though that market is probably the most competitive market for good bread in this country, they sell every loaf they bake, and sell much of it at a retail price without having a retail store or any employees. They have had laudatory write-ups in newspapers and magazines, and now bakers travel thousands of miles to meet them and see their bakery. They continue to make small changes in their operation—not to expand it, but to keep their business congruent with the way they want to live. The entire operation, including oven, bakery racks, proofers, mixer, structural and plumbing modifications—and even the van used to deliver the bread—cost less than most bakeries pay for an oven alone. Yet Chad and Liz produce more than 300 loaves of bread a day (on average), in addition to an increasing array of pastries. I hope that an introduction to Chad and Liz will help you to use consideration in both your baking and your life—whether you plan to bake for your family in the backyard or for the public on a larger scale.

Point Reyes Station, West Marin County, California

Point Reyes Station is a small town about an hour north of San Francisco, at the southern end of Tomales Bay—a long shallow saltwater basin that formed where an earthquake fault met the sea and broke the coast apart. To the west lies the Point Reyes peninsula, a National Seashore where large dairy ranches have been established for over a hundred years. To the east are the ranch and farm lands of West Marin, the least populated part of the county that holds Mill Valley, Sausalito, Novato, and San Rafael.

Growth in West Marin is tightly regulated by open space regulations, so finding a place for a bakery at a reasonable rent is not easy; in fact, most of the real estate in Point Reyes is owned by just a few families. The coastal towns are full of tourists on some days of the week, however, and many of them want to get a nice loaf of bread, a piece of cheese, and a bottle of wine. The large population centers in San Francisco, the East Bay, and southern/eastern Marin are also only an hour away, easily accessible for selling bread or to go out for an evening of great jazz.

The Bay Village Bakery

The Bay Village Bakery occupies a converted potter's studio in back of a small, old-style California coast house on a small street just off the main drag through Point Reyes Station: Route One, the coastal highway. Chad and Liz rent the place from a member of one of the old local families. The house is two stories, with white-painted redwood novelty siding, paneled inside with beaded board. It has never been renovated, so it keeps a decided late-19th/early-20th century look about it. Nothing fancy.

The wooden studio/bakery is small, too—just 219 square feet, with two longer and two shorter walls. There is a big 6 x 8-foot Alan Scott oven sticking out from one of the long sides like a large lens on a small camera. Inside the bakery, the hearth and brick facade of the oven occupy the left half of their wall, while a table about 7 feet long (for working with dough) takes up the rest of it, underneath a window. On one of the short walls there are floor-to-ceiling wooden shelves where the loaves Chad bakes each day cool slightly before they are piled into slatted, stackable wooden crates for delivery. The floor of the bakery is made of old softwood boards, while overhead there are wrought-iron racks that hold peels, rakes, and mops for the oven.

When production first started in this space in May of 1997, the other short wall had a stainless steel sink and a big window, while the other long wall had the bakery door and a series of steel standards for wrought-iron shelf brackets. These brackets held boards that supported rows of round proofing baskets and folded linen *couches* full of proofing *batards*. There was no mixer and no proofing box in the bakery, just a stack of thick plastic rectangular kitchen tubs used for mixing, hand kneading, and fermenting all of the dough for the two hundred loaves Chad and Liz made each day.

Things have changed in the past year, though. Although they have increased their production by about fifty percent, Chad has cut down on the amount of physical effort he puts into the dough, Liz has cut down on the time she puts into distributing the bread, and they have set aside more time for themselves, away from the bakery.

For the bakery, they first bought a mixer that duplicated the kind of hand mixing Chad had been doing (an ancient diving-arm mixer, imported from Europe); this machine now sits between the sink and the big table. They also bought two climate-controlled proofing boxes that replaced the wrought-iron racks and boards where loaves used to proof.

Next, they negotiated with the farmer's markets they serve, agreeing to slightly later bread deliveries. They stopped deliveries to stores on Saturday, and began a barter arrangement with two other small business-people so that the store deliveries are shared, with a consequent reduction in the overall number of trips each week.

The changes on the recreation side include scheduling free time for the two of them several nights a week, building in a routine of breakfast and dinner "out" on one of their busiest days, and scheduling a regular overnight stay in San Francisco every six weeks.

As part of the barter, a neighbor bakes loads of Danish whole rye bread several days a week as the oven is cooling, and another neighbor uses the side yard of the house and bakery to grow cut flowers which she sells in stores in more populated parts of the county. The little plot of land on the edge of town has turned into a regular beehive!

The People at the Bay Village Bakery

Chad and Liz met at culinary school in New York state. Liz's parents are artists, and she grew up in Brooklyn and in Garrison, New York. She is older than Chad—she is in her mid-30s and he is in his late 20s. Before she went to culinary school, Liz started college (concentrating on painting and video art) but left to study acting, first in an academic setting, then with Lee Strasberg in New York. In college she had a catering service with a friend, and in New York she waited tables—the classic starving actor. Eventually she spent a year and a half at the School of Visual Arts in New York in a documentary photography program that prepared her (in one sense, anyway) for a long trip to the Alaska/Canada border country, to a wilderness hamlet called Boundary. There she made a photo essay about members of a pioneering family who still keep in touch with Liz. She then moved to San Francisco and worked as a cook and baker until she applied to the Culinary Institute of America program, in Hyde Park, New York. At that time (1991) the CIA program in California hadn't started, and Liz wanted a longer, professional-level course at any rate, as she had a realistic idea of the technical requirements of fine baking and pastry work.

Chad is from Texas. He attended a well-known private school in Houston, spent a summer at Exeter, and generally qualified himself for a conventional career path he chose not to tread. Instead, he followed his interest in food by going to work for and then managing a large natural foods store, then working as a pastry chef at the Four Seasons hotel (in Houston), before applying to the Culinary Institute. Chad's parents have accepted his career choices well: they understand craft work and the craftperson's life better than many modern Americans. Chad's father has owned his own business, for example, and Chad's mother is from a family of custom bootmakers in San Angelo, Texas. They make the kind of boots that people just have to wait for, as all of the work is done by hand. Much like Chad's bread.

Learning the Trade

Both Chad and Liz had a lot of baking experience before culinary school, but their introduction to the kind of baking they now do came through a teacher who asked them to come along to visit Dan Leader's Bread Alone Bakery and then to visit Richard Bour-

don at his famous bakery in the Berkshires of western Massachusetts. The visit to Bread Alone (and their meeting with Dan Leader) was something of a bust, but their visit with Bourdon changed their lives. His Berkshire Mountain Bakery is a must-see destination for artisan bakers who want to learn to work with extremely wet whole grain doughs, and Chad and Liz were awed by Bourdon's bread, his methods (the bread was all handmade), and the life choices he had made—to leave a career in classical music and make bread that incorporates some of the principles of macrobiotic cooking. (One of these is to include enough water in the food to render grain as fully digestible as possible.) They stayed all day with Bourdon, and before leaving arranged to work with him while continuing at CIA in the evening course. One index of Chad's intensity at the time is the schedule he established for many months (Liz kept it up for two months before getting pneumonia): school from 2 P.M. to 10 P.M., wake at 2 A.M. and drive to the Berkshires (about an hour and a half), work 4 A.M. to noon, then drive back to school.

The work at Bourdon's involved a lot of heavy physical labor, carrying boards loaded with loaves in a double proofing process designed to ensure that they are fully fermented and hydrated before they are baked. This is a process that Bourdon developed from techniques he learned while studying with Patrick Le Port, at Le Port's bakery in the Alps—famous in France for the taste and texture of its rustic breads. After four months of this double schedule of school and work, Chad took a few weeks off, then returned to work with Bourdon for a year and a half, while Liz worked in the kitchen at the Canyon Ranch spa in Lenox, Massachusetts, often with low-fat and/or flourless pastry recipes.

The tradition in crafts, of course, is of a progression from apprentice to journeyman, then to master. This means that when one is proficient in the work done by one's original master, it is time to work for shorter periods with other masters of the trade, journeying from place to place to do so. In the course of these stays one learns additional skills and ways of doing things, which one hopes will lead to a synthesis in which the new whole (the new master) is greater than the sum of its parts. When journeying time came for Chad and Liz, they went to Chico, California for eleven months. Dave Miller (who had worked with Bourdon and Le Port, and others) had taken over the Poncé bakery. After eleven months in Chico, they felt they were ready to travel to the source—to France and Patrick Le Port's *Boulangerie Savoyarde*. There Chad could continue to bake bread while Liz made pastries in a wood-burning oven somewhat like the one they eventually hoped to have. As it turned out, there were lifestyle lessons to be learned in six months in France, as well: that the best bread is made by people who not only work hard, but who stop from time to time for conversation, good wine, good food, and a stroll downtown!

After stops at several other French bakeries, including that of Daniel Colin, Chad and Liz came to California to talk to Alan Scott about building an oven for a bakery that would join all that they had learned in both America and France. They found that Alan wanted an agreement with them based on character and a handshake, not on legal niceties. Under such a gentleman's agreement, however, he would help them in every way he could to start a bakery—by building an oven, by using his contacts in the area, and by carrying some debt for them until they could make a go of it.

They began by staying at his house for three months, starting to bake bread several days a week in his oven so they could begin to build a trade before they had to meet the overhead of a separate operation. They were fortunate to find a house that was ideally situated, with a building available for conversion to a bakery—reducing but certainly not eliminating the bureaucratic hoops they needed to clear to start their own operation. They moved into the house but continued to bake at Alan's until their oven was ready.

Evolution of a Bakery

The changes that Chad and Liz have made in their operation and facilities over the past year have been made to preserve the quality of their lives, in the spirit of the lessons they learned in France. Let's look at their work and lives in the fall of 1998.

MIXING

The Bay Village Bakery dough process takes place in rectangular polyethylene tubs that are large enough to hold twenty or thirty kilos of dough. These are the same tubs that most artisan bakers use for fermenting and retarding mixed doughs, and Chad realized that they are similar in many ways to the wooden kneading troughs that village bakers used for centuries before the arrival of mechanical mixers—with the advantages that they are rugged, are exceedingly easy to clean, can be easily moved about, come with convenient plastic lids, and are accepted by the Health Department without question.

Chad still uses these tubs for his fermentations, and he used them to hand-knead all of his doughs until the spring of 1998. He did this both because he hadn't rounded up the money to buy a mixer and because he wanted to preserve dough qualities that he thought he might lose with mechanical kneading. That word, "kneading," might not be the best word to describe his technique, actually—Chad's action is more of a stirring, stretching, and turning motion. When he kneads by hand he has several tubs going at once: at first he only works in each one for a few minutes, long enough to thoroughly mix all the ingredients, wet all the flour, and to allow rough, coarse gluten strands to develop. He lets the dough sit a while (this is an *autolyse*, but with the leaven already added; conventionally the term is used for a hydration step before the leaven is added), then comes back to it several times briefly, wetting his hands in a bowl of water every few strokes to keep the dough from sticking. Each time he returns to the dough it becomes less clumpy and stringy; it comes together and smooths out under the stretching he gives it. It is not nearly so developed or worked as most machine-mixed dough.

Chad's dough ferments in the tubs for four hours (he uses a brief two-hour final stage of leaven expansion before he mixes up his dough). As it ferments, he returns to "turn" the dough in the tubs, giving just a few stretching and folding strokes with his wet hands every hour or so, strokes similar to but less vigorous than those he uses in kneading. After this treatment, his fermented doughs are wet but cohesive. They are extensible in shaping and tolerant in proofing and they spring beautifully in the hot oven Chad prefers, forming a dark, chewy crust and a flexible, open crumb.

Chad knows that mechanical mixing could disturb the balance of forces in his dough so that he might lose the qualities he wants to bring to his bread. That is why he went to the extent of importing an old mixer himself, when he realized he needed one. He wanted to be sure he could get the same results as he had gotten by hand, the same results that European bakers got, fifty or more years ago, by using diving-arm mixers. The most basic mixer of this type has ony two visible moving parts (a bowl and a paddle), and their movements have a stately, deliberate quality not at all like the mad whirling and rushing of a vertical planetary mixer hook, or the dental-drill percision of a spiral mixer's probe. Instead, a metal paddle drops to the middle of the bowl, pulls back to the rim, lifts up, moves over, and drops back to the center of the bowl again. It continuously lifts, stretches, and turns over the dough as the bowl moves around and around at a moderate speed. There is almost no tearing of the developing gluten net with this kind of mixer, little heating of the dough, and minimal aeration and oxidation.

Before he got the mixer, Chad was baking 80 loaves an oven load, three loads a day. Each load of 80 loaves represented 60 kilos of dough, and several formulas—country bread, cardamom/currant bread, and polenta bread, for example. Each formula represented at least one batch of dough to be kneaded by hand, perhaps two. It wasn't the time it took as much as it was his sheer exertion that led to the mixer. Now Chad has mechanically reproduced his hand-mixing method, except that he can handle a full 60 kilos (80 loaves) in a batch. That not only shortens his kneading time (by half, because he can process twice as much at a time) but also leaves him fit to shape and bake twice as many loaves as he could previously.

Let's look at the timeline for a typical load of loaves he will bake tomorrow. Chad starts the process at 8 A.M. today, when he mixes his final intermediate leaven. He starts to mix the final dough at about 10 A.M. today, first putting all the ingredients or all of them except the leaven into the mixer and running it for two to three minutes at 45 to 50 revolutions a minute. He then lets it sit for fifteen to thirty minutes, adds the leaven if necessary, then mixes it for four to five minutes before dumping it into a tub to ferment. At that point it is in the same partially developed state that he achieved with hand kneading. Over the next four hours he will turn, stretch, and fold the dough several times with wet hands, just as he did with his hand-kneaded dough.

At 2 P.M. Chad will again turn the first batch of dough, then dump it out on the table for division by weight. Since his table is wooden and the dough is quite wet, he uses flour on his hands and table, but he doesn't try to get perfectly formed loaves, just rounded lumps. After they rest for fifteen minutes, he shapes the loaves with a series of quick, sure movements. The dough is wet enough that the loaves will not become stiff with flour as he shapes them; he sifts a mixture of wheat and rice flour into his *bannetons* and onto his *couche* cloths before the loaves go in.

PROOFING CABINETS

Chad has installed climate-controlled proofing boxes in his bakery for several reasons. The most important one is that he wanted to get his schedule closer to Liz's, so they can spend more time together. Probably the next most important goal was to reduce the amount of time he spent in the bakery in the early morning hours—the hours before dawn. A significant related reason is the climate in Point Reyes, which is often too hot in the summer to allow the loaves to ferment and proof as long as he would like, for the flavor he wants to develop. Initially he had installed an air conditioner in the wall of the bakery to control the proofing temperature, but air conditioners don't last when you run them on full cold all the time, and they will not cool a space to below their lowest setting, which is still too warm to completely retard rising dough. They also extract most of the moisture in the air they cool, which can dry out the surface of the dough too much. Of course, in Chad's setting, the air conditioner not only cooled down the loaves, it refrigerated the whole bakery (expensive, in a bakery that contains the facade of a masonry oven!) and there wasn't any way to shut it off automatically and warm the loaves (and the bakery) up again, a specified number of hours before they go in the oven.

Now the loaves proof in the bakery at about 80 degrees Fahrenheit (remember, the facade and door of the oven are in that little room, too!) for two hours (to perhaps 6:30 or 7:00 P.M.), then go into the proofing boxes at 55 degrees Fahrenheit for eight to ten hours (say, 2:30 A.M.), at which point the temperature in the boxes will automatically be raised to 65 degrees Fahrenheit. Chad will then be able to start baking when he gets into the bakery at 4:30 to 5:00 A.M. Although he first started baking three loads a day, he is now able to bake six loads a day—the equivalent of more than 450 loaves.

Selling the Bread

Chad and Liz do not sell bread at the bakery. There are usually a few people with whom they are bartering, and those people may stop by for a few loaves, but almost all the bread is sold elsewhere, at stores or farmers' markets. Where it goes, the type of bread delivered, and the way it is delivered all vary with the day of the week. About 30 percent of the total sales at this point are from pastries, for which there is terrific demand and for which the profit margin (not to mention the labor margin!) is more favorable.*

Most of the bread that Chad and Liz bake, though, is sold at farmer's markets. These are often ideal situations for artisan bakers, with low fixed overhead, enthusiastic regular customers, and (usually) retail pricing. Bay Village bread goes to two farmers' markets, two days a week each at market: Tuesday and Saturday in Berkeley, and Thursday and Sunday at the Marin County Civic Center in San Rafael. In Berkeley Liz sells from a stand she sets up in front of her van, while in Marin the bread is sold by the staff of a concession store that also sells baked goods made by others, including large artisan bakeries. In both places, though, their bread sells out long before the market closes, and this has brought up issues that Chad and Liz have had to negotiate with the organizations that sponsor the markets.

For instance, the market in San Rafael opens at 8 A.M., and the sponsoring organization would like to reward the people who come early by having plenty of goods there for them to buy. But getting fresh bread to San Rafael at 8 A.M. would mean that Chad would have to bake all night and that Liz would have to spend the pre-dawn hours preparing to deliver and delivering bread. She would also be out on the road well before the other stores that sell her bread are open; the situation in Berkeley is similar. On Tuesday the market in South Berkeley opens at 1 P.M., while on Saturday the market at the center of town opens at 10 A.M. Recently, Chad and Liz have negotiated that they will have their bread in San Rafael by 10 A.M. (two hours after the market opens) and in Berkeley by 3 P.M. (Tuesday) or 11:30 A.M. (Saturday). Although this kind of change may seem small, the impact on their lives is large.

Financially, their best bread profit is at the Berkeley Farmers' Market, because they get a retail price. They sell out of basic 22-ounce *batards* at $4.00—itself a significant premium over other loaves available in Berkeley, but those other loaves are neither organic nor brick-oven baked, as are those from Bay Village. (Bay Village loaves with more expensive ingredients such as walnuts sell for as much as $5.50.) Although there is certainly an expense associated with the drive to Berkeley and back and the time spent at the market, it is more than justified by the 45 percent greater income it produces, and by the friendships Liz has developed here.

Food stores that get the bread are Tomales Bay Foods, the Bolinas Market, The Palace Market, Toby's Feed store, the Woodlands Market, and The Good Earth, all in

*Currently Liz makes *frangipans* (an almond cream pastry), about the same number of *galettes* (fresh fruit tarts), *croquants* (toasted almond and lavender flower cookies, similar to biscotti, but more thinly sliced), bags of oven-toasted muesli, candied orange and currant *sablés* (egg-washed almond flour cookies), and she is starting to make flourless chocolate cakes made with fresh Scharffenberger chocolate from California.)

Marin County. However, none of them get it every day of the week, and they all sell out, with customers getting to the store when the delivery is due to be sure they get a loaf. The same thing happens at the Marin County Farmers' Market, where there is now a sign-up sheet to guarantee that early shoppers will get a loaf when they arrive. Although there would probably be plenty of business selling to restaurants if there were more loaves to sell and a way to get them there, their two current restaurant customers (Manka's, in Inverness, three miles away, and the diner across the street in Point Reyes) are willing to pick up bread at the bakery.

Another way that Bay Village bread is delivered is by barter, the same way that the Rabins (Upland Bakers) get some of their bread delivered. One of their barter partners, Marianne, a restoration architect in her native Denmark who has lived in northern California for years, is a long-time friend of Alan Scott's, and for some time used Alan's oven (she now uses the Bay Village oven) to bake a type of Danish whole rye bread not usually available in this country. At first she did it because she wanted to eat that kind of bread again, and she couldn't get it here. Then she baked to meet the challenge of getting it "right," as the exact recipe and the conditions for making the bread (grain, milling, fermentation, and baking) were quite elusive. Marianne had to import Danish bread pans (with nearly vertical sides, a high-temperature silicone rubber coating inside, and ganged together with thick wire) before she got the result she wanted. Now she bakes thirty-two large loaves (each three pounds, although some of them are later cut into smaller loaves) two days a week in the Bay Village oven, at the end of the day when the heat has fallen enough for the slow baking and full gelatinization her dough needs. She delivers the Bay Village bread to Bolinas; Liz takes Marianne's bread to the markets in Berkeley.

Recently they have started another barter, with a flower farmer named Cathy who is using the side yard of their house to grow cut flowers. They have arranged with her that she will deliver bread several days a week when she delivers her flowers for sale—as if just having a flower farm next to one's house isn't enough!

The Bay Village Bakery now encompasses a web of relationships among a variety of people striving to create earth-friendly businesses and sustainable lifestyles. It is a participatory web, from oven to bread to flowers, from production to distribution to consumption. It's about living in harmony with your values. And it takes a lot of hard work.

A Week in the Life of a Village Baker

Monday (*Getting ready for Tuesday bakes*)

Chad—At 8 A.M. Chad mixes leavens for the doughs he will make that day, then has breakfast and takes a stroll.

Chad mixes a series of doughs from 10 A.M. to 3 P.M., enough for five to six 80-loaf oven loads. He divides and shapes those loaves from 2 to 6 P.M. After they have each proofed for two hours at 80 degrees Fahrenheit the batches will be cooled to 55 degrees Fahrenheit and held for baking early the next morning.

Chad fires the oven from 11 A.M. to 7 P.M. He uses almond and walnut firewood from the Central Valley of California, from trees cut out as groves are replanted or lost to development. He burns a steady fire from beginning to end, although he does move the fire from the middle to the back corners of the oven toward the end of the burn. He leaves the ashes in the oven overnight with the oven door in place. At the end of the burn the temperature one inch into the dome masonry is about 900 degrees Fahrenheit; early the next morning the interior temperature of the dome is 650 to 680 degrees Fahrenheit and the hearth is 530 to 575 degrees Fahrenheit before he rakes out the ashes, mops lightly, and starts to bake.

Liz—Preps pastries from 3 to 5 P.M. This involves mixing batches of basic pastry and cookie doughs, toasting nuts, and cutting biscotti. Since some of the products (such as biscotti) have a long shelf life, she may only deal with certain preparations once a week or once in two weeks.

Tuesday (*Chad describes this as a "crazy day" due to the number of people involved and the places they go*)

Chad—Bakes from 5 A.M. to 10 A.M., both bread and pastry. Then he delivers bread to stores in Point Reyes (The Palace Market gets twenty-five loaves, Toby's Feed Barn gets twenty loaves). Chad uses the early afternoon to thoroughly clean the bakery—mopping and scrubbing.

Liz—Starts at 7 A.M. by cutting fruit and forming (then baking) the pastries for the day. She also prepares and loads the boxes of bread that will be distributed that day. Liz leaves Point Reyes in time to get to the Berkeley Farmers' Market by 3 P.M., and is there until 7 P.M., with a drive home that takes over an hour.

Cathy—Delivers flowers and bread to stores, starting at 10 A.M.: the Woodlands Market in Kentfield (twenty-five loaves), The Good Earth in Fairfax (thirty loaves), in addition to stores that get flowers but not bread.

Marianne—Bakes from 10 A.M. to 12 noon, but while her bread bakes, she delivers to the Bolinas market (at least forty loaves for Bay Village, in addition to her own bread, baked on a previous day).

Wednesday (*Chad tries to stick to the schedule and finish up as early as possible, so he can have a quiet time with Liz. Maybe they will work together on something special for dinner.*)

Chad—Makes leaven at 8 A.M. He fires the oven from 11 A.M. to 7 P.M., and mixes doughs from 10 A.M. to 3 P.M. He divides and shapes from 2 to 6 P.M.

Liz—Does general business, both for bakery and household matters.

Thursday (*This is a day when they may be able to get done early enough to go out for the evening, either in Marin or San Francisco.*)

Chad—Bakes from 5 A.M. to 9 A.M., then tries to nap until noon, when Liz returns and they can spend time together.

Liz—Delivers from 9 A.M. to 12 noon, taking bread to the Marin County Farmer's Market, to Woodlands, and to The Good Earth. She also takes Cathy's flowers. Can spend time with Chad in the afternoon.

Marianne—Bakes from 10 A.M. to 12 noon, then delivers to Bolinas.

Friday (*Chad says this is a "big mellow work day." They put so much energy into the bread and pastry that they don't have the strength left to cook for themselves. Chad and Liz eat breakfast and supper out, somewhere in Point Reyes.*)

Chad—Mixes leaven at 8 A.M. He fires the oven from 11 A.M. to 7 P.M. He mixes doughs from 10 A.M. to 3 P.M. He divides and shapes from 2 to 6 P.M. Chad makes the same five to six loads as on other days, plus a full load of flat bread (*fougasse*) on sheet pans that can be baked just before the loads of loaves are started on Saturday.

Liz—Preps pastries all day, in preparation for the Saturday morning Berkeley market, which is their biggest day for pastry.

Saturday (*Because this is such a busy day at the Berkeley market, they don't deliver to stores. The stores in Point Reyes each send someone over to pick up the orders.*)

Chad—Bakes from 4:30 A.M. to 11 A.M., baking the last loads for the local trade after Liz has left for Berkeley. He mixes leaven at 8 A.M., mixes dough from 10 A.M. to 3 P.M., fires the oven from 11 A.M. to 7 P.M., and divides and shapes from 2 to 6 P.M.

Liz—Makes and bakes pastries in the early morning, then sells at the Berkeley Farmer's Market from 11 A.M. to 4 P.M. She does the bulk of their weekly shopping at the market and at stores in the Bay area on her way back to Point Reyes.

Sunday (*Chad bakes on Sunday because the Marin County Farmer's Market is held that day. However, the evening is like Thursday evening because they can go out if they want, and don't have to be back in the bakery until 8 A.M.*)

Chad—Bakes from 5 A.M. to 9 A.M.

Liz—Delivers from 9 A.M. to 12 noon, taking bread to stores as well as the concession at the Marin Market in San Rafael.

Once every six weeks: Chad and Liz let the Marin market and the stores know that there will be no bread on Sunday. They get done Saturday at noon, then meet at the north side of the Golden Gate as Liz returns from Berkeley after the Saturday market. They go into San Francisco—to art shows or museums, for city walks, dinner, theater or music, then spend the night at a hotel or inn. They return home mid-afternoon Sunday. Chad may do a short oven firing to maintain a stable temperature in the oven, but otherwise they are "off" until Monday morning. These overnights away from the bakery spread some of their needed decompression time through the year, with minimal disruption of the work of the bakery.

Natural leavens. Masonry ovens. Small-scale bakeries. Right livelihood. Amen.

BAKERS' RESOURCE:
SOURDOUGH MICROBIOLOGY
(with Michael Gänzle)

While I was working on this book I had long conversations (by e-mail) with Michael Gänzle, at that time a graduate student in Sourdough Microbiology at the University of Hohenheim, in Germany. His answers to my questions were so clear and so much more useful than the material I found in the literature that I (with his permission) abstracted them and posted them to the rec.food.sourdough newsgroup in early 1997. In our conversations, Michael summarized a range of current research that would not have otherwise been available to me. He sent me pre-publication versions of a book chapter he wrote with his professor, Dr. Hammes, and in the spring of 1998 Michael read a draft of *The Bread Builders* and commented on it in such detail that I changed several areas of the text.

Although this book may have seemed exceptionally technical, it in fact is a review summary of a great deal of information that is even *more* detailed, not just about fermentation, but about all aspects of baking. Because there may be some readers who would like to see more of the details, especially about fermentation, I have revised some of the exchanges I had with Michael, to present them here.

—*Daniel Wing*

A Conversation with Michael Gänzle

DW: Is there any benefit of speeding up the fermentation process?
MG: I strongly feel that the "time equals money" equation is not true for sourdough bread or any kind of fermented foods—wine, soy sauce, cheese, vinegar, fermented sausage: they usually get better if they are fermented for a long time (the definition of "long" varies, though, with the different foods).

DW: What are the stages of development in a leaven or dough? Why do most processes call for a tripling of the leaven in each of a series of three stages?
MG: There is a microbiological explanation for the three-stage sourdough process, since microbial growth can be divided in three stages. When

the organisms are transferred to a new environment (e.g. by refreshing a sourdough that has been in the refrigerator), they take some time to adapt: no growth occurs initially in the "lag phase," but once the organisms are familiar with the new environment, they start to grow exponentially, meaning one doubling of cell counts in a given time (the "generation time"). This is the "logarithmic phase." Eventually, the culture will become static, when the organisms have run out of food or are inhibited by their metabolic end-products. For effective sourdough fermentation, one needs a lot of metabolically active cells. After three or more refreshments, the organisms quickly enter "log phase"—they will reliably start to grow soon after inoculation and will produce enough carbon dioxide to raise the bread.

Things are different with yeasted dough, though: there simply are so many cells that these have to cough only once to raise the dough.

DW: Please explain the major factors that affect microbial growth in a leaven or dough.
MG: We've been doing quite some work to figure out which factors affect microbial growth in sourdough. I've done some work in vitro (Gänzle et al., "Modeling of growth of *Lactobacillus sanfranciscensis* and *Candida milleri* in response to process parameters of the sourdough fermentation," *Applied and Environmental Microbiology*, July 1998); and a colleague of mine, Markus Brandt, has looked at actual dough fermentation. Taken together, one can state the following:

A. The optimum temperature for sourdough lactobacilli is 32–33°C. Above and below that range, for instance at 37°C and 20°C, the generation time is twice as long.
B. At 39°C and 15°C, the generation time is four times as long.
C. At 41°C and 4°C, no growth is observed.

For the yeasts, the figures are as follows:

A. 28°C (optimum growth)
B. 32°C and 20°C (double generation time)
C. 34°C and 14°C (fourfold generation time)
D. 35°C and 8°C: no growth.
   (These data are graphed on page 53.)

So: if several refreshments are done above 32°C, the yeasts will gradually drop out.

The optimum pH for lactobacilli is 5.0–5.5 (which is the initial pH of a sourdough with 5 to 20 percent inoculum), while their minimum pH for growth is 3.8 (they usually produce acid until pH 3.6 is reached). Lactic or acetic acid concentrations don't affect the growth of lactobacilli very much if the pH of the dough is held constant: this is the reason the buffering capacity of the flour is so important for these organisms (a high buffering capacity in high-ash flours means that the lactobacilli produce more acid before the critical pH is reached). It also means that in doughs that are continuously given a high inoculum (more than about 30 percent), you'll find more yeasts and fewer lactobacilli. Eventually, the lactobacilli flora may change, with more acid-tolerant lactobacilli (e.g. *L. pontis*) prevailing: no *L. sanfranciscensis* is found in such doughs.

Yeasts are different: they don't mind low pH at all, but are strongly inhibited by acetic acid, and to a much lesser extent by lactic acid. Sourdough yeasts such as *C. milleri* are exceptionally tolerant of acetic acid. Increasing salt concentrations inhibit growth of lactobacilli, but yeasts tolerate more salt. In German baking processes no salt is added to the sourdough until the final bread dough.

So much for the in vitro theory. Markus has found most of the predictions come true for rye dough. The effect of variation of the inoculum size was interesting: if he reduced the inoculum size by one half, he had to wait almost exactly one generation time (one doubling time of the lactobacilli) longer until the dough reached the same cell count, pH, and titratable acidity as the dough with the higher inoculum. This was true for inoculum sizes between 1 percent and 20 percent at a 50 percent inoculum, when the pH is so low that the lactobacilli don't really grow well, and at an inoculum size of 0.1 percent, when the pH and the oxygen pressure in the dough are so high that the cells have a prolonged lag time. The generation time of *L. sanfranciscensis* in rye dough at 28°C is a little less than an hour, so if the inoculation size is reduced from 20 to 2.5 percent, it will take about three hours more until the dough is ripe.

One question is whether these findings are true for all flours and for all organisms. The *L. sanfranciscensis* strain isolated by Kline and Sugihara does not differ very much from the two strains I've been looking at. All the literature available tells me that, as long as we're looking at sourdoughs with a tradition of continuous propagation, the system behaves the same way. There might be differences between rye flour and white wheat flour, though, as the amylase activities in wheat flour (when not fortified with malt) are so low that the organisms may run out of food before the critical pH (for lactobacilli) or the critical acetic acid concentration (for yeast) is reached.

DW: Worldwide, rye is second to wheat as a bread grain. What are the special considerations in baking with rye?
MG: Remember that rye quality depends heavily on the weather conditions during the harvest: if it is very humid before and during the harvest, sprouting starts, leading to increased amylase activity. In a dry year, the amylase activities may be rather low, so there is less necessity for acidifying the dough. It may also be noted that rye not only has a higher amylase activity, but also a higher protease activity, which is important for flavor development through the Maillard reactions.
DW: Most authors state that the organisms in natural leavens come from the air, which I don't believe is true. In fact, isn't there some doubt about these organisms coming from grain or fruit, also?

MG: Sourdough organisms are certainly cultured from the environment—*L. sanfranciscensis* and the yeasts must come from somewhere—but these organisms most probably do not originate from the air, the grain, or the flour. Marco Gobbetti, whom I mentioned earlier, has been looking for *L. sanfranciscensis* on all kinds of Italian wheat flours, and he has not found any. No other scientist has been able to isolate *L. sanfranciscensis* from any other source than sourdough, but most sourdoughs contain this organism as the dominating flora. A possible source may be the humans who maintain the cultures: there are all kinds of lactobacilli thriving in the mouth, the intestines, etc. But, wherever *L. sanfranciscensis* comes from, it most probably does not come from the flour. Some yeasts may.

DW: How stable are sourdough cultures over time, and is there any difference between the stages of a sourdough expansion that justifies calling each stage by a different name?
MG: Some sourdoughs are quite close to infinity, as far as the generations go. The dough we've been working with, a rye starter that has the reputation of being one of the best rye starters available, is well above fifty years "old." It is fascinating that the culture we use *has not changed* in the past thirty years, since people started to do microbiology with it. There are still two strains of *L. sanfranciscensis*, and one yeast, *C. milleri*. Remarkably, the two strains of *L. sanfranciscensis* react almost identically on changes of pH, temperature, etc. So the definition of a "three-stage sourdough process" makes no sense—one may think of each of the "sourdough stages" as just a link in an infinite chain of repeated inoculations. But most of us will still continue to use the traditional terms to describe them!

DW: Do you agree with Dr. Sugihara's answer, when asked whether sourdough cultures could be contaminated with commercial yeast? He said not if you have a stable culture that is continuously maintained with the same conditions and ingredients.

MG: Dr. Sugihara is certainly right here. There was an experiment done by a Dutch group: baker's yeast didn't survive more than two refreshments. I think that it's the acetate that kills the commercial yeast, as it's less acetate-tolerant than sourdough yeasts.

DW: Many knowledgeable people are surprised when I tell them it is possible to raise dough with bacteria, in the absence of any kind of yeast.

MG: We've done the experiments, it works quite well without yeast. The volume is somewhat smaller, though. Markus Brandt has estimated the contribution of yeasts and lactobacilli to gas production in a normal sourdough: about 50 percent comes from lactobacilli and yeasts each. The yeasts are fewer in numbers, but larger in size. Lactobacterial fermentation releases plenty of CO_2.

DW: Bakers are interested in the acids produced by leaven microbes because much of the distinctive flavors are products of fermentation. Can you tell us what factors influence this process?

MG: The production of lactic acid in dough is determined mainly by the buffering capacity of the flour, i.e. the ash content. Dough hydration and temperature are much less important, as far as Spicher's investigations go. I think that the higher lactic acid content he measured in doughs fermented at higher temperature or lower hydration is due mainly to the faster rate of fermentation in these conditions. (This holds true if you calculate the lactate produced on the amount of flour in the dough: this ratio is fairly constant.)

The amount of acetic acid produced is controlled mainly by the availability of fructose. *Lactobacillus sanfranciscensis* produces lactic acid, ethanol, and carbon dioxide from maltose or glucose. If the organism wants to produce the more oxidized end-product (acetic acid) another substrate must be reduced. *L. sanfranciscensis* can reduce 2 moles of fructose to mannitol per mole of acetic acid formed, and the ratio of mannitol to acetic acid found in sourdough is about 1:8, fairly close to the theoretical value of 2 which would be found if fructose were the only co-substrate reduced. During fermentation, *L. sanfranciscensis* starts to produce lactic acid and acetic acid first, and forms lactic acid and ethanol only if fructose is depleted. There is a lot of fructose in dough, but not all of it is available for the lactobacilli. Yeasts liberate some of the fructose bound in gluco-fructans—it thus becomes available for the lactobacilli. If you go too high with the temperature, you slow down yeast growth, and the acetic acid levels in the dough decrease.

For bakers, an easy way to increase acetic acid content is to add sugar (that is, sucrose, a molecule consisting of glucose and fructose). This won't increase the total titratable acidity, though, as that is determined by the buffering capacity. Sugar addition (not too much, 1 or 2 percent) may speed up fermentation in white wheat flours: as mentioned above, in contrast to whole wheat flour and rye flours, the amylase activities and thus the sugar concentrations in white flours are rather low and may limit microbial metabolism.

As far as the influence of acetic acid and lactic acid on flavor go: lactic acid has no influence on aroma, only on taste, while acetic acid is an aroma volatile. So, I think it is not so much the ratio of lactic to acetic acid, but more simply the acetic acid content that matters in bread aroma.

DW: What do you think accounts for the breakdown of phytate in fermentation systems?

MG: The reason it is broken down at low pH is not that the wheat and rye enzyme (phytase) is most active at low pH, but because CaMg-Phytate is insoluble at higher pH and thus not available for enzymatic cleavage.

DW: How essential is oxygen to fermentation?
MG: Yeasts in dough don't have to rely on oxygen for growth: if that were the case, they wouldn't be there, as oxygen is quickly depleted.

DW: Do you feel leavens are best stored in a stiff, refrigerated form?
MG: Such leavens may keep up to three months. German commercial sourdough cultures are distributed as a stiff, refrigerated product. The supplier does not guarantee storage stability of more than four weeks, though.

DW: There is much debate in the U.S. about the proper conditions for "starting" a fresh culture. What conditions do you think are important?
MG: I think it does not matter if the first batch of a new sourdough "stinks"—the good bacilli will come out eventually, and they may come faster if fermentation is done around 25–30°C. (As mentioned earlier, the temperature optimum of L. sanfranciscensis is 32–33°C). There has been nice work done in Rudi Vogel's lab on the microflora of a freshly started sourdough: first, there are enterobacteria (Escherichia coli, Salmonella, Enterobacter), highly undesirable organisms that stink terribly. Then there are homofermentative lactobacilli (good lactic acid producers, but they don't produce gas or acetic acid), then acid-tolerant, heterofermentative lactobacilli that make lactic and acetic acid, as well as CO_2. I think this took about forty-eight hours at 30°C in Vogel's study. The stink at the beginning does not matter, as the organisms will be diluted out or die eventually. No L. sanfranciscensis appears by forty-eight hours, though: these will occur only after repeated refreshments. Peter Stolz told me that it takes about two weeks of repeated inoculations to get a good "sanfranciscensis" sourdough. I don't know whether or not this process was sped up in his case as, due to his workplace, his skin is probably all covered with L. sanfranciscensis!

DW: Many new sourdough bakers in the U.S. are intimidated by recommendations by some authors to work with large volumes when new cultures are propagated. This isn't sensible, is it?
MG: I agree with you: one gram of dough is one billion lactobacilli and ten million yeasts: more than enough to sustain the culture. In the lab, I'm doing most experiments on a 1/10 ml scale. For dough refreshments at home, it does not get much smaller than 10 grams (2 teaspoons): it's difficult to handle smaller amounts.

DW: How often must cultures held at room temperature be refreshed to maintain the sourdough flora?
MG: The main requirement for sourdoughs containing L. sanfranciscensis is repeated, frequent refreshment (not counting storage in the refrigerator). Peter Stolz said that one refreshment every twenty-four hours will suffice. If intervals are much longer than that (let's say more than three days), different, more acid-tolerant organisms may evolve (e.g., L. pontis).

DW: I assume that at any given temperature a thinner starter will ferment faster than a thick one and will reach a lower pH but will not contain as much acid.
MG: Faster, yes, but if you calculate the amount of acid produced on the weight of the flour rather than the dough weight, the outcome (lactic acid per grams of flour) should be independent of dough consistency over a relatively wide range of consistencies. So, the pH will be the same.

DW: Caramels and Maillard products are responsible for much of the flavor and aroma of fresh yeasted bread, although of these two, Maillard products are much more intensely aromatic. What effect does fermentation have on these products?
MG: These are the important compounds in both yeasted breads and sourdough breads; however, it is important to note that whatever chemicals are

reacting with each other during baking must be formed during dough fermentation. (Schieberle in Munich has done several nice studies: he supplied doughs with amino acids and demonstrated that the levels of aroma compounds in the bread were increased). So, formation of aroma precursors during dough fermentation is crucial for the Maillard reaction, leading to some of the distinctive flavor of well-fermented bread.

Other Notes from Michael Gänzle:

1. Sourdoughs are a continuum from beer to bread, raw to cooked. There are stages in between: raw, liquid sourdoughs are consumed in some societies (Africa, Turkey, Scotland).

2. Although continuously propagated sourdoughs are usually dominated by *L. sanfranciscensis*, *L. brevis*, or *L. pontis*, only *L. brevis* is among the fourteen lactic bacteria commonly recovered from wheat flour. It is clear that not all organisms can compete in the environment of a continuously maintained sourdough culture—one organism is usually dominant to the tune of five or six orders of magnitude.

3. Although *C. milleri*, *C. holmii*, and *S. cerevisiae* predominate as the yeast components of sourdoughs, of these only *C. saccharomyces* routinely metabolizes maltose, the preferred substrate of *L. sanfranciscensis* (which will use glucose to any extent only when there is no maltose, and then starts to use it slowly, and switches back to maltose when it is available).

4. *L. sanfranciscensis* begins to die off at about pH 3.6, and eventually more acid-tolerant bacteria will predominate. *L. sanfranciscensis* is relatively more susceptible to drying than some other common sourdough lactobacilli, although there are now strains that may be successfully freeze-dried.

5. Comparison tastings show that bread fermented with *L. sanfranciscensis* is the most flavorful, because of the spectrum of dough volatiles produced: ethanol, heptanol, 2-methyl-1-pentanol, 1-heptanol, 1-octanol, 3-methyl-1-butanal, heptanal, 1-trans-2-hep-tanal, octanal, nonanal, and acetic acid. There is comparatively little ethylacetate (or isobutyrate, according to Calvel). The yeast species present does affect the volatile profile to some extent.

6. Fermentation vigor and gas production by yeast and bacteria vary with temperature along the same lines as their reproductive activity (data from Spicher and from Brandt). The "temperature window" for CO_2 production, however, is slightly greater than that for growth, and the maximum fermentation temperature is one to two degrees Celsius higher than the maximum reproduction temperature.

RECOMMENDED SOURCES

Alton-Spiller
P.O. Box 696
Los Altos, CA 94023
barmbaker@aol.com
Leaven kits and The Barm Bakers' Book.

American Institue of Baking
1213 Bakers Way
Manhattan, KS 66502
(913) 537-4750
webmaster@aibonlin.org
*An organization for professional bakers of all
types, with academic programs and presentations
and an online bibliography.*

Bread Bakers Guild of America
P.O. Box 22254
Pittsburgh, PA 15222
(412) 322-8275
www.bbga.org
*Comprehensive resource on artisan baking, with
membership and seminars.*

Brick Institute of America
11490 Commerce Drive
Reston, VA 20191-1525
(703) 620-0010
www.bia.org

Charley's Greenhouse Supply
17979 State Route 536
Mount Vernon, WA 98273-3269
(800) 322-4707
charleysgreenhouse.com
Foggit spray nozzles.

Consulting and Marketing Services
  (San Francisco Baking Institute)
390 Swift Avenue
South San Francisco, CA 94080
(415) 589-5784
*Professional baking supplies, but will sell
to individuals; comprehensive consultation
services for artisan bakers. Also offers academic
presentations.*

Dietmeyer, Ward, and Stroud
P.O. Box 323
Vashon Island, WA 98070
(206) 463-3722
dwstroude@ptinet.net
Masonry heaters and small externally-fired masonry ovens.

Earthovens (Heather Leavitt)
4207 Broad Brook Road
South Royalton, VT 05068
(802) 763-8780
www.Earthovens.com
Masonry oven baking workshops, oven books.

Earthstone
1233 North Highland Avenue
Los Angeles, CA 90038
(800) 840-4915
www.miraclemile.com/earthstone/
Modular ovens.

Expanded Shale, Clay, and Slate Industry
  Association
2225 East Murray-Holladay Road, Suite 102
Salt Lake City, UT 84117
(801) 272-7070
www.concreteworld.com/escsi

Foggit Nozzle Company, Inc.
2308 Vicent St.
San Francisco, CA 94116
(415) 665-1212
Fogg-it spray nozzles, spray wands, shut-off valves.

Charles A. Hones, Inc.
607 Albany Avenue, P.O. Box 518
Amityville, NY 11701-0518
(516) 842-8886
Gas burners.

FBM
RD 3, Box 799, Cranbury, MD 08512
(800) 449-0433
Professional bakery supplies, but will sell to individuals.

W.R. Grace & Co.
(617) 876-1400
Vermiculite manufacturer.

Giusto's Specialty Foods
241 East Harris Avenue
South San Francisco, CA 94080
(888) 873-6566
www.guisto.com (planned for 5/99)
Wholesale source of organic grains and flours.

Harbison-Walker Refractories Company
  (formally A.P. Green)
Green Boulevard, Mexico, MO 65265
(573) 473-3626
www.apgreen.com
Refractory concretes and mortars.

King Arthur Catalog Store
RR2 Box 56
Norwich, VT 05055
(800) 827-6836
www.kingarthur.com
Comprehensive supplies and literature for home and small commercial bakers, carries La Cloche.

LaFarge Calcium Aluminates
9033 Laurel Branch Circle
Mechanicsville, VA 23111
(800) 524-8463

Marine Salt Traders
236A West East Ave., Suite 167
Chico, CA 95926
(530) 877-1892
seasalt98@hotmail.com
Clay pan evaporated sea salt from Brittany.

Masonry Heater Association
www.mha.org

Mugnaini Imports
340 Aptos Ridge Circle
Watsonville, CA 95076
(888) 887-7206
www.mugnaini.com
Modular ovens.

National Concrete Masonry Association
2302 Horse Pen Road
Hemdon, VA 20171-3499
(703) 713-1900
www.ncma.org
Information on concrete block construction.

Ovencrafters
5600 Marshall-Petaluma Road
Petaluma, CA 94952
(415) 663-9010
www.nbn.com/~ovncraft
Oven plans and consultation, cast iron doors for clay ovens, grain mills, oven books, oven tools, English-style prefabricated ovens, thermocouples and meters.

Perlite Institute
88 New Dorp Plaza
Staten Island, NY 10306-2994
(718) 351-5723
www.perlite.org
Information on perlite, including technical data and source companies.

Raytek
1201 Shaffer Road
Santa Cruz, CA 95060
(800) 866-5478
www.raytek.com
Infrared pyrometers.

Refractory Institute
650 Smithfield Street, Suite 1160
Pittsburgh, PA 15222-3907
(412) 281-6787
e-mail: triassn@aol.com
Technical assistance and source lists for refractories.

Renato's
2775 West Kingsley Road, Garland, TX 75041
(800) 876-9731 or (972) 864-8800
www.Renatos.com
Modular ovens.

Sasafrass Industries:
1622 West Carroll Avenue, Chicago, IL 60612
(800) 537 4941
Manufactures La Cloche.

Sourdoughs International
Box 670 Cascade, ID 83611
(800) 888-9567
www.cyberhighway.net/~sourdo/
Distinctive natural leavens from around the world.

Strong Systems, Inc.
(800) 255-9057
Vermiculite and perlite manufacturers.

Walnut Acres
P.O. Box 8, Penns Creek, PA 17862
(800) 433-3998
www.walnutacres.com
Organic grains and flours.

Williams-Sonoma
Box 7456, San Francisco, CA 94120
(800) 541-2233
www.williams-sonoma.com
Comprehensive home cooking and baking equipment supplier, carries La Cloche.

GLOSSARY

This glossary does not include definitions of the various types of masonry materials, as there is a chapter devoted to those definitions.

ATCC: American Type Culture Collection (www.atcc.org), a source for pure strains of microorganisms, including those that predominate in natural leavens.

absorption: The ability of a flour to take up and hold water. Higher for high-gluten flours and those with relatively high damaged-starch levels.

acid: A solution containing free hydrogen ions, or a substance that will release them when dissolved in water.

acid pH: Since pH is a measure of the acid/base state of a solution, "acid pH" indicates that the solution in question is acid, and has a pH of less than 7 on a scale of 14.

acid tolerance: The ability of a microorganism to grow in acid conditions.

active starter: A leaven that has recently reached its equilibrium yeast and bacterial population. If thick, it will be spongy, tenacious, and gassy. If thin, it will be frothy and bubbly.

all-purpose flour: White wheat flour. May be bleached or unbleached. Unbleached all-purpose flour from national companies or northern mills is suitable for bread, but that from southern mills may not be suitable for bread due to low protein content.

amylases: A class of enzymes present in grain but also supplemented by millers when malted barley is added to flour. Amylases break starch down to sugars and dextrins.

Anfrishsauer: The first stage (first expansion) of the traditional German baking sequence, made from *Anstellgut*, water, and flour.

Anstellgut: The inoculant to the first stage in the three-stage sequence of expansion of a leaven culture in the traditional German bakery. It is a portion of the ripe sourdough from the previous day.

ash content: The mineral content of flour.

autolyse: A rest during kneading to allow a dough (usually of flour and water only) to continue hydrating and the developing gluten to relax before kneading is resumed, leaven and salt are added, and the gluten is taken to full development. Usually done when dough is being machine-mixed. (French)

autolysis: The process by which yeast and bacterial cells break up when the medium in which they are growing becomes toxic. Dying cells release into the growth medium a variety of substances (proteolytic enzymes, glutathione) that interfere with gluten.

bacteria: Single-celled organisms, usually smaller than yeasts. Though some may be harmful to animals or plants, most are not, and they are present in vast numbers in our environment, serving many useful functions that allow us to live on Earth. Some bacteria ferment sugars, but they don't make CO_2 in the same amounts as yeast under typical conditions—they make organic acids instead.

baguette: A white flour, yeasted long French loaf, weighing about 250 grams.

bake: Heat to an internal temperature of at least 195 to 200 degrees Fahrenheit in a dry environment. For hearth loaves the environment should be humid initially, then dry.

baker's yeast: Yeast descended from top-fermenting brewer's yeast, but now selected and commercially produced for raising dough. A variety of types are available.

banal oven: An oven under the control of a feudal lord, who regulated and charged for its use. Peasants were forbidden to use any other oven.

banneton: A basket, usually lined with linen, that holds a proofing loaf. Baskets can be used without cloth if the bread and baskets are floured, especially with a mixture of wheat and rice flour, which is less sticky. (French)

barm: An English term for a natural leaven, often derived from brewery dregs.

bassinage: Adding water to a stiff dough to adjust its texture. Much easier than adding flour to a dough that is too soft. (French)

bâtard: A "bastard" or oval loaf, halfway between a *boule* (round loaf) and a *baguette*. (French)

batter: A thin mixture containing flour and water, with a hydration of more than 100 percent. Batters often contain air after they are mixed, and mixing a batter before adding it to a dough increases the small air cell content of the dough.

beer yeast: Brewer's yeast selected for making beer.

biga: Originally the same as a natural leaven but now usually refers to a sponge raised with commercial yeast. (Italian)

bleaching: Intentional oxidation of flour.

boule: Ball of dough or round hearth loaf. (French)

bran: The outer coating of cereal kernels, containing most of the fiber in the grain.

bread flour: Usually refers to white wheat flour, bleached or unbleached, with a greater protein content than the all-purpose flour made at the same mill, but less than the high-protein flour made at the same mill. Bread flour is often added to all-purpose flour doughs when rye flour or whole wheat flour are added. Approximately the same percentage of bread flour will "correct for" the rye or wheat, if the baker wants to maintain light loaves. Bread made with all bread flour may be very light but does not have the wonderful taste and supple crumb of bread made with slightly lower-protein flours.

brewer's yeast: Yeasts used to make beer and ales. Most, but not all, are strains of *Saccharomyces cerevisiae.*

bottom-fermenting yeast: A type of brewer's yeast (lager yeast, *Saccharomyces uvarum*) which forms its initial fermenting mass in the bottom of a vessel of liquid.

buffer: A substance that reduces the swings in pH in a solution as acid or base is added. The minerals in flour tend to serve as a buffer.

burn-out: The end of the oven fire, when it has burned to the far end of the oven.

caramelization: The result of a series of high-temperature chemical reactions among the breakdown products of sugar, contributing to crust browning and flavor.

carbohydrates: Chemical compounds of carbon, hydrogen, and oxygen such as sugars, starches, celluloses, and pentosans.

centering: The framework that holds an arch in place until the mortar of the brickwork sets up.

chef: A piece of a previous batch of dough kept over to inoculate a new flour/water mixture, which will then become a leaven, starter, sponge (synonyms).

coburg: An English term for a round hearth loaf with a cross slash in the top.

coking: Heating wood in an oxygen-poor environment until the water in the wood and many of the volatile compounds have been boiled off. Charcoal is wood that has been completely coked.

commercial yeast: A term for baking yeast, as opposed to natural leavens. Natural leavens contain yeast, but usually different species or varieties that can compete in acid media.

couche: A length of linen cloth that is puckered up to hold individual loaves (usually *baguettes* or *bâtards*) as they proof. (French)

crumb: The interior of the loaf; everything that is not crust.

culture: As a noun, refers to a batch of microorganisms in a nutrient medium, such as a flour/water mixture. Could be "pure" (one type of organism) or "mixed" (more than one type of organism).

damaged starch: Starch granules that have been broken in milling and are therefore accessible to water and to amylase at temperatures below the gelatinization temperature, when all starch will be accessible to water.

denaturation: The point at which protein is inactivated, whether by heat or other chemical changes in the medium.

Desem: Name given to a leaven originally started from whole wheat flour, initially propagated at low temperatures. Also the name given to 100 percent whole wheat bread made from such a starter.

détente: French term for the rest period loaves get between the rounding of the dough balls at the end of the fermentation stage and the shaping of the loaves.

development: In this context it means to work the dough so as to fully hydrate, link, and then condition the dough, making it strong and extensible.

dextrins: Soluble short-chain carbohydrates produced as a byproduct of the cleavage of starch by amylases.

directly-fired oven: One in which the heating fire burns in the the same chamber where the bread is baked.

dividing: Cutting the dough mass into loaves.

docking: English synonym for slashing loaves.

dough: A mixture of flour and water in which the weight of the water is in or near the range of 60 to 75 percent of the weight of the flour.

dough yield *(Teigausbeute):* Common expression in bakery books and articles. It is a measure of the amount of water in the dough, as in the baker's percentage. The difference is that the weight of flour (100 parts) is added to the weight of water used (x parts) to give dough yield. For example, a dough yield of 171 means a hydration of 71 percent.

draft door: A door that can be placed into the oven mouth after the fire is well established and producing much less smoke. It is used to slow down the fire by reducing its oxygen supply.

durum: The type of very hard wheat from which pasta is made. Kamut is a large-kernel wheat similar to durum.

einkorn: German for "first grain"—a native wheat of the Middle East and probably the first grain to be domesticated. The kernels are smaller than those of emmer and most modern wheats. Protein percentages are higher than for common wheat. About 20 percent of strains are suitable for making bread.

elasticity: The springiness that allows dough with well-developed gluten to stretch and return to its previous shape.

emmer wheat: The staple grain of prehistory, principal grain of Egypt, probable ancestor of durum wheat and, by ancient hybridization, bread wheat. Tolerates hotter climates than einkorn wheat.

extensibility: The quality (seen in wheat doughs especially) that stabilizes the gas cells of a rising dough and prevents the cells from breaking. This life-like quality can be felt in the way a good dough complies with handling. It is due to thin-film strain hardening, a property of gluten/starch suspensions.

extraction rate: The percentage of the total

weight of grain milled that is recovered as flour. As the extraction rate increases, the percentage of bran and germ in the flour increases. The lowest extraction flours may be referred to as "patent" flours.

fermentation: Usually means the conversion of sugar to carbon dioxide, alcohol, organic acids, and organic volatiles.

fermentation stage: Usually refers to a stage in breadmaking after dough is mixed and before loaves are divided and shaped. Sometimes referred to as "first proof," "first rise," or "bulk fermentation."

ficelle: A "needle" or extremely thin *baguette* of 125 grams.

fleurage: French for the flour used to prevent dough from sticking to the counter or the peel. Often based on rice flour.

foccacia: Itatian equivalent of *fougasse;* a flat bread often flavored with herbs, olive oil, coarse salt, or vegetables.

fougasse: French equivalent of *foccacia;* a flat bread often flavored with herbs, anchovies, or bacon.

four: Oven. (French)

fungi: Plants that lack chlorophyll, ranging from yeasts and molds to mushrooms.

gas cells: The bubbles in dough that form the small holes in the crumb of a baked loaf.

gelatinization: Uncurling and hydration of starch chains to form a gel. Occurs as a suspension of starch granules is heated.

genetic engineering: The creation of life-forms containing genetic material from other species or genetic material altered in test tubes and reimplanted into cells.

gluten: A protein complex prominent in wheat doughs. It is formed by the association of two precursor proteins, glutenin and gliadin, and by its strength, elasticity, and extensibility determines the structure of the dough.

gluten flour: Usually used to refer to a flour that is made by separating out a high-protein fraction of wheat flour. Occasionally used to refer to powdered vital wheat gluten, which is a water extraction of wheat flour.

Grundsauer: Third stage of leaven expansion in German baking.

hearth: The floor or sole of a masonry oven, the surface on which hearth breads are baked.

heat: In this context refers to the quantity rather than the intensity of heat present. The term "temperature" refers to the intensity of heat.

hootch: The liquid layer that can accumulate in the top of a container used to store a thin (very liquid) leaven.

humidity: The amount of water vapor (dampness) present in air.

hydration: Several meanings in this context: (1) The weight of water in a leaven or a dough, relative to the weight of flour. Therefore, a dough at 70 percent hydration is 41 percent water, and a leaven at 100 percent hydration is 50 percent water; (2) The capacity of a flour to absorb water (usually called absorption); (3) The quantity of water in flour (which is related to environmental humidity).

incubate: Encourage growth in a culture by maintaining conditions that favor the growth of the organisms in the culture.

inoculate: To introduce a microorganism to an appropriate medium for its growth.

knead: To continue mixing a dough beyond the point when the ingredients are uniformly distributed. This first causes abrasion of flour particles, then suspension of starch granules, and then hydration and linking of flour proteins. Professional bakers who use mechanical mixers use the term "mixing" to include kneading.

lactobacilli: Rod-shaped bacteria that typically produce lactic acid as the major end-product of their fermentation.

lame: A special kind of knife (or razor blade holder) used to slice loaves. (French)

lean dough: Without fat, sugar, or emulsifiers. Rustic hearth loaves are made from lean dough.

leaven: That which raises bread by producing carbon dioxide. In this context, it is a batter, sponge, or dough that contains a mixed culture of yeast and bacteria that has been continuously maintained by a series of inoculations and incubations.

levain: French for leaven.

Levain de tout point: The final leaven in the sequence of leaven expansions in traditional French baking; used to make up the dough.

lievito naturale: The usual Italian term for a natural leaven.

lintel: A piece of metal that holds up the masonry above an opening that is not arched.

liquid medium or media: A mixture of nutrients and water, in which organisms may be propagated. For example, a flour/water suspension such as a leaven or dough.

madre: A leaven, especially one similar to a *chef.* (Spanish)

Maillard reactions: A set of high-temperature chemical reactions involving the breakdown products of both sugars and proteins. The end products produce much of the dark color and pleasant flavor of fresh bread.

malt: Dried and ground sprouted barley, high in amylase, that is added to flour to guarantee that plenty of sugar is available to fermentation. More important for yeasted-dough processes than naturally leavened doughs. If excessive, leads to excessive dextrin formation, and thus to slack doughs, gummy crumb, and gummy crust.

miche: A large round French loaf weighing from a kilogram to four or more kilograms.

mix: Used by professional bakers to include both mixing until the dough mixture is blended and for what others call kneading.

mock-up: A quick trial fitting of the elements of a piece of construction, to help the builder visualize the finished piece.

molding: Synonym for shaping loaves.

mother sponge: A storage leaven.

mutation: A change in the genetic makeup of a strain of organisms, which may lead to a change in structure or function.

mycologist: A scientist who studies fungi.

old-dough method: The method of mixing some pre-fermented dough with a new batch of dough to improve its flavor and extensibility.

oven spring: A rapid increase in the volume of a loaf that occurs early in the baking of a well-made loaf.

over-proof: To allow the last stage of rising to last too long for the temperature and fermentation activity of the dough. Makes slack loaves, often with poor volume, shape, and crumb texture.

pH: A measure of the hydrogen ion concentration (on a logarithmic scale) in a solution, from 0 to 14. Values less than 7 are acidic, while values over 7 are basic.

pain de campagne: A French hearth loaf (round or oval in shape), rustic in appearance, with a floured crust. Usually made from high extraction flour or from a mixture of white and whole wheat flour, sometimes with a small amount of rye flour added.

parchment: Baking parchment is heat resistant, non-stick paper used to line pans or to support proofing (and baking) loaves.

pâte: Dough. Spoken of as *p. batarde, p. douce, p. ferme* for normal, soft, and stiff doughs. (French)

pâte fermentée: The old-dough method. (French)

peel: A paddle-shaped, long-handled tool used to load and unload hearth loaves. A **transfer peel** is a thin slat used to move long loaves from a *couche* to an oven peel.

phytic acid: A chemical that holds phosphate, it is found widely in plants. It can interfere with calcium absorption if it is not broken down in fermentation.

pointage: The first rising after mixing (usually called the fermentation stage, first rise, or first proof). (French)

polymer: A molecule formed of linked, repeated units, as starch is formed from sugars.

poolish: Sponge. (French)

proof: Usually means the final stage of rising, after the loaves have been shaped. Sometimes used ("first proof") to refer to the rise after kneading and before loaves are shaped (fermentation stage), or to a test done by the baker to see whether commercial yeast is still alive.

r.f.s.: Rec.Food.Sourdough—Usenet group about natural-leaven baking.

refreshment: Adding water and flour to a leaven

to increase its volume and feed its culture.

retained-heat oven: One in which the bread is baked with heat retained by a masonry mass, rather than a continuous fire.

retarding: Cooling dough to slow down the rate of fermentation.

retrogradation: Partial recrystalization of starch. One of the factors that makes stale bread feel dry and stiff.

Sauerteig: Sourdough. (German)

scuffle: A baker's mop. A metal ring is attached to another ring on the end of a pole; a rag is fed through the outer ring and may be dunked in water, then rung out for swabbing the hearth.

selective breeding: Traditional genetic manipulation by selection and propagation of organisms with desired characteristics.

slashing: Cutting the top of a loaf (on an angle, $^3/_8$ to $^1/_2$ inch deep) to allow for oven spring without bursting of the crust of the loaf. Necessary for most wheat-based hearth breads, unless proofed and baked at very high humidity.

sole: Synonym for hearth.

sour: In this context, means a leaven, dough, or bread high in lactic, acetic, and other organic acids.

sourdough: Dough or bread raised with a natural leaven, in which the bacterial component of the leaven culture has produced acid which gives the bread a tangy taste, good keeping qualities, and (usually) an open crumb and firm crust.

spelt: A large-grained soft wheat that was a predominant grain, along with emmer wheat varieties, in traditional European agriculture.

sponge: A thick batter or thin dough with hydration from 75 percent to 100 percent.

sponge leaven: A sponge that has been inoculated with a leaven culture, then inoculated until it is ripe.

sponge method: The process of making yeasted bread after a long (four to eight hours) pre-fermentation stage, utilizing about one-quarter the usual amount of yeast, the water in the recipe, and enough flour to form a sponge.

spring wheat: Wheat that is planted in the spring and harvested in the fall.

stable culture: One that has been propagated through many generations and is not changing in its microbiological composition.

starch: The strong carbohydrate polymer of plants. In wheat, starch is tightly arrayed in granules, which break open as they are heated.

starter: Something that can be used to inoculate a sourdough culture. Essentially the same thing as a leaven. In American sourdough baking, the term "starter" has been used to describe all storage, starter, and sponge leavens. This is sometimes confusing, although it does reflect the fact that all of these leavens contain the same culture (microorganisms) and are differentiated only by their intended purpose and (sometimes) by their consistency, which can be thin or thick depending on the process used by the baker.

starter leaven: Could be used to describe a new sourdough culture, being propagated from an infusion of flour (or fruit) in water, but not yet strong enough to raise a dough.

starter sponge: A ripe leaven of sponge consistency.

storage leaven: One that is used to preserve the culture from one baking session to the next. Usually kept in a refrigerator.

straight dough: Common method of making yeasted bread by mixing all ingredients at nearly the same time.

strong flour: High-gluten flour.

symbiotic association: In this context, two microorganisms that have complementary metabolic needs and products, with resistance to toxic chemicals that the other symbiont produces. This makes their mixed culture more robust and less susceptible to disruption by a third organism that may be introduced.

temperature: In this context refers to the intensity as opposed to the quantity of heat.

template: A full-size pattern that can be used to adjust a construction layout.

thermocouple: A bimetallic temperature probe that can be wired to a remote meter to show the temperature of any part of an oven.

time: In this context usually refers to the duration of a process or a phase of a process, as in rising, kneading, heating time.

titratable acid (TA): The amount of acid present, regardless of the pH of the solution, also called Total Titratable Acidity (TTA). The TA may be higher than expected if the buffering effect of ingredients (flour with a high ash/mineral content) is high.

tolerance: In this context, the ability of a dough to tolerate handling by the baker and delays (or advances) in the baking schedule, while still producing acceptable loaves. Greater for naturally leavened bread, as fermentation and proofing times are longer to begin with. In French, *tolérance.*

top-fermenting yeast: Brewer's yeast (ale yeast, *S. cerevisiae*), which forms its initial fermenting mass in the top of a vessel of liquid. The progenitor of commercial bread yeasts.

Venturi: A narrowed tube in which a fluid (liquid or gas) is accelerated, creating a vacuum into which another liquid or gas can be drawn and mixed.

vielle pâte: Another term for old dough (*pâte fermentée*).

viscoelasticity: The property of behaving both like an elastic solid and a flowing liquid. A rubber band is the classic elastic solid. Water and honey are viscous fluids, but honey is more viscous than water. Neither of them are elastic. Dough is viscoelastic, and the key characteristic of viscoelastic materials is that added time tends to increase their viscous behavior, and taking away time (acting on them quickly) tends to increase their elastic behavior.

volatile organic compounds: Molecules that contain carbon (hence organic in the chemical sense) and evaporate easily (hence volatile) with structures that classify most of them as ketones, enols, aldehydes, and esters. Many of them have distinctive odors. Even when present in small proportion, they give flavor to fruit, wine, bread, and other foods.

Vollsauer: The third and last stage of leaven expansion in German baking. Some of this is saved to become *Anstellgut*, and the rest is used to prepare the dough.

weak flour: Low-gluten flour.

white oven: Externally fired oven, so called because there is never any soot inside the oven.

whole grain flour: Should contain everything that was originally in the kernel.

wild yeasts: Used casually to refer to the yeasts in sourdough leavens and doughs. They are not truly "wild" when they are part of a stable culture, but the term is used to differentiate them from commercial yeasts.

winter wheat: Wheat planted in the fall and harvested the next year.

yeast: Single-celled fungi that ferment sugars and produce CO_2, alcohol, and other organic products. There are many species, usually differentiated by their metabolic/biochemical characteristics.

BIBLIOGRAPHY

Author's note:

I have consulted many wonderful primary, secondary, and tertiary sources to gather the material for this book. Where facts or concepts are mentioned in only one of those sources, and seem to arise from that source, I have tried to credit the author(s). However, I have found few such facts or concepts, and most of those were in scientific articles. Most other works (like this one) offer information that is not in any sense unique. I have been careful not to quote without attribution, but I feel that most of the concepts and facts do not require such attribution—they have proliferated over generations like kernels of grain. If you wish to buy one other book about hearth breads, I recommend Jay Ortiz's *The Village Baker*. If you want another book about whole grain baking, get *The Laurel's Kitchen Bread Book*. For inspiration, get Jerome Assire's *The Book of Bread*. (DCW)

Ackroyd, W. R., and Joyce Doughty. *Wheat in Human Nutrition*. Rome: FAO, 1970.

Alford, Jeffrey, and Naomi Duguid. *Flatbreads & Flavors.* New York: William Morrow, 1995.

Assire, Jerome. *The Book of Bread*. New York: Flammarion, 1996.

Barden, Albert and Hyytiainen, Heikki. *Finnish Fireplaces: The Heart of the Home*, 2nd edition. Helsinki: The Finnish Building Center, 1993.

Bell, George. *Permanent and Field Ovens*. United States Army Comissary Service, c. 1880s.

Boily, Lise, and Jean-François Blanchette. *The Bread Ovens of Quebec*. Ottawa: National Museums of Canada, 1979.

Brady, George, and Henry Clauser. *The Materials Handbook*, 13th ed. New York: McGraw-Hill, 1991.

Bread Bakers Guild of America Newsletter. Box 22254, Pittsburg, PA 15222.

Calvel, Raymond. *Fermentation et Painification au Levain Naturel.* (Extract of a series). Paris: Le Boulanger-Patissier nos. 5, 6, 7, 8, 10, 1980.

———. *The Flavor of Bread.* New York: Chapman and Hall, 1997.

———. *Le Gout du Pain.* France: Editions Jerome Villette, 1990.

Cereal Chemistry (journal). American Association of Cereal Chemists, St. Paul, Minnesota.

Corrither, Shirley. *CookWise.* New York: William Morrow, 1997.

David, Elizabeth. *English Bread and Yeast Cookery.* Newton, Mass.: Biscuit Books, American Edition, 1994.

Delacretaz, Pierre. *Les Vieux Fours a Pain.* Yens-S/Morges, Switzerland: Editions Cabedita, 1993.

Denzer, Kiko. *Build Your Own Earth Oven.* Blodgett, Ore.: Earth Ovens, 1998.

Hoseney, R. Carl. *Principles of Cereal Chemistry,* 2d ed. St. Paul, Minn.: American Association of Cereal Chemists, 1994.

Iott, Nancy. *"A La Recherche du Pain D'Antan."* Hanover, N.H.: Unpublished Thesis, Baker Library, 1992.

Jacob, H. E. *Six Thousand Years of Bread.* Garden City, N.Y.: Doubleday, Doran, 1944.

Jaine, Tom. *Building a Wood-fired Oven.* Prospect Books, Devon, 1996

Leader, Daniel, and Judith Blahnik. *Bread Alone.* New York: William Morrow, 1993.

Leonard, Thom. *The Bread Book.* Brookline, Mass.: EastWest Health Books, 1990.

Lyle, David. *The Book of Masonry Stoves.* 1984. Reprint, White River Junction, Vt.: Chelsea Green, 1997.

McGee, Harold. *On Food and Cooking: The Science and Lore of the Kitchen.* New York: Macmillan, 1984.

Ortiz, Joe. *The Village Baker: Classic Regional Breads from Europe and America.* Berkeley, Calif.: Ten Speed Press, 1993.

Pomerantz, Yeshajahu, ed. *Wheat: Chemistry and Technology.* St. Paul, Minn.: AAAC, 1970.

Pyler, Ernst. *Baking Science and Technology,* 2 vols. Merriam, Kan.: Sosland Publishing, 1988.

Rambali, Paul. *Boulangerie.* New York: Macmillan, 1994.

Robertson, Laurel, et al. *The Laurel's Kitchen Bread Book.* New York: Random House, 1984.

Selker, John, and Eric Shirey. "Design Principles of Simple Ovens," *Cookstove News* 5, no. 1 (1985).

Shirey, Eric, and John Selker. "Testing Commercial Ovens for Efficiency and Overall Performance," *Cookstove News* 6, no. 1 (1986).

Sicher, Gottfried, and Hans Stephan. *Handbuch Saurteig.* Hamburg: BBVW, 1982.

Silverton, Nancy. *Breads from the La Brea Bakery.* New York: Villard, 1996.

Spiller, Monica. *The Barm Bakers' Book: Breadmaking with Whole Grain Flours and Lactic Leavening Barm*, 2d ed. Los Altos, Calif.: HRS Press, 1992.

Wood, Edward. *World of Sourdoughs from Antiquity.* Sourdoughs International Inc., P.O. Box 1440, Cascade, ID 83611.

INDEX

THE BREAD BUILDERS

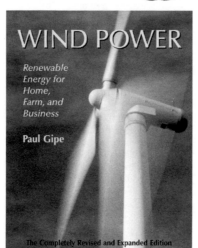